D0461358

# Fantastic Antone Succeeds!

# Fantastic Antone Succeeds!

## Experiences in Educating Children with Fetal Alcohol Syndrome

EDITED BY
JUDITH KLEINFELD AND SIOBHAN WESCOTT

UNIVERSITY OF ALASKA PRESS
FAIRBANKS

*Library of Congress Cataloging-in-Publication Data*

Fantastic Antone succeeds! : experiences in educating children with
fetal alcohol syndrome / edited by Judith S. Kleinfeld and Siobhan
Wescott.
    p. cm.
    Includes bibliographical references (p. ) and index.
    ISBN 0-912006-71-4 : $30.00. -- ISBN 0-912006-65-X (pbk.) : $20.00
    1. Mentally handicapped children--Education--Alaska--Case studies.
    2. Indians of North America--Alaska--Education--Case studies.
    3. Fetal alcohol syndrome--Alaska--Case studies.        I. Kleinfeld,
Judith. II. Wescott, Siobhan.
    LC4632.A4F36    1993
    371.92'8'09798--dc20                                    93-8839
                                                            CIP

First printing, 1993, 5,500 copies
Second printing, 1994, 3,000 copies
Third printing, 1996, 5,000 copies
Fourth printing, 2001, 3,500 copies

International Standard Book Number: cloth, 0-912006-71-4
                                    paper, 0-912006-65-X

Library of Congress Catalogue Number: 93-8839

Printed in the United States of America by Edwards Brothers, Inc.

This publication was printed on acid-free paper that meets the minimum
requirements for the American National Standard for Information Science—
Permanence of Paper for Printed Library Materials ANSI Z39.48-1984.

Publication coordination by Pamela Odom, University of Alaska Press.
Book design and production by Paula Elmes, Publications Center, Center for Cross-
    Cultural Studies.
Cover design by Dixon Jones, IMPACT/Graphics, Rasmuson Library.

To my parents, Benjamin and Leona Smilg, who gave to me the intense love and care that the parents who wrote the chapters in this book have given to their children.

—Judith Kleinfeld

To Michael Dorris who, in his efforts to raise his child with FAS, was like the lone bicycle racer bearing the full brunt of the wind on his shoulders. A pack of bicycle racers, on the other hand, can spread the burden of adversity, creating less resistance for each member. I hope this book is a step towards bringing together all those individuals raising children with FAS.

—Siobhan Wescott

# Contents

---

### PART I
### HOW PRENATAL ALCOHOL EXPOSURE
### AFFECTS CHILDREN AND THEIR FAMILIES

# PART III
## TEACHERS' TECHNIQUES

# PART IV
## WORKING WITH FAMILIES OF ALCOHOL-AFFECTED CHILDREN

# Acknowledgments

THE PARENTS, TEACHERS AND OTHER PROFESSIONALS who wrote these papers on helping alcohol-affected children and their families have shown extraordinary generosity in reflecting on their own experience, thinking through what they have learned, and offering their practical wisdom to others. Such thinking and writing can be painful, as well as enlightening, and is very difficult to do. We appreciate their willingness to reveal their frustrations as well as their successes, and we hope that readers will honor their efforts and their trust.

We thank the University of Alaska for inviting parents and teachers to work with university researchers in constructing practical knowledge on how to educate alcohol-affected children. The Northern Studies Program in the College of Liberal Arts at the University of Alaska hosted the First International Conference on Educating Children with Fetal Alcohol Syndrome in the spring of 1991. During the following year, the university provided time for Professor Judith Kleinfeld, director of Northern Studies, to work with Siobhan Wescott, a Dartmouth graduate and specialist in fetal alcohol syndrome, in editing these papers. Since many experienced teachers and therapists are not professional authors, some of the papers required substantial collaborative work with the editors.

We appreciate as well the care and attention of Sue Mitchell and Paula Elmes of the Center for Cross-Cultural Studies Publications Center and of Pam Odom and Debbie Van Stone of the University of Alaska Press in preparing these papers in final form. We also thank Barbara and Russell Tabbert in their fine preparation of the index.

We express our gratitude to many organizations for the financial support which made both the conference and the publication of these papers possible: the Alaska State Legislature; the President's Discretionary Fund at the University of Alaska; the Alaska Department of Education; the Tanana Chiefs Conference; and the Governor's Council for the Handicapped and Gifted in Alaska. We especially appreciate the support of the Licensed Beverage Information Council, since their flexible funding permitted us to continue this work.

The Steering Committee for the International Conference on Fetal Alcohol Syndrome helped select speakers for the conference and the authors of the papers published in this book. Steve Saiz, a founder of the Alaska Fetal Alcohol Syndrome/Fetal Alcohol Effects (FAS/FAE) Parent Support Group, generously shared his experience and knowledge from the perspectives of a teacher, adoptive parent, and researcher. Chris Jackson-Maiak, FAS coordinator for the Regional Center for Alcohol and Other Addictions at the Fairbanks Native Association and public health nurse at the Chief Andrew Issac Health Center for Tanana Chiefs, provided invaluable suggestions and insightful perspectives. Terry Rovig, previously with the Yukon-Koyukuk School District and now with the Fairbanks North Star Borough School District, suggested useful resources and approaches based on her professional expertise in special education.

We thank as well for his inspiration and support former Alaska state senator Johne Binkley, who has done more than any legislator in the United States to bring the issue of alcohol-related birth defects to public attention and to introduce relevant legislation.

In the interest of continuing to support FAS research and education, we are donating our royalties from the sales of this book to FAS organizations.

While we thank the many people who contributed to this effort, the content of this book is entirely the responsibility of the authors.

# Introduction

JUDITH KLEINFELD

AFTER MUCH THOUGHT AND WORRY, Sally Caldwell decided to tell her adopted son Antone why he had so many learning problems. She told him about his diagnosis—fetal alcohol syndrome.

"What does *F A S* mean, Antone?" she asked, sensing his boredom with her long explanation.

"Fantastic Antone!" was her son's clever reply.

"And what about the *S*—it's FAS," said Sally. They agreed on *"FAS*—Fantastic Antone Succeeds!"

## ANTONE

Antone is indeed fantastic. He has the small and spindly body, flat midface, and distinctive facial features of fetal alcohol syndrome. He has the characteristic learning and behavioral problems. Paying attention is difficult for him. He has great trouble adapting to change in routine. He slides into purposeless, repetitive activity. He is hypersensitive to touch.

"Many nights I would look down at him, sleeping soundly in his bed, and just cry," his adoptive mother writes. "His bloated belly and bony legs are sprawled out in the bed. There is nothing that can make the reality of FAS disappear from his life."[1]

Despite FAS, Antone at nine is thriving. He attends regular classes in school and was elected student council representative.

---

1. Quotations without references in this introduction come from the chapters in this book. For ease of reading, I have not included citations and page numbers in these cases.

He scored above average on the school's achievement tests—reaching the fifty-fourth percentile in reading and the seventieth percentile in mathematics. Antone also scored above average on a standardized measure of practical living skills.

What delights his mother is not his competence but his character. Antone has had the same best friend, a boy his own age, for more than five years. "They run for help when the other gets hurt, and they get angry and make up," says his mother. "They figure out how to solve problems and encourage each other to do the right thing. They laugh belly laughs until tears roll down their cheeks."

But there is no doubt about the diagnosis—fetal alcohol syndrome. Antone must try so hard to keep himself together. School presents the greatest stress. As the week goes by, staying in control becomes out of his reach:

> On Monday, he comes home from school and is willing, focused, responsive, affectionate, sympathetic, able to work and complete tasks independently. By Friday, he is resistive, scattered, inattentive, unable to follow even simple, single command instructions independently, and is failing at any attempt to use techniques that ordinarily help him focus. Sharp, repetitive sounds erupt from him at inappropriate times. . . . Like a stuck record, he repeats phrases and loses his train of thought.

Fortunately, Fridays give way to Sundays, a honeymoon day when Antone becomes himself again. Antone's average IQ scores, together with other signs, such as his above average scores in mathematics, raise the possibility that his biological brain damage may be less severe than his physical appearance suggests. While such an explanation is possible, usually external physical damage, especially in the face, is a sign of damage to the brain. Much of the credit for Antone's success must go to his mother, who has carefully observed her son's reactions and figured out just how to help him. She has done graduate work in special education. She brings to Antone both a professional's skills and a parent's passion. Antone defies the stereotypes—the stereotype of the child with FAS who is failing in school, the child without friends, the child without a conscience.

## CINDY

Cindy is also fantastic. Although diagnosed at a young age with moderately severe FAS by pioneer researcher Dr. David Smith, her mother believes FAE better describes Cindy, since she lacks all of the distinctive physical features of fetal alcohol syndrome. Cindy earned an associate of fine arts degree from the Institute of American Indian Arts. Her adoptive mother describes her graduation and the honors she received:

> On a sunny day in May of 1992, my husband and I watched with button-bursting pride as our daughter Cindy walked across the platform to receive her associate of fine arts degree from the Institute of American Indian Arts. Actually she walked across the platform twice, once to collect her diploma and once to accept the Azalea Thorpe New Memorial Award for Fiber Arts. She also stood to receive recognition from the Educational Testing Service Talent Roster, the National Dean's List, and the IAIA Dean's Honor List. Like every graduate, Cindy wore her traditional tribal regalia, a buckskin dress she researched, designed, and created.

I met Cindy when she enrolled as a junior at the University of Alaska. Her mother, Anne Gere, learned that I was working on fetal alcohol syndrome and wrote to find out about the university's mathematics requirement. As for many children with FAS/FAE, mathematics had been Cindy's nemesis. "Learning the basic facts of addition and subtraction took years," wrote her mother, "and she could never be sure that what she struggled to memorize on Monday would be hers on Wednesday."

Cindy dropped in to see me at my office, and I asked her to have lunch with me at the faculty dining room. Cindy jotted down the appointment on a torn page of her notebook, and I wondered if she would even remember it. A week later, the day before our scheduled lunch, Cindy came by my office again. She had wondered if I had forgotten about our lunch and was just checking. On the appointed day she came into my office wearing not her usual jeans but a black dress, hose and heels, and a magnificent coat of her own design. She had made it from a traditional Indian blanket. The stunning coat reminded me of a coat with an Indian theme modeled at a university benefit earlier that year. I would have bought it from Cindy on the spot. This young woman could go into business in clothing design, I thought. If math is a problem, she can hire an accountant. At lunch, Cindy talked about meeting her birth mother in Alaska and developing her Indian identity. I told her about my efforts to help my own children develop a Jewish identity. Cindy pointed out that my children might have an easier time developing a Jewish identity in Israel, just as it was easier for her to claim her Athabascan heritage in Alaska. Cindy seemed a bit more open and sociable than other college students I had taken to lunch. I thought about the noted researcher Ann Streissguth's point that the sociability and superficial verbal ability of young people with fetal alcohol syndrome often makes people overestimate their skills.[2] Perhaps I was making this mistake. Perhaps, though, Cindy was every bit as competent as she appeared, and it was the label of fetal alcohol syndrome that was leading me astray.

That semester Cindy made the Dean's List.

## NEGATIVE STEREOTYPES ABOUT CHILDREN WITH FETAL ALCOHOL SYNDROME

Why do we not see features about alcohol-affected children like Antone and Cindy? Television and radio programs broadcast stories about young men with fetal alcohol syndrome who end up in jail or adopted children who turn wild and destructive because alcohol "poisoned" their brains.

Our images come from the worst-case scenarios, presented as if they were typical outcomes. We continually receive the message: Alcohol-related brain damage is severe, permanent, and irreversible, and nothing can be done.

Part of this message is correct. Alcohol abuse during pregnancy indeed can result in permanent damage to the brain and central nervous system of the developing fetus. Both animal studies and

---

2. A. Streissguth, R. A. LaDue, and S. P. Randels, *A manual on adolescents and adults with fetal alcohol syndrome with special reference to American Indians*, 2d ed. (Seattle, Wash.: Dept. of Psychiatry and Behavioral Sciences and U.S. Dept. of Health and Human Services, 1988).

autopsies of human brains demonstrate clearly that alcohol exposure in utero can cause serious brain malformations. Summarizing the research, Petrakis concludes, "Alcohol or a metabolic product may cause excessive cell death in the developing central nervous system and may interfere with cell migration, a process essential for the proper development and organization of the brain, skull, and face."[3]

The damage, however, is not always severe. "The results may range from brain tissue disorganization that is detectable only under a microscope (for example, abnormal termination of nerve fibers in the hippocampus)," Petrakis observes, "to gross malformation of some brain structures."[4] Many children of mothers who abuse alcohol escape damage entirely. Some show only slight effects. The impact of alcohol on the developing fetus depends on many different factors—such as how much alcohol the mother drank, what fetal structures were developing at the time, and the genetic makeup of the mother and the baby.

The messages we have received about fetal alcohol syndrome serve an important purpose—to warn the public about the potential harm of drinking during pregnancy. But it is not true that all children prenatally affected by alcohol are severely damaged. Nor is it true, as the cases of Antone and Cindy demonstrate, that nothing can be done for them. Maternal alcohol abuse has an enormous range of effects on children. While many are mentally retarded, other have IQs in the normal range. While some have such serious learning disabilities that they need special classes, others can manage in a regular classroom. Ironically, as we become more and more aware of the subtle effects of prenatal alcohol exposure, we will identify more and more children who are only mildly affected.

Such mildly affected children, often diagnosed as FAE, often have more serious difficulties than children with the full syndrome.[5]

---

3. P. L. Petrakis, *Alcohol and birth defects: The fetal alcohol syndrome and related disorders* (Rockville, Md.: U.S. Department of Health and Human Services, Public Health Service, National Institute on Alcohol Abuse and Alcoholism, 1987), 43.
4. Ibid.
5. Streissguth, LaDue, and Randels, *A manual on adolescents and adults with fetal alcohol syndrome.*

Since the children look like anyone else, no one suspects that they disobey because they cannot remember things and they cannot remember things because of organic brain damage. Instead, they may be labeled as "willful, lazy, or stubborn." Their caregivers have to fight the same battles over and over again because the child "looks perfectly normal."

## The Powerful Impact of *The Broken Cord*

Nothing has had such a powerful effect on people's images of alcohol-affected children as the bestselling book, *The Broken Cord*. Michael Dorris, a Native American professor formerly at Dartmouth College who later turned his gifts to writing, tells the story of adopting a son, his desperate search to find out what is wrong with his son Adam, and his discovery that his beloved son has fetal alcohol syndrome. No matter how much he loves his son, no matter how much his effort and devotion, Dorris cannot make Adam whole or even teach him the most elemental skills. "After seven years of formal education, most of that with intensive professional tutoring, he was unable to make change for a dollar, avoid a mud puddle if it lay in his path, or discriminate between a clean and dirty dish."[6]

The brilliance of Dorris' writing and the intensity of his passion make the image of Adam spell-binding. *The Broken Cord* awoke people to the dangers of alcohol abuse during pregnancy and moved them to action. The book's publication, and the television movie based on it, caused an outpouring of legislation aimed at warning people of the dangers of drinking during pregnancy, conferences and programs to educate people about fetal alcohol syndrome, and a host of other efforts to prevent alcohol abuse among pregnant women.

But *The Broken Cord* also drew the portrait of Adam with such clarity that people often see no other child. "People think if they've

---

6. M. Dorris, *The broken cord* (New York: Harper and Row, 1989), 120.

read *The Broken Cord*, they know what FAS/FAE looks like," one social worker told me. "You forget that it presents one case and a poor case outcome at that. You forget there is a range."

In the most dramatic scene of the television movie, Dorris learns what is wrong with Adam. Visiting a treatment center for children on the Pine Ridge reservation, Dorris enters a room filled with children who bear an uncanny resemblance to his son.

Pulling from his wallet a photograph of Adam, Dorris thrusts the photograph into the hands of the director showing him around. "I have a son!"

"That's it all right. FAS . . . See, the eyes, how wide-set. I'm sorry," the director says. "Your wife an alcoholic?"

"No, he's adopted." Dorris replies. "They say when he was born it smelled like he was steeped in wine. I've been trying so hard for so long to help him."

His voice grows desperate, "Tell me what to do, what finally works for these kids!"

"What works for them? What works?" says the director. "Not a damn thing!"

This unfortunate message—"What works for them? Not a damn thing!"—has seeped into the public consciousness with the image of Adam. But the message is overdrawn.

Dorris' account suggests that Adam suffered severe biological damage as a result of his mother's alcohol abuse. His mother died of alcohol poisoning soon after his birth. Adam had brain seizures which continued into adulthood. His learning disabilities were substantial in every area. At five years of age, for example, he was still not potty-trained.

Adam also had a difficult early start. Dorris did not adopt him until he was three years of age. Tied to his crib as a baby, malnourished, sick with chronic pneumonia, Adam lacked the advantages of a strong foundation. Nor did he enjoy the benefits of an early diagnosis or early intervention. Dorris did not understand Adam's problems and had expectations that Adam could not meet.

## FOLLOW-UP STUDIES ON
## CHILDREN WITH FETAL ALCOHOL SYNDROME

When Dorris wrote *The Broken Cord,* Adam appeared to be representative of children with fetal alcohol syndrome. In an act of extraordinary generosity, Dorris makes public the family matters that most of us would prefer to keep private. He offers his own son as a "face to paste on all those pages of statistics."[7]

The major follow-up study of the characteristics of adolescents and adults with FAS/FAE had been done by the prominent researcher Ann Streissguth and her colleagues at the University of Washington. Adam seemed quite representative of the sixty-one adolescents and adults with FAS/FAE she and her colleagues had studied.[8] "It was uncanny," Dorris points out, "how her composite results paralleled my own experience."[9]

In adolescence and adulthood, these sixty-one children with FAS/FAE had an average IQ of sixty-eight (the mentally retarded range), although their IQ scores varied from twenty (severely retarded) to one hundred and five (normal). Only six percent attended regular school classes without special help. On the Vineland Adaptive Behavior Scale, their average level of life skills was seven years, even though their average age was seventeen years.

This study, reported in the *Journal of the American Medical Association,* and widely publicized in the media, has shaped our understanding of what the future holds for children with FAS/FAE.[10] But a closer look at the study shows what Streissguth herself points out—the error of generalizing from what happened to this particular group of children to other children who have the benefits of early diagnosis, early intervention, and stable families.[11]

---

7. Dorris, *The broken cord,* 243.
8. Streissguth, LaDue, and Randels, *A manual on adolescents and adults with fetal alcohol syndrome.*
9. Dorris, *The broken cord,* 240.
10. A. P. Streissguth et al., "Fetal alcohol syndrome in adolescents and adults," *Journal of the American Medical Association* 265, 15 (1991): 1961–1967.
11. A. P. Streissguth, "What every community should know about drinking during pregnancy and the lifelong consequences for society," *Substance Abuse* 12, no. 3 (1991): 114–127.

Streissguth and her colleagues examined adolescents and adults who had been diagnosed as having FAS or FAE in the early 1970s and 1980s when fetal alcohol syndrome was first identified. The major study defining the syndrome was published in 1973.[12] Since the syndrome was new, those identified may have been the more obvious and severe cases.

Streissguth and Randels point out this possible problem of referral bias:

> We note that there is a possibility that subject selection factors have influenced these results. It may be that the patients who are referred for evaluation, both in the screening studies and the two FAS follow-up projects, are those with the greatest problems. If this is so, it would bias the results toward poor performance for this population.[13]

Another problem in applying the results of this study to children who have grown up in different circumstances is that about half the subjects came from screening studies on Indian reservations. The particular conditions of reservation life—cultural change and cultural conflicts, economic hardship, social problems—may account for some part of the young people's difficulties and test scores.

Furthermore, these adolescents and adults had grown up in extraordinarily difficult circumstances. As Streissguth and her colleagues point out, "These patients came from remarkably unstable family environments; they had lived, on average, in five different principal homes in their lifetimes (not counting receiving homes or temporary shelters)."[14]

Even more telling, eighty-six percent of the sample had suffered from child neglect, fifty-two percent had suffered from

---

12. K. L. Jones and D. W. Smith, "Recognition of the fetal alcohol syndrome in early infancy," *Lancet* 2 (1973): 999–1001.
13. A. P. Streissguth and S. Randels, "Long term effects of fetal alcohol syndrome," in G. C. Robinson and R. W. Armstrong, eds., *Alcohol and Child/Family Health* (Vancouver, B.C.: University of British Columbia, 1988): 135–151.
14. Streissguth et al., "Fetal alcohol syndrome in adolescents and adults," 1965.

physical abuse, and thirty-five percent from sexual abuse.[15] Such circumstances do not necessarily predict what will happen to alcohol-affected children who grow up in more nurturing homes.

This influential study demonstrated clearly and persuasively that fetal alcohol syndrome does not just go away as patients grow into adolescence and adulthood. Since the distinctive physical characteristics of the syndrome fade at adolescence, some people had thought that fetal alcohol syndrome itself faded with age. As Aronson and her colleagues found, even when children are raised in good foster homes, the low IQ scores and other neurological damage persists.[16]

The fundamental point is that a diagnosis of FAS or FAE does not carry an inevitable sentence of school failure, a jail term, or any other outcome. The effects of prenatal alcohol damage vary enormously in individual children, and we do not have any research which carefully examines the effects of excellent education and care.

Streissguth herself makes this point with eloquence in a later analysis of her own study:

> The wide variation in intellectual levels in this group of patients confirms what we have known since the beginning, namely that the diagnosis of FAS does not carry with it any particular guarantees or inevitabilities about IQ or about academic achievement levels. **Diagnosis of FAS does not mean that a person cannot graduate from high school or even attend college** [emphasis added]. It does mean that some degree of brain damage has been sustained and that the manifestations of this will be apparent in the persons' adaptive behaviors.[17]

In short, our images of children with fetal alcohol syndrome and the future that lies before them have been shaped by research

---

15. R. A. LaDue, A. P. Streissguth and S. P. Randels, "Clinical considerations pertaining to adolescents and adults with fetal alcohol syndrome," in T. Sonderegger, ed., *Perinatal substance abuse: Research findings and clinical implications* (Baltimore: The Johns Hopkins University Press, 1992): 104–131.
16. M. Aronson et al., "Children of alcoholic mothers," *Acta Paediatr Scand* 74 (1985): 27–35.
17. A. P. Streissguth, "Fetal alcohol syndrome: Early and long-term consequences," in L. Harris, ed., *Problems of drug dependence 1991: Proceedings of the 53rd annual scientific meeting*, NIDA research monograph number 119 (Rockville, Md.: U.S. Department of Health and Human Services, 1992): 129–130.

with children who were probably more severely affected, grew up in difficult circumstances and received little help. We do not know what the future holds for alcohol-affected children where the biological damage is less severe. Nor do we know what will happen to children who have the benefits of early diagnosis, early intervention, loving and informed parents, and appropriate education.

Just as we should not overestimate the damage of prenatal alcohol abuse, we should not minimize it. Loving and intelligent care can do a great deal but cannot fix the fundamental damage. The experience of parents and teachers in this book in no way implies that if only the parents were more astute or the teachers devoted more time to the children, all would be well. Quite the contrary, what many parents and teachers are describing are ways to cope with severe problems.

Sometimes all you can do is have a sense of humor.

"Tell her this story," one mother said to my research assistant. "My husband has expensive black shoes that he always keeps perfectly shined. One winter morning, he stuck a foot into a black shoe and felt toward the toe—dog poop! I rounded up my adopted son, who has FAS, and asked, 'Do you know anything about this?'"

"Nope, nothing," he insisted.

"Dog poop may be frozen when you bring it in," his mother pointed out. "But when it warms up, it gets gushy."

"I never thought of that!" her son said in all innocence.

## THE EXPERTISE OF EXPERIENCE: DEVELOPING *FANTASTIC ANTONE SUCCEEDS*

My own interest in fetal alcohol syndrome began when friends of mine adopted a baby. The birth mother, wiser than she knew, selected them above all her other choices. Since they were teachers, the mother thought they could give her child the best beginning in life.

When I heard the news, I invited them over to dinner so I could meet the new baby. Shutting the door against the black winter, I peered into the quilt, eager to find a fuzzy head.

"What a darling!" I said, as the baby emerged, tiny and still. The baby's birth mother had a history of alcohol abuse.

But this gorgeous child, I hoped, had escaped the problems. Even mothers who drink heavily, I knew, have only about a one in three chance of having a baby with the full syndrome. I was not going to breathe a word about fetal alcohol syndrome that happy winter evening.

Before we sat down to dinner, I suggested that we put the baby on a quilt in my bedroom. Nothing could harm him and we could easily hear his cries. We ate salmon in honey sauce and listened for the baby who cried not at all.

"Such a good baby!" I said, trying to dispel my growing unease. With my three children, I never ate dinner without rushing to retrieve a squalling infant. But babies are not alike, I reminded myself, and nothing at all may be wrong with this baby.

When I talked to my friends a few months later, the diagnosis was clear. They had known it all along. He had all three signs of fetal alcohol syndrome. What would the future hold for him? As a university professor with a Harvard doctorate in human development, I wanted to know what educational strategies might help him. I too had read *The Broken Cord*.

As a researcher, I recognized that this book told only one story, an account of one father's experience with one child. From fascinating research on how the mind works, I knew that people seize on such vivid examples and believe they are far more typical than they actually are.[18] We vastly overestimate the frequency of emotionally interesting events—like plane crashes. Cognitive researchers call this mistake the problem of "availability" and "ease of representation." Such cognitive errors are hard to shake.

The picture of Adam in *The Broken Cord* is just such a vivid representation. But what happened to Adam did not necessarily predict what would happen to my friends' boy. They had a diagnosis and knew what they were dealing with. They had gotten their

---

18. A. Tversky and D. Kahneman, "Judgment under uncertainty: Heuristics and biases," *Science* 185 (1974): 1124–1131.

child soon after birth and could start immediately to build a strong foundation. Furthermore, their child might have sustained far less neurological damage. No one knew.

What would provide people in their situation the most help? I began to write a research proposal to describe best case scenarios—how alcohol-affected children fared in excellent homes. But such a formal research study seemed premature. First, we had little idea of what a best case scenario looked like for alcohol-affected children. My own parenting style—a warm but busy household with lots of commotion and freedom for children—was not necessarily best for alcohol-affected children. Indeed, I later learned that my own preference for rich, open, and unstructured environments was exactly wrong for children with FAS/FAE.

Second, the type of formal research I was proposing would take many years to complete, from writing the grant proposal through instrumentation through data collection through data analysis through publication. I was probably looking at a six-year project.

Formal research would be necessary before we could come to any scientifically grounded conclusions about probable outcomes for alcohol-affected children with different levels of physical damage who grew up in different types of environments. But before undertaking formal research, scientists often start out with a period of informal, exploratory work. This exploratory stage is not intended to prove anything. It is intended to develop ideas, to come up with hypotheses, to figure out what line of research is likely to bear fruit.

At the time, I was doing research in an area known as the *wisdom of practice* in teacher education. As Kaestle points out in "The Awful Reputation of Educational Research," educational researchers had failed to come up with general rules defining effective teaching that improved upon common sense.[19] Researchers were finding it far more fruitful to identify expert teachers and describe just what they did.[20]

---

19. C. F. Kaestle, "The awful reputation of education research," *Educational researcher* 22, 1 (1993): 23–31.
20. D. C. Berliner, "The nature of expertise in teaching," in F. K. Oser, A. Dick and J. Patry, eds., *Effective and responsible teaching* (San Francisco: Jossey-Bass, 1992): 227–248.

What we needed to understand how to teach children with fetal alcohol syndrome, I thought, was just such experts—parents and teachers who had many years of experience working with alcohol-affected children. They could describe what they had tried with their children and what the results had been. When any of us talk about our own experiences in this way, we tell anecdotes or stories. We tell about the time when. . . .

Such stories, I knew from my own research in trying to capture the wisdom of practice of expert teachers, contained the practical knowledge that practitioners had gleaned.[21] Through stories, practitioners indeed told more than they knew. The stories told of what they had tried, with what hopes, in what circumstances, and what had happened and why. The stories were vivid and memorable and drenched with emotion. Moreover, such stories did not claim too much. A story did not say "this works for ever and always." A story made a more modest and far more useful claim "this worked for me in this circumstance and might also work for you."

The first step would be to locate and bring together expert parents and teachers—people who had experience and stories. Many agencies were willing to contribute funds toward such a conference. I wanted to invite people on the front lines, teachers who had spent years working with alcohol-affected children, parents who had devoted themselves to the children's well-being, therapists who had worked with many cases and had some sense of what could and could not be done. What could experienced practitioners, who did not usually write in professional journals, tell us about how to raise alcohol-affected children and what the future might hold for them?

Finding such experienced people proved to be far easier than I expected. My friends told me they had placed their baby in an early intervention program and the teacher's techniques were helping. When I called this teacher, she told me that she had worked with alcohol-affected children for more than ten years. Many children could come close to appropriate age levels on developmental

---

21. J. S. Kleinfeld, "Getting it together in teacher education: A 'problem-centered' curriculum," *Peabody Journal of Education* 65, 2 (1988): 66–78.

tests by age three, she believed, if the parents worked with the children with single-minded energy. She suggested other experienced people to contact, and they suggested other people who said they had found helpful approaches.

After a month of telephone calls, I had located some highly experienced people. Jan Lutke in British Columbia had adopted eight children with FAS/FAE and had founded a political advocacy group that was bringing about change. Nancy Harrison in the Northwest Territories had adopted three children with FAS and had been foster parent to thirteen children with FAS/FAE. When her daughter with FAS was falling behind in school and the teachers did not even notice, she prevailed upon a retired teacher, Beulah Phillpot, to start an alternative private school in her living room.

Phillpot did not rely on standard behavior modification techniques, which many parents and teachers were saying had mixed success. She was finding it far more effective to teach alcohol-affected children structured routines so they could guide themselves through an academic task. In her school, the children talked out loud, as they studied, guiding themselves through the task. When they had internalized the routine, they no longer talked out loud. Her school reminded me of a religious Jewish school, where the children learned by chanting out loud.

In a northern rural community, I located another teacher, Patrice Winick, with an inventive answer to a concern of many teachers: Am I supposed to modify my entire classroom to fit the needs of one alcohol-affected child? By using more concrete and active approaches to learning, Winick improved education for all the children, not just the child with FAS. Danielle, a fifteen-year-old girl, was a star example of what can be accomplished even with a severely affected child. She worked as a preschool aide during part of the school day, keeping herself organized through a structured checklist of activities. Winick showed a videotape of Danielle teaching preschool. Danielle could not remember the letter V which she was teaching on Valentine's Day. But she handled the situation— sliding her finger along the alphabet line behind her until she came to the V.

The experiences of another child, Jeffrey, are discussed in one chapter from the perspective of the teaching specialist, Jan Hinde, who worked with him and in another from the perspective of his parents, Stephen and Michele Saiz, who explain why they chose to home-school their son.

About twenty parents, teachers, and highly regarded researchers, such as Dr. Ann Streissguth and Dr. Barbara Morse, came to the University of Alaska Fairbanks in 1991 for an international conference on educating children with fetal alcohol syndrome. They described their own experiences with alcohol-affected children and the approaches that they had found effective.

Two crucial ideas began to emerge. First, many experienced researchers, parents, and teachers were reporting outcomes far better than what had been portrayed in the sensationalized accounts of the media. Some children indeed resembled these negative stereotypes, but others did not. We heard of cases of young people with FAS/FAE in college. Moreover, even the alcohol-affected children who had been placed in special education classes did not resemble the lonely, depressed, unhappy children of the media. Many had friends, enjoyed their pets, and were happy in youth organizations, and in their schools and families.

Second, many experienced practitioners had come up with helpful educational techniques. What was especially interesting was that so many people—who lived in different regions of the United States and Canada and who had never talked to one another—had come up with the same techniques. Several teachers and parents, for example, told of their success with using photographs to remind a child with FAS/FAE of a chore or routine. If children could not remember what they were supposed to do after school, for example, parents took photographs of the child doing each step and displayed the photographs in sequence on the wall.

What would be of great help to other teachers and parents, we realized, would be just this day-to-day experience—the *wisdom of practice*. I asked those attending the conference to write papers for other parents, teachers, and therapists. The conference had also pointed out other types of practical experience we needed. Many parents at the conference, for example, were adoptive parents or birth mothers with considerable education. We needed information about how to work with other kinds of parents. We needed detailed descriptions of alcohol-affected children who were going to college. After the conference, I found such authors. Rodger Hornby describes in valuable detail how to develop trust and rapport with natural parents of alcohol-affected children, based on his twenty years' experience working with Native American and other families. Anne Gere describes how she and her husband raised Cindy, now a junior in college.

To write about raising an alcohol-affected child is an emotionally wrenching endeavor. "I just had to put the paper down," one adoptive mother said to me, after she pulled out the first psychologist's report which predicted an IQ in the fifty to sixty-five range for her baby. To write about the experience is to live again through all the pain, as well as the progress. These parents, like Michael Dorris, have shown extraordinary generosity in making public their private lives.

Capturing the expertise of practice is difficult as well because of the nature of expertise. As the philosopher Michael Polanyi points out, we know more than we can say.[22] As we gain expertise in any field, our knowledge becomes more and more tacit, a deep understanding that defies our efforts to capture it in words. An expert diver cannot tell us exactly how he or she executes a flawless dive. An expert teacher cannot tell us precisely how he or she runs the classroom. To help parents and teachers tell even a part of what they knew, required close collaboration between the writer and an editor. To the editor fell the task of reading early drafts and asking for clarification, for description, for examples.

I was fortunate in locating an experienced coeditor, Siobhan Wescott, a graduate of Dartmouth College. An Athabascan Indian, Ms. Wescott had already published on fetal alcohol syndrome, especially as it affected Native American groups. She brought to her work not only her fine writing skills but also an extraordinary tact and warmth.

---

22. M. Polanyi, *The tacit dimension* (Garden City, New York: Doubleday, 1967).

## PARENTS AND TEACHERS OF
## CHILDREN WITH FAS/FAE AS NATURALISTS

Many parents and teachers of children with FAS/FAE reminded me of great naturalists. Like Charles Darwin, who developed the theory of natural selection through his five-year voyage on the *Beagle*, they were careful observers. Charles Darwin "was not a trained mind in the academic sense; the early notebooks illuminate the fact that it was nonetheless a self-disciplined mind guided by one dominating purpose: to explain from observed evidence the biological and geological sequences of the earth."[23]

These practitioners were also not formally trained researchers. But they too had a dominating purpose. They wanted to help their children grow up to be not only competent but also caring people. "Although my son's brain has been irreversibly damaged by alcohol, his soul has not," writes Sally Caldwell.

Caldwell, for example, noticed that her son had strikingly different reactions to different types of preschools. In one type of preschool, her son would not join the group. Once he even sat outside in the snow crying and refusing to enter the building. In another type of preschool, her son adjusted quickly, excelled, and looked forward to each day. Like a researcher doing a case study, Caldwell systematically analyzed the differences between these two school environments, down to subtle differences like the teacher's facial expressions. In the preschool where her son thrived, the teacher used obvious visual cues, like a broad smile, while in the other preschool, the teacher's expressions were subtle and hard for her son to understand.

Many of these parents, teachers, and children with FAS/FAE became kitchen-table inventors. When one child had trouble writing a summary of a story for school, Antonia Rathbun figured out how to build on the child's visual style of thinking. Rathbun taught her to draw pictures of the three main scenes of the story, write a short caption below each picture, and end up with—Eureka!—a

---

23. N. A. Barlow, *Charles Darwin's diary of the voyage of the H.M.S.* Beagle (Cambridge: University Press, 1933): v.

one-paragraph summary just like the teacher wanted. Diane Malbin's daughter would miss the school bus or wait outside a long time because she could not read a clock. Her daughter solved the problem for herself by writing down the target time on Post-it paper and putting the paper next to the numbers on the digital clock. When the numbers matched, she left for the bus.

Many of the most inventive practitioners have professional training in education and especially special education. They are avid readers of the research literature on alcohol-related birth defects and learning disabilities. Their observations and inventions, just as those of researchers, build on the relevant research. Several parents and teachers, for example, point out that Feuerstein's work on mediated learning, originally developed in Israel for disadvantaged children, appears to be especially fruitful for alcohol-affected children.[24] Behavior modification techniques, they say, often do not work for their children. If promised a reward for emptying the dishwasher, one mother told me, her daughter does not do the job more often— she just does not remember it. But teaching her daughter routines for remembering things and solving problems, based on Feuerstein's work, seems far more effective.

Her daughter raises chickens who sometimes escape from their coop and huddle underneath it. Her daughter, diagnosed with FAS, will go out to feed the chicks and see that they have escaped from their cage. But she does not see the problem—the chicks could freeze or starve if they are not put back in their coop. Her mother handles the situation with Feuerstein's approach. She teachers her daughter a routine to use in spotting problems. Her daughter has learned routinely to ask herself two questions: "First, what's wrong with this picture? Second, what can I do about it?" Her daughter is gradually learning to use this routine on her own. Now she will come in the house and say, "Do you know that the animal has no water?"

While we have edited these chapters to avoid some repetition, we have deliberately allowed much of the repetition to remain. We

---

24. R. Feuerstein, *Instrumental enrichment: An intervention program for cognitive modifiability* (Baltimore: University Park Press, 1980).

do so to underscore a crucial point: Many parents and teachers who have not communicated with each other have come up with similar techniques which they find effective for alcohol-affected children. We need careful, controlled studies of the effectiveness of educational programs based on such techniques. But the need for scientific knowledge should not stop us from celebrating and using the wisdom of practice that parents and teachers offer.

## CONCLUSION

The climate of pessimism that surrounds alcohol-affected children is unwarranted. Many of the children described in these chapters are thriving. My friends' baby, now a preschooler, glows with well-being. And why should he not? He has doting parents who give him intense attention, praising his every accomplishment—his new ability to sit still during a lesson, his skill with a computer program, his expanding sentences. He has a new adopted baby sister who appears to have entirely escaped damage from her mother's alcohol abuse. His mother has taken a year off from her teaching position to stay home and teach him. No one knows what the future may hold for him or, for that matter, for any of us. The happiness of the moment should not be taken lightly.

*The Broken Cord* has given us one face with which to understand the reality of fetal alcohol syndrome. But Adam's face is not the only face of an alcohol-affected child. Other children have sustained far less biological damage. We are only beginning to understand the nature of their learning problems and how to educate them. As we learn more, we will be able to create different futures. We need other faces, including the face of "Fantastic Antone who Succeeds."

# PART I

## HOW PRENATAL ALCOHOL EXPOSURE AFFECTS CHILDREN AND THEIR FAMILIES

# Information Processing
## Identifying the Behavioral Disorders of Fetal Alcohol Syndrome

BARBARA A. MORSE

*Barbara A. Morse, Ph.D., is an assistant research professor of psychiatry (psychology) and program director of the Fetal Alcohol Education Program, Boston University School of Medicine. She has conducted research and educational programs on the identification of women at risk for substance abuse, prevention and treatment of FAS, diagnosis of FAS, and the development of children with FAS. Dr. Morse has published widely in this area.*

IN THE SEVENTEEN YEARS SINCE FETAL ALCOHOL SYNDROME (FAS) and fetal alcohol effects (FAE) were identified in the United States, several thousand papers have been written describing the clinical signs and how children are damaged from prenatal exposure to alcohol. While there is still much to be learned, the scope of our understanding of the effects of alcohol addiction during pregnancy is impressive. Alcohol's capacity to damage the developing fetus is indisputable. I intend to explore an area that, to date, has received considerably less attention: the specific developmental problems of children with FAS. My goal is to identify strategies that can help overcome the broad range of effects occurring in children exposed to alcohol in the uterus.

It could be argued that intervention strategies cannot be devised until we have clearly defined the problems of children and the

23

mechanisms which underlie them. However, the needs of children and their families demand that intervention strategies be tested now.

## CHARACTERISTICS OF ALCOHOL-AFFECTED CHILDREN

In spite of society's current focus on cocaine, alcohol remains the most commonly abused substance in the United States, and one of the most powerful teratogens, causing malformations of the fetus. The three major signs that comprise FAS are impaired growth, changes in facial structure, and central nervous system abnormalities. Children are smaller, both before birth and after. Children with FAS grow more slowly than ninety percent of other children and, although development is progressive, the deficit is permanent. FAS is distinguished by unusual but consistent facial characteristics, including flattened mid-face, short up-turned nose, small eye openings, drooping eyelid (ptosis), smooth area from the base of the nose to the upper lip (philtrum), and thin upper lip (see below).

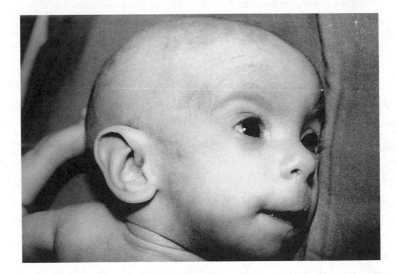

Damage to the central nervous system results in many problems. The average IQ of children with FAS is seventy, although a broad range from less than fifty to greater than one hundred and fifteen has been reported. Other signs of central nervous system damage include slower development, problems with perception, hyperactivity, learning disabilities, and behavior disorders caused by damage to the brain.

When these three signs—slow growth, identifying facial features, and central nervous system damage—are seen in conjunction with maternal alcohol abuse during pregnancy, the diagnosis of FAS is justified. When a child has one or two of these signs and maternal alcohol consumption can be confirmed, then the child is said to have FAE or alcohol-related birth defects (ARBD).[1] FAS is estimated to occur in 1.9 per thousand live births, or approximately 7,000 a year in the United States. FAE is believed to occur three to four times as often as FAS.[2]

Children with FAS may also show multiple abnormalities in other areas of the body.[3] Those areas include the ears, eyes, mouth, heart, liver, skeletal system, and urogenital (genital-urinary) systems. These associated abnormalities are nonspecific to alcohol exposure, and can also result from a wide variety of other factors. Since the human body has limited ways to react to stress, the timing of the insult in fetal development, rather than the agent, determines the precise effect. Knowing the mother's alcohol history is critical to diagnosing alcohol-related birth defects accurately.

While growth and physical problems characterize children with FAS, the problems presented by central nervous system damage are the most serious. The list of documented abnormalities is lengthy: extreme irritability and restlessness in infancy, perceptual problems, delays in learning to talk, hyperactivity, fine and gross motor abnormalities, learning disabilities, intellectual impairment, clumsiness, fearlessness, inappropriate social behavior, memory deficits, and eating disorders. Lemoine, Harousseau, Borteyru, and Menuet described this list of behaviors more than twenty years ago and they

---

1. H. L. Rosett, "A clinical perspective of the Fetal Alcohol Syndrome," *Alcoholism Clin Exp Res* 4 (1980): 119–122; R. J. Sokol and S. K. Clarren, "Guidelines for use of terminology describing the impact of prenatal alcohol on the offspring," *Alcoholism Clin Exp Res* 13 (1989): 597–598.
2. E. Abel and R. Sokol, "Incidence of Fetal Alcohol Syndrome and economic impact of FAS-related anomalies," *Drug and Alcohol Dep.*, 19 (1987): 51–70.
3. H. L. Rosett and L. Weiner, *Alcohol and the Fetus: A Clinical Perspective* (New York: Oxford University Press, 1984.)

have been observed repeatedly in numerous subsequent studies.[4] Observations by individual clinicians suggest additional behavioral problems, including failure to learn from mistakes, lack of judgment, lack of remorse for misbehavior, lying, immature behaviors, persistent sleeplessness, extreme mood changes, unusual aggressiveness, and wide variation in learning abilities at different times.

These children give an illusion of purposefulness. For example, they may remember information that is important to them but forget other items easily. Parents report frequent lying, but done in such a way that the lie is transparent. This leads to the idea that children with FAS or FAE are naughty, devious, lazy, willfully disobedient, or otherwise intractable.

## Diagnosing FAS/FAE:
### Most Children Do Not Have Severe Problems

We are just beginning to develop systematic, effective intervention for children with FAS or FAE. The lack of abundant clinical experience and research hampers the development of effective intervention strategies. The important first step in treating FAS/FAE is an accurate diagnosis. Yet the diagnosis remains elusive. As we have no biochemical tests to confirm FAS, diagnosis is based on the clinical judgment of the examiner. Assessment is difficult in newborns when central nervous system anomalies cannot be documented and facial dysmorpholgy may not be obvious.

It is even more difficult to make the diagnosis because children with FAS or FAE are not all alike. The different effects of alcohol exposure are due to a number of variables. Foremost among these is dose. The risk to the fetus increases in both incidence and severity with the amount of alcohol consumed. Timing of exposure also accounts for variability of effects. Exposure during the first trimester poses the greatest threat to organ development. Exposure during the last trimester is most likely to affect central nervous system development.

---

4. P. Lemoine et al., "Les enfants de parents alcooliques: anomalies observees. Apropos de 127 cas," *Ouest Med* 21 (1968): 476–482.

Individual differences in children also result in varying effects. Alcohol causes a decrement from the optimal; children's abilities will be less than if they were not exposed. However, it is also important to remember that not all of the problems seen in affected children are a result of alcohol exposure. The development of the child is also affected by genetics, maternal characteristics, and lifestyle. Additional studies are needed in which the IQ of the biological mother is taken into account in analysis of children with FAS, as mother's IQ is one of the strongest predictors of the child's IQ.[5]

Illness, nutrition, and other drug exposures in the mother must also be considered when evaluating the effects of alcohol on a child. It is not uncommon for women to combine cocaine, alcohol, marijuana, and other drugs during one pregnancy. Very little data on the effects of multiple exposures exists. Mothers may also seek alcohol in non-beverage substances such as Lysol, cough syrup, and antifreeze. These exposures undoubtedly contribute to adverse infant outcome as well.

Just as risks from prenatal alcohol exposure increase with dose, risks also increase with number of pregnancies. This factor is independent of age. In a survey by Abel, the risk of a younger sibling of a child with FAS also having FAS (assuming equal or higher consumption of alcohol during second pregnancy) is seventy-seven percent.[6]

FAE is estimated to occur three to four times as often as FAS, although it is much less frequently recognized. Behavioral issues are usually the primary feature of this disorder. To some, the problems presented by FAE are even more frustrating than those of FAS. Children often appear normal, more is expected of them, and they are less likely to qualify for special services.

Another impediment to the development of treatment strategies is the poor description of problems that children with FAS have. With a few exceptions, the literature has repeated the first

---

5. T. Greene et al., "Prenatal alcohol exposure and cognitive development," *Neurotoxicol Teratol* 13 (1991): 1.
6. E. Abel, "Incidence of anomalies among siblings of FAS cases," *Neurotoxical Teratol* 10 (1988): 1–2.

identified list of problems, rather than enlarging our understanding of the problems and their scope. The most severely affected children have been described, rather than the problems of the majority.

Many health care professionals have limited experience with FAS and FAE. Often they have been exposed only to research papers describing severely affected children who make little or no progress, even with excellent homes and comprehensive intervention. When physicians are suspicious about the diagnosis of FAS in a patient, they frequently have only this literature as a reference. If the child does not exhibit the symptoms of one who has been severely affected, the diagnosis of FAS may be inappropriately discarded.

Only ten to twenty percent of children with FAS may have effects as severe as those represented in the medical literature. Most have subtler effects, and improvement is seen over time.[7] Among the families who work with the Fetal Alcohol Education Program at the Boston University School of Medicine, the majority have children who are in regular classes in the public schools. Some may attend resource centers several times a week. A few attend special education classes entirely.

Two families associated with our program for many years have young adult children who are employed or attending community college. In each case, the children have remained in their biologic family homes. Some of the children were diagnosed in infancy and the others at school age. Both mothers have been in recovery for many years. Perhaps the single greatest factor that accounts for the success of these children is not the severity of their condition (there is wide variation), but the intensive intervention and advocacy that the families have provided and continue to provide. In many cases, the intervention required changing schools frequently when the resources of one had been exhausted. In some cases residential

---

7. H. L. Spohr and H. C. Steinhausen, "Clinical, psychopathological and developmental aspects in children with the Fetal Alcohol Syndrome: a four year follow-up study," in *Mechanisms of Alcohol Damage* in Utero, Ciba Foundation Symposium 105 (London: Pittman, 1984).

schools were used for a time. Parents remained actively involved in advocacy and in choosing the most appropriate educational program. Because there were no precedents for these families, instinct and parental knowledge guided them.

Success stories like these have not been described in the scientific literature. Since medical journals represent the primary source of information for most physicians, it is not surprising that the literature heavily influences their prognoses. Broadening the information that physicians receive about FAS can have dramatic effects on the identification rate. We were able to demonstrate this effect on identifying children with FAS in an informal telephone survey of local clinics serving children with birth defects. Initial inquiries found only one or two children with FAS per clinic. Follow-up consultations with one clinic describing both the wide variation in the expression of FAS and specific techniques to use when questioning parents increased the number of identified children twelve-fold over a two- to three-month period. The medical director realized that they had been serving children with FAS all along; however, the representation in the literature of portraying only severely affected children caused FAS to be overlooked as a diagnosis.

The misperceptions about children with FAS have been fed by the mass media, which has described individual case histories as though they represent the majority of children. A sensationalist account of children with FAS in trouble with the law on a national television program generated innumerable telephone calls to our program from parents who wished to return their adopted children if this was the future they could look forward to. To date, there have been no scientific studies following children with FAS to determine if they have more trouble with the law than other groups, nor studies in prisons to see if there are disproportional numbers of inmates with FAS.

Inability to diagnose FAS also results from the physician's lack of experience with substance abuse in general. Medical education about addiction remains inadequate. Many clinicians are uncomfortable asking a parent about alcohol use. Determining an accurate maternal alcohol history is difficult; exact amounts consumed during pregnancy can never be obtained, nor the relationship of that consumption to children's behavior verified. In the case of children living with adoptive or foster parents, maternal alcohol histories are often not available. This lack of information leaves physicians dubious about calling a cluster of symptoms FAS. In a study we recently conducted among Massachusetts pediatricians, knowledge of the diagnostic signs of FAS was high. However, few had diagnosed FAS. This is surprising, since FAS is believed to occur as often as Down's syndrome across the entire population and much more frequently in special populations. Health care professionals and educators require ongoing training to help them recognize the various manifestations of FAS throughout childhood and adolescence and to help them work with families.

Finally, many physicians report that without a specific treatment protocol, FAS need not be specially diagnosed and should be treated like any other central nervous system disorder. They are reluctant to apply a term that is seen as pejorative in some settings (such as schools), when few perceived benefits result. When intervention strategies are developed, accurate diagnosis becomes more meaningful.

## An Information Processing Framework for Understanding the Behavior of Alcohol-Affected Children

Currently we must rely almost entirely on clinical observation of children's behavior to understand their difficulties and to attempt intervention. Research is needed to answer questions about specific central nervous system damage and behavior in children. Understanding that the behavior of alcohol-affected children is a manifestation of physiologic damage rather than willful misconduct emphasizes the need to provide treatment. In animals (rodents, dogs, and monkeys), we know from experimental research that alcohol damages specific brain sites during prenatal development and results in disturbed behavior. In particular, damage to the hippocampus has been implicated in learning and memory deficits, and damage to the cerebellum may affect motor control.[8]

Two examples may help to illuminate the kind of neuro-be-havioral problems typically encountered in children with FAS. In one circumstance, a child is asked to turn on the porch light. Either he/she runs to the porch and then cannot remember what to do, or goes to a room other than the porch and turns on that light. In either case, the child is fully aware that he/she is not doing something right but cannot determine the appropriate response. Often when asked to repeat the instruction, the child will do so word for word but still cannot complete the task.

In another instance, a child is asked to return to the front hall and hang up a coat. She willingly starts back towards the hall. Halfway there, she stops and looks all around the family room. Cushions from the couch are on the floor, so she stops and picks them up. Then she walks a bit further, stopping to pick up all of her toys. Finally, she turns around and looks at her mother, who asks her if she remembers what it was that she was going to do. She says no. The mother reminds her, and she hangs up her coat.

Now consider a third example. A child is asked to get dressed in the morning. He takes off his pajamas, folds them up, then five minutes later, puts them back on again. If asked, he will tell you that he is supposed to get dressed and does not know why he put his pajamas back on.

In the first two instances, most people would interpret the situation as the children trying to do what they are told to do. The children are clearly trying to be compliant, but have apparently lost the means to translate what has been said to them into appropriate action. In circumstances more similar to the third example, however, children may be considered naughty and inattentive. Yet the mechanisms that are responsible for each of the behaviors may be essentially the same. Children appear to understand information (in these

---

8. E. Riley, "The long-term behavioral effects of prenatal alcohol exposure in rats," *Alcoholism Clin Exp Res* 14 (1990): 5; J. R. West, C. R. Goodlett, and J. P. Brandt, "New approaches to research on the long-term consequences of prenatal exposure to alcohol," *Alcoholism Clin Exp Res* 14 (1990): 674–689.

cases, requests to do something), yet are not able to process or act on the information in an appropriate way. The link between the information and the action is defective; these children have severe information-processing deficits.

Information processing deficits were first defined in the 1960s to represent learning disabilities in four domains: input, integration, memory, and output. Input represents the recording of information from the senses. Memory represents the storage of information for later use. Integration is the process of interpreting the input. Output requires appropriate use of language and motor skills.

Many people have a learning disability in one or two areas; children with FAS seem to have processing deficits in all areas. They have difficulty recording, interpreting, storing, retrieving, and using information. Many children will function well one day and poorly the next. A malfunctioning word processor offers an analogy to understand how these deficits affect a child's ability. Although full sentences are typed into it, only pieces of the sentences can be retrieved. Some information has not been saved or has unwittingly been stored in an inaccessible place. Special cues may bring it back, or perhaps one day it will suddenly reappear after hitting a random key. When only pieces of sentences are available, it is very difficult to understand the full meaning of the typed text. In the case of the situations described above, the children have grasped part of the request but not enough to complete it. Input, integration, and memory are all affected. The children may not have recorded the original information, or have recorded only pieces of it. They may have forgotten the request as they moved from one room to the next.

In some cases, parents will try to ensure compliance by asking a child to repeat directions. In our society, we often use a person's language skills as a measure of their abilities. Children with FAS often have very good expressive language—they talk a lot and seem social. But expressive language is not an accurate measure of receptive language, the ability to comprehend what other people say. Simply asking a child to repeat a direction does not ensure understanding. Without understanding there can be no compliance.

Both research and clinical reports have also suggested wide variation in learning abilities at different points in time. Periods of easy learning may be followed by periods of difficult learning.[9] From a parent's or teacher's point of view, such a child is very frustrating. He or she knows the alphabet perfectly one day, does not know it three days later, but is proficient again in a week or two. The information has been stored somewhere in the brain, but is not accessible to the child. These children are often inaccurately labeled forgetful and lazy. They are accused of being able to remember only what they want, not what others want.

In addition, alcohol-affected children are observed to repeat misbehaviors, suggesting that they never learn from their mistakes. However, the child with FAS may interpret information very concretely and be unable to generalize, to see the similarities and differences between situations. When we ask a child not to ride a bicycle in the street, we assume that the child can make certain observations about the situation; for example, that all streets are similar or that there are dangers from cars on all streets. A child with FAS may not pick up the cues which allow generalizing information from one street to another. In one case from our experience a six year old was discovered to be awake most nights, wandering the usually busy street down to his friend's house. He thought it perfectly conceivable that the friend would be available to play at 4 A.M., even though the cues that would make this nonsensical to us were all there. It was dark, no one else was on the street, and he had not eaten breakfast. If you had asked him if it was dark, he would have said yes. But he was unable to connect the relationship between the darkness and the availability of a playmate.

Another manifestation of this inability to see similarities and differences between situations may be the child's similar behavior towards both familiar people and strangers. We assume that the differences between people you know and those you do not are

---

9 M. Aronson and R. Olegard, "Fetal Alcohol Syndrome in pediatrics and child psychology," in *Alcohol and the Developing Brain*, A. Ryberg and E. Engel, eds. (New York: Raven Press, 1985).

obvious. But if you cannot pick up on the cues that tell you who is familiar and who is not, then you may treat everyone the same way.

Recognizing information-processing deficits suggests a shift in thinking about many behaviors which children with FAS show. First, the concept of a naughty, willful child diminishes. Instead, children are seen as misinterpreting what they hear or only being able to process certain pieces of information. They try to make sense out of what their brain is telling them, but that seldom makes sense to the rest of the world. The child who dresses for summer in a turtleneck and wool sweater is not just trying to be funny or willful. More likely, she simply has never made the connections between temperature, season, weather, and clothing.

As our understanding of the nature of the disabilities improves, our approach to teaching also changes. Rather than relying on the standard teaching method that emphasizes verbal learning, activity-based learning becomes more important. Using all of the senses for learning increases the likelihood of successful input. Anecdotal reports suggest that using pictures, music, and kinesthetic activities can improve learning for children with FAS.

This model further explains why a structured environment is so important to alcohol-affected children. Children with FAS do best with a highly consistent routine because such structure reduces the demands on the brain to process and respond to new information. In school, a consistent routine helps the child to concentrate on learning something new. The same activities should occur at the same time each day. Children benefit from having assigned seats in school that do not change during the year. Activity areas should be clearly marked. When changes in schedule or set-up need to occur, advance preparation eases the transition.

A familiar routine acts as an external structure for children who have difficulty internalizing behaviors. When the external structure remains relatively constant, children learn to count on it and are able to focus their energies on learning.

The following examples show how this theory might be translated into classroom techniques.

In the classroom, alcohol-affected children may:

**Become confused with directions involving more than one step.**
*Suggestion:* Give only one step at a time; put pictures on a small chart to represent all the stops involved in a process, e.g., getting ready for snack.

**Appear to know something one day, forget it the next, and then know it again after several more days. This will happen less often for events that the child is really interested in.**
*Suggestion:* Recognize that they are not intentionally forgetting but have lost the ability to retrieve information. Help learning take place in as many different modalities as possible (visual, tactile, auditory). Songs are learned more easily because the words are repeated and are reinforced by the music. Provide cues, prompts, and lots of rewards. Use tools such as typewriters, computers (that are consistent and predictable), and tape recordings to help compensate for poor memory.

**Repeat exactly what you have asked them to do, but they still cannot (or at least do not) complete the task.**
*Suggestion:* Recognize that their expressive verbal skills are better than their receptive ones. Rather than assuming willful defiance on the part of the child, try restating your request or breaking it down into smaller steps. Even better, demonstrate what you want, so the child has a visual image.

**Have difficulty doing anything that involves arranging, sequencing, or taking turns.**
*Suggestion:* Know that the concept of order is often something the child just cannot understand. Provide ongoing visual cues to make learning easier. Recognize that these children may require multiple repetitions of information before they know it.

**Repeat words, questions, or actions over and over.**
*Suggestion:* Some children perseverate or get stuck in their thoughts or actions because their brain has difficulty processing information. It may also be a sign that their central nervous system has been overloaded. No matter how much you try to explain, they will be unable to absorb the ideas at this time. Try not to add any additional stimulation.

## Conclusion

Alcohol exposure *in utero* is associated with a broad range of central nervous system abnormalities. The resultant problems with information processing help to explain the neuro-behavioral problems that children with FAS may have and offer a useful framework in which to understand these problems while we begin to develop therapeutic strategies.

Fetal alcohol syndrome is a frustrating, complex disorder. In the midst of this frustration, it is important to focus on the abilities of children with FAS rather than the disabilities. Learning may occur differently and slowly, but it does occur. Collaboration among parents, clinicians, and researchers will ultimately provide the key to understanding the complexities of this disorder. Together we will move towards maximizing the potential of all alcohol-affected children.

# Growing with FAS
## Parent to Parent Advice
### PAMELA GROUPE GROVES

*Pamela Groupe Groves and her husband Stan have adopted
six children, including in 1984 an infant girl and her brother, a
toddler, both with a diagnosis of fetal alcohol syndrome. They
have been foster parents to many children with disabilities. In
1989, Ms. Groves started a newsletter,* Growing with FAS, *to
overcome the isolation of those caring for children with FAS/
FAE and provide a way to exchange ideas. To ask questions or
share your thoughts and successes, write: Pamela Groves, 7802
S.E. Taylor, Portland, Oregon 97215 U.S.A. To receive a sample
copy, please include a self-addressed stamped envelope.*

"WILL YOU TAKE THEM?"

That is what the caseworker asked me. One child was an infant girl on the edge of "failure to thrive." Her brother, a toddler
with serious developmental delays, showed such odd behavior that
his current foster mother complained she could not handle him.
Almost as an afterthought, the caseworker mentioned that both children had a diagnosis of full FAS.

I had read one newspaper article about FAS and probably knew
as much about it as the caseworker did. My husband and I soon
discovered that parenting these children was unlike anything we
had experienced as adoptive and foster parents, even though we
had cared for many children with developmental delays, learning
disabilities, and emotional complications. But we bonded together
and adopted them.

37

We had read everything we could find about FAS/FAE but found that most of the information was about prenatal and infancy issues. We wanted to know what FAS would mean in the long term and how to help our children reach their potential. We did not know anyone else parenting children with FAS and stumbled along, trying to find techniques that helped. We knew others must also be struggling along, feeling isolated, searching for answers. The idea for a newsletter germinated, and in 1989 we published the first issue of *Growing with FAS*.

In this chapter, I will describe the problems, feelings, and ideas that readers of this newsletter have shared with me. Some letters are from parents struggling to cope with their children's needs and their own worries and emotions. Other letters come from grandparents or relatives who suspect a loved child has FAS/FAE. Some writers offer their own exciting discoveries such as a strategy, a medication, or an emotional attitude that has made a great difference for them and may make a difference for someone else. In this uncharted territory, we all benefit from communicating with others who have traveled this terrain.

## Getting the Diagnosis: Knowledge is Power

Many people write about the pain and frustration of finding a diagnosis, but all agree that the search for a knowledgeable diagnosis is well worth the effort. Diagnosing FAS/FAE can be difficult. Children with many other disabilities, including hyperactivity and attention deficit disorder, show similar symptoms. Some of these problems, such as lead poisoning, can be remedied with proper medical attention. A diagnosis of FAS/FAE, on the other hand, means irreversible brain damage. But the diagnosis creates understanding and begins the process of acceptance and adjustment.

We had the benefit of knowing from the beginning that our two children had a diagnosis of FAS. We were not really aware what this diagnosis would mean for all of us, but at least we knew we would encounter special needs along the way. Many parents have not had this advantage. They often face a difficult time of suspecting, denying, seeking a diagnosis, and then accepting and learning. I have received many letters from parents[1] in various stages of this process:

> We took our son in for an evaluation and I really wasn't impressed. I went very well prepared with photos, school reports, data on biological parents, daily logs, and so on. The doctor didn't seem interested in much of it.
>
> In the beginning he asked about IQ and I explained my son is not a good test taker. I told him various behaviors lower his score drastically.
>
> After a five minute examination, the doctor concluded that there was no chemical imbalance or FAS/FAE. How he could determine that is beyond me!
>
> His theory was that my son's problems stem from a low IQ. He said that he does have FAE-like characteristics but due to the fact that he is not short in stature, FAE is ruled out. I explained to him that from all the literature I had read, being small is a supporting characteristic, not a determining one. He disagreed.
>
> I left that appointment very frustrated. Why wouldn't he listen to all the facts for the past nine years? Why wasn't he interested in the school reports? How could he conclude all of our son's problems are caused by low IQ? He thought I was just a hysterical mother who didn't know what she was talking about.
>
> All I know is that I can't live like this any longer and my only option is to send him off to a place that can help him. More and more people are telling me that I've got to do it and the pressure to just wash my hands of him is almost unbearable. They say that I've done all that is humanly possible and it's time to give up.
>
> Darlene A. Clark

*My Response to Darlene*

Unfortunately you have experienced first hand one of the problems in finding a diagnosis. It can be difficult to locate an experienced specialist.

I have no way of knowing whether this doctor's diagnosis is accurate. I do know you have reservations about the examination and results. If I were you, I would trust that instinct and look for another diagnosis.

Try to obtain referral from someone working in the field of FAS/FAE or a parent with a child who has FAS/FAE. If you cannot

---

1. These letters are used with parents' permission. We have used the parents' name or "anonymous" as they have requested. Identifying details have been changed in many instances.

find someone to give you a referral, investigate and interview beforehand, behavioral pediatricians, developmental pediatricians, and dysmorphologists. Try a nearby university with a medical school. You may have to travel to another city.

In the meantime, please take care of yourself, too. It will not benefit anyone if you burn yourself out! Some mothers say they are revitalized by going out for morning coffee alone or taking a bubble bath when everyone is off for the day and indulging in a good cry, if needed, while soaking in the bubbles. Some make a long distance telephone call to a friend, browse in a favorite bookstore or write a letter to *Growing with FAS*. Working mothers say it's worth the income loss to take a half a day off.

Not only parents seek diagnosis. I have gotten many letters from grandparents and relatives who suspect children have FAS/FAE. Some fear to say anything. They know that the adopted child was so desperately wanted. One grandmother wrote that she could see her grandchildren only through the babysitter:

> One thing that may set me apart from other grandparents is that I do not have free access to my grandsons with FAE. The parents deny me any involvement, considering me an ogre for noticing that something is wrong with them. I believe my daughter-in-law is FAE. There is no characteristic I've heard of that she doesn't possess.
>
> Anonymous

*My Response*

I understand totally your temptation to self diagnose your grandsons and your daughter-in-law as FAS/FAE. You may be correct or incorrect. It is important that we do not get into self diagnosis. Only a professional can diagnose with accuracy. The problems may be FAS/FAE or may be from another source.

Even though you are not currently in a position to secure or encourage diagnosis, you can use what you know about FAS/FAE to deal with the symptoms. Your knowledge of FAS/FAE can better help you understand how your daughter-in-law operates and thinks. If she has FAE or even if her effects are from some other condition, she is operating from a different perspective than you are in all areas of life. Understanding this may help you to relate to her better and find ways to communicate. If you can mend the relationship, you will have better access to your grandsons. You will be able to assist them in their development, and, if the parents become open to FAS/FAE, you will be there to offer support and information.

Some grandparents find that patience brings results. Over time, their son or daughter stops denying the problem and they are able to provide information and support of great value to their grandchildren:

> I am the grandmother of three affected girls. Their mother stayed on alcohol and drugs the entire nine months of pregnancy with each of them. My son has remarried this last year and now has his girls with him. They bought a home and live close to me. He found a wonderful lady who is working very hard to help these three granddaughters of mine. Our biggest problem has been for my son to admit that they have a problem. Things got so bad that he finally had to ask for help. I begged him to seek some type of counseling.
>
> The seven-year-old is the most affected. She is such a pretty little girl and so loving. At other times she can be a total mess. She can disrupt the family to the point of almost making all of us crazy. It is so hard to look at my granddaughters and tell myself that there are things that are never going to be better.
>
> I went to the school last year and took some of your FAS newsletters with me. I wanted the school to know that my granddaughter had problems so they should not treat her as a mean, lying, cheating child. I wanted her treated as a child with special problems. The special education teacher read the newsletters and asked me to bring in *The Broken Cord*. My granddaughter's teacher chose not to read the materials and now I am glad she is out of her classroom. We are now trying to get help for her.
>
> I cannot tell you how glad I was to find your newsletter. At first my son just glanced at them and denied that this was his kids' problem. But now he reads every article very carefully and sometimes takes them for the school counselors to read.
>
> Marie Fetters

*My Response to Marie*
> I appreciate your sharing, openness and dedication to your granddaughters. Now that your son is getting out of the denial stage I urge both of you to begin investigating where you can go for an official diagnosis. You can give the diagnosis to the schools, which will mean easier access to services.

## GETTING OTHERS TO ACCEPT AND REMEMBER THE DIAGNOSIS

Even when you have a diagnosis, others may not accept or even remember it. My own daughter's well-meaning special education teacher kept insisting her slow cognitive pace was just laziness. Her memory problems also became an issue, and it took more than half a year to convince the teacher that my daughter was not forgetting the multiplication tables on purpose. What it took to change this teacher's awareness was time, my own educational efforts, the teacher's experience with my daughter, independent testing results, and conferences with evaluators and the special education supervisor. But it was worth it. When the teacher's understanding of the situation changed, my daughter's attitude toward this teacher and school itself improved.

A diagnosis of FAS/FAE is especially hard for others to accept because the children are so sociable and inconsistent in their behavior:

> My four-year-old grandson was in an Early Intervention Program and then went into a special needs class. He is bright and charming. Because he has had constant one on one attention from my husband and me, he can fool a lot of people into thinking he can do more than he can. We have become very frustrated trying to make people aware of some of his problems, especially when it comes to his safety.
>
> Anonymous

> I know our daughter was diagnosed FAS, but I seem to keep trying to convince myself that maybe it is FAE because she functions well most of the time. I am still confused as to the symptoms.
> She is almost six and has lived with us nearly two years. In that two years, she has many times displayed symptoms that I guess were caused from FAS. All along my husband and I have been doubting that it truly is FAS that is causing her to act the ways that she does. Two days ago she experienced her first time at truly "losing it." As I write, I am having so much difficulty fighting back the tears. I want so much to be able to help her, but I don't know how.
>
> Shirley Hogan

*My Response to Shirley*
Many parents write to me saying they have to continually remind themselves that the child has FAS/FAE. As the child

grows, the natural inclination is to expect the child to take on new responsibilities but often the child cannot meet all of the new challenges and parents have to relearn the child's strengths and weaknesses.

If parents forget, can we really be surprised when teachers, extended family members and friends "forget" and expect more than can be given?

Here are some suggestions my readers and I have come up with to help parents work with the school system:

- Do not overlook your child's teacher in helping you maneuver through the school system. Cultivate this relationship and make it as positive as possible. Many parents have found the classroom or special education teacher to be their best ally.
- Educate yourself on the special education guidelines, regulations and laws of your school district and state and federal agencies.
- If you are having trouble getting a teacher to understand a particular issue or disability, schedule a conference with the teacher and a special education supervisor in the district and ask the specialist to explain the condition and how to work with it.
- Seek an outside evaluation if necessary and request specific suggestions on how to work with your child. Set up a conference and take the results directly to the school yourself rather than have the results mailed to the school. If the agency is slow in getting the evaluation into written form, ask for a written summary and a contact person the teacher can telephone for details.
- Many organizations offer parent advocate services and other assistance in helping you learn of your child's educational rights and help that may be available. Some can refer you to attorneys who specialize in the school issues. Contact your school district office or local Association for Children with Learning Disabilities to ask if your area has an advocacy association.

You can also contact national agencies. Some suggestions are located in Appendix II.

## Getting Support: On the FAS Path

When we moved to an urban area from a small rural community, I thought to myself, "This is great! In this large district, professionals will be well educated in how to work with children with FAS." At our first special education team meeting, I could have fallen off my chair when one of the school specialists said, "This is the first child with FAS we have worked with." Later in the school year, after I had educated my son's teacher fully on the effects of FAS, I could have cracked my head on the table when she said, "Well, he had a choice to make about the appropriate behavioral decision."

**Blaming the Parents**

Not only will people not understand the children's problems but they may also blame you:

> I went to the school on the day our adopted daughter entered special education. I talked to her teacher, gave her articles explaining FAE and explained how our daughter might act out. The teacher said that she understood. The first time our daughter acted out we were told that she behaved in this manner because of her upbringing in our home and we were presented as neglectful parents.
>
> Lawrence Gellerstein

> Our adopted son is five years old. We have been subjected to untold abuse and attempted exploitation by others. Our marriage counselor told us our marriage was on the rocks. Otherwise, why was our child so bad off—despite the fact that we have two happy, healthy birth children.
> The last time we went out and carried on our behavior modification program of removing the tantruming child from the store (too much stimulation) and then ignoring him until he was ready to cooperate, we got turned into child protective services! We must be monsters to have such an angry child.
>
> Anonymous

*My Response*

You are definitely not alone in having been confronted by social service agencies speculating on child abuse. I receive many letters on this topic. My suggestion is to be prepared ahead of time with copies of evaluations and the diagnosis as well as information on FAS/FAE to be kept in a specific file.

When you are in public and he has a tantrum or behaves inappropriately, you might say something such as, "I know you are mad because you cannot have that toy today. We will come back in when you feel better." It is crucial to remain calm and in control of yourself.

One mom wrote to me that she was worried about what the new neighbor would think the first time she heard her daughter have one of her temper tantrums. I suggested she take a welcome-to-the-neighborhood baked treat over, and, in the conversation, work in the fact that she has adopted children with special needs and explain the behaviors. It turned out the new neighbor had personal experience with special needs and both found a friend.

### Handling Your Own Emotions

One moment my own son can be so endearing and act in such constructive ways, I wonder if there has been no brain damage, no ill effects of alcohol, that he is almost average. Then the next moment his behavior reminds me that he is on his own railroad track. His track is laid down next to mine and at times connects with mine but the pattern is his own. For me, this is the crux of the problem: finding the connections so our tracks meet as often as possible and traveling along peacefully when they do not.

Some of my most valuable letters show the ways in which parents have learned to hang on as they ride this emotional roller coaster:

> Our twenty-year-old adopted son is living away from home in not the best circumstances but we have had to let go for our sanity and his. He has been in jail and picked up for warrants on unpaid fines. He walked out of high school one day and said he wasn't going back. He had graduated but we had him staying longer to take vocational education classes.
>
> We are still supportive but with a new focus. He knows we care and calls when things have hit bottom. This is hard on me, especially, but I'm becoming a better parent to him when each day isn't filled with chaos.
>
> Diane

> I believe everything happens for a reason. I thank God we have our son. I think giving him up was the ultimate act of love for his mother.

I try not to think about the future. We deal only with today, with the thought that our child is loving and kind as well as difficult to live with at times.

Whatever alcohol has done to him, it has not taken away his ability to love and be loved.

Annie Fitzgerald

### Giving Yourself a Break

Parents on the FAS path need respite care, and it is hard to come by. Here are suggestions the readers and I have come up with:

- If you cannot find someone to babysit while you leave the house, hire a young teenager to help at home while you are there or take with you if you go out. The teenager's sole duty is to supervise and occupy the child.
- Contact all the special needs agencies in your area to find a respite care center or organize respite care through an FAS/FAE support group.
- Look for a summer camp that provides services to children with special needs. Check the camp guides in your library.
- Contact your local university to see if students may need to work with a child with special needs as part of their educational experience.
- Contact scouting programs or religious and community service programs to see if a leader is willing to work with your child or be a mentor. Because children with FAS/FAE are often gullible and susceptible to abuse, select a mentor with care. Stay involved and provide some supervision. Appear occasionally without prior notice.
- If you are church attendees, call churches to see if there is a church in your area with a program for people with special needs.
- If your child is adopted under an adoption subsidy, ask if you can add in costs for respite care or summer camp. Your child might also qualify for social security disability. Contact social security in your area.

## MEDICATION: THE BIG QUESTION

In their desperate search for solutions, some parents have turned to medication with the assistance of a knowledgeable doctor. A number of specialists in the field actively discourage medication. Some fear parents will latch on to medications as a quick cure and ignore other techniques valuable in the long run, including developing support systems and coping skills. Those specialists who do turn to medication usually recommend as well the use of other techniques such as behavioral management. All caution that medication is not an option for everyone and that finding the right medication and dosage requires trial and error.

When our son was attending first grade in a small rural school, his teacher had the time and temperament to work with his attention deficit. He could rarely sit in the chair at his desk for more than a couple of minutes. He was constantly in movement—slouching over the back of his chair or reclining over his desk, on his desk, or under his desk. During silent reading time, he did not read books. He played with them as if they were blocks. His only successes were recess and math when the class used manipulatives.

When we moved to an urban school, I worried because the teacher probably would not be able to deal with his attention deficit in a large class. By coincidence we had scheduled a developmental examination at a medical university for late August. To handle his moderate to severe attention deficit disorder, the specialists recommended medication together with behavior management. Fortunately, our pediatrician was willing to try medication, a low dose of ritalin, with the goal of increasing my son's attention span. The results were impressive and immediate. My son was able to sit and focus through a lesson. He was able to follow through on assignments. In fact, many people started to compliment him on his excellent study skills.

Now in fourth grade, my son still takes medication on school days, but he does not use it during vacations. The doctor would like to phase him off in a year or two. Right now, we are continuing with the medication. His teacher says he can definitely tell when my son forgets to take it.

Other parents write of similar turn-arounds:

When our son first came to live with us at the age of three, he put pennies in the toaster, cut holes in our water bed, and made money and possessions disappear. By the time my son was ten, he was shoplifting, taking things from classmates and family, and having destructive temper tantrums. He kicked holes the size of a dinner plate in his bedroom walls. He played with matches and lit "torches" on the school bus with matches and hair spray. He attempted to forge a check. On one of his more interesting escapades, he took $200 from my dresser and purchased a RAT from one of the neighbor children!

Most of his peers ostracized him. Notes from his teachers said, "He is not trying . . . won't make a consistent effort . . . is easily distracted . . . has no respect for others' property. . . . "

Finally and hesitantly we decided with our behavioral pediatrician to try medication. The doctor advised us of the possible side effects: appetite loss, dizziness, and stomach pains were among them. She also cautioned us, "This doesn't always work for the child with FAS/FAE."

In his case the positive effects from the time release Dexedrine were almost immediate. His peers began to trust and include him in activities. He was not longer disruptive in the classroom and his teacher became his ADVOCATE!

People are quick to tell me, "He is too thin." He was once my best eater, choosing fruits and vegetables over junk foods. His appetite is missing and his healthy eating habits have all but disappeared.

Still, the benefits outweigh the complications. In the beginning, the changes were strictly behavioral, but, in time, his school grades began to improve. His ability to concentrate and stay on task made the difference.

There will always be personal battles he must face, but we haven't had a single $200 rat in the house since he began.

My son made an important distinction early in the process. "Mom," he said, "don't call these drugs. It's medicine. I don't take drugs."

I sometimes feel guilty having him medicated all the time. Am I keeping him from being himself?

Penny Line

*My Response to Penny*
> I do not think you are keeping him from being himself. I think you are freeing him to be himself.

Some professionals worry about the side effects of medication. Our daughter was on phenobarbital to control seizures, and I found it difficult to tell if there were side effects. When she was transitioned to tegretol, it was as if she had been in a dulled state. She gained a new sparkle and zest for learning after the phenobarbital was phased out. Many specialists have legitimate concerns about medication so approach it with care, expect a period of trial and error, and maintain constant supervision.

## COPING WITH ADULT CHILDREN

Parents find they must continue advocating for their child far past the time most children are becoming responsible for themselves:

> Our son is now nineteen years old and a high school graduate, whew! There were times I thought we would never make it that far. He actually finished school on a real positive note, having joined the marching band and learned to play five instruments. The experts said he could never do it. We have always fought the school's effort to limit him, always hoping he could reach some of his dreams. While reality clearly shows his limits, I am glad we withheld our doubts and fears and allowed him to try the band. The doctors always told us that musical instruments would prove too frustrating for him, but he proved the doctors wrong.
>
> I guess I thought once we got him through school, some of the hard work would ease up. Boy, was I wrong! The challenges of having an "adult" child with FAS are even bigger than school struggles. At least the school environment provided a little buffer zone of security. We have had a year of our son being battered by a world that can not or will not try to accept him. He doesn't want pity and there is no mercy, not in the job market or any place else!
>
> He finally found a job this summer at Disneyland and we're hoping it will continue into fall. The world expects him to act like an adult and his brain doesn't know how. It is heart rending to watch him try to function socially and suffer rejection and misunderstanding.
>
> Marilyn Moore

*My Response to Marilyn*

You could brainstorm ideas on how he might use his skill and enjoyment in music. Could he be a tutor, assist a band instructor, help in a music store?

Employment can be a problem for many adolescents and adults with FAS/FAE. Many are highly motivated but have difficulty learning the routines and behaviors required.

Try contacting Team Work, a program which recruits and trains mentors to help youth with disabilities prepare for, find, and stay on jobs. Team Work programs are available in cities like Washington, D.C.; Duluth, Minnesota; Boulder, Colorado; and Miami, Florida, and the program is spreading rapidly. Contact Team Work, Foundation for Exceptional Children, 1920 Association Drive, Reston, Virginia 22091 703-620-1054.

## PARENTS' DISCOVERIES

Our greatest source of knowledge is each other. Parents themselves make discoveries like these, beginning with my own:

### Sign Language

Our youngest girl is severely delayed in language and speech. We discovered by accident the benefits of sign language. She was in a developmental preschool with two deaf children where sign language was used all the time. Our daughter soon began using some of the simple signs for words she did not say. The sign seemed to provide a bridge between nonverbal and verbal language expression. Soon afterward, she would replace the sign with the verbal word. As her speech developed, we encouraged her to use impromptu gestures of her own design to help her communicate her message. She uses them as a bridge and drops them when her developing speech makes the gestures obsolete.

### Eye Contact

Eye contact was my most exciting discovery. When I want my son to understand, I raise his chin so he no longer is looking at the floor. When he looks at me, nothing else seems to interfere.

Anonymous

**Making Abstractions Concrete**

As my child enters adolescence, I am finding that his needs in the area of abstractions can not be overemphasized. When he is anxious about an upcoming event, we've found it helpful to use his visual skills. We hang a calendar in a conspicuous spot and let him "x" off the days beforehand. Other times we use the calendar, with a piece of candy attached to each day, to ease his tension through a difficult period and help him visualize the final date.

Recently my husband found another way to apply this principle. He took the video camera to one of our son's soccer games and kept the camera on our son throughout the game, rather than on the soccer ball or plays. On that tape, our child was involved in one significant game play. Afterwards, we rewound the tape to that spot and played it repeatedly in slow motion.

Seeing himself on video gave him a confidence in his ability that our words had been unable to communicate. I realized we had stumbled onto another means of turning an abstraction into a concrete visualization that he could understand.

Penny Line

## EMPHASIZING STRENGTHS

Parents write about the difficult behaviors of children with FAS/FAE, but they also express a fundamental respect and admiration for their toughness and their strengths. These clusters of strengths seem to appear often in children with FAS/FAE. I cannot stress enough, however, that each child is unique. You must observe your child to determine individual abilities and ways to build on them. The result may be a life-long hobby or possible employment.

**Athletic Abilities**

Many children with FAS/FAE thrive in individual sports including swimming, gymnastics, dance, and track. For some children, the repetitive motion in activities such as swimming provide a soothing effect similar to the stress reduction obtained through perserveration. Taking part in athletics uses excess energy, builds self-esteem, develops a life-long enjoyment, and provides opportunities for social life. Try to find a mentor in your child's sport, taking care to provide some supervision to prevent taking advantage of the child's vulnerability.

## Creative Talents

Many children with FAS/FAE have creative talents in different areas, perhaps because they see the world differently. Often children have musical abilities, like the boy who learned to play five instruments when the doctor thought he could not. Some children have artistic abilities in drawing and pottery. Creativity may be expressed in inventing things, storytelling, and even in cooking. Adapt to what the child can do. Many parents have children with FAS/FAE use the microwave or make food that does not require cooking over a hot burner. If the child has trouble getting thoughts into writing, provide a tape recorder and share the tapes with willing listeners such as grandparents or save them for future memories.

## Manipulating Objects

Often children with FAS/FAE are good at building and constructing with Legos, blocks, and anything they can take apart and put together. My children adore hammering and building so we provided them with the frame of a playhouse and materials which they use to build, tear down, and rebuild the walls. Many enjoy gardening with its watering, raking, weeding, and planting. Children can garden in your yard or window box, assist neighbors, or work in a community garden project.

Keep the strengths of the children in mind. Even though children with FAS/FAE may have severe memory problems and some cannot remember the multiplication tables or follow lengthy directions, they often have an excellent long-term memory for events and activities. My children often astound me with their memories of past family activities and our previous homes.

Even though children with FAS/FAE are said to lack conscience, many have great empathy for others and a deep sense of justice, especially before hard experience forces them to build a barrier around themselves. The child with FAS/FAE is often the one who identifies with the scapegoat in the classroom or the child unjustly treated by the teacher. My son loves and identifies with the beast who is saved from death when he learns kindness in *Beauty and the Beast*, the handicapped son of the gangster mother in *Goonies* who comes to be loved and accepted by the Goonie gang, and the baby dinosaur in *Land Before Time* who finds a family to love him.

Children with FAS/FAE are often devoted and loyal to their pets, friends, family, and spouses. They are often socially engaging, verbal, and enjoy knowing a variety of people, especially if negative reactions resulting from inappropriate behavior have not caused them to withdraw. They will often make friends with other children who have been left out of the group because they are different. These friendships can be difficult for parents to supervise but can be rewarding for the child.

The letters I receive contain many words of frustration, confusion and pain but they also express love, hope, and commitment. The parents and family members I hear from are the most dedicated people I have ever known. They have looked inside themselves at their own values, experiences, abilities, and history. They, as well as their children, are growing with FAS.

# Cindy's Story
## FAE and College
### ANNE RUGGLES GERE

*Anne Ruggles Gere, a professor of English and professor of education at the University of Michigan in Ann Arbor, has combined parenting and professional life for the past twenty years. She received her B.A. from Colby College, her M.A. from Colgate University, and her Ph.D. from the University of Michigan. She lives with her husband and children in Farmington Hills, Michigan.*

I will tell you something about stories,
[he said]
They aren't just entertainment.
Don't be fooled.
They are all we have, you see,
all we have to fight off
 illness and death.
You don't have anything
if you don't have the stories.[1]

ON A SUNNY DAY IN MAY OF 1992, my husband and I watched with button-bursting pride as our daughter Cindy walked across the platform to receive her associate of fine arts degree from the Institute of American Indian Arts (IAIA). Actually she walked across the platform twice, once to collect her diploma and once to accept the Azalea Thorpe New Memorial Award for Fiber Arts. She also stood to receive recognition from the Educational Testing Service Talent

---

1. Leslie Marmon Silko, *Ceremony* (New York: Penguin, 1977).

Roster, the National Dean's List and the IAIA Dean's Honor List. Like every graduate, Cindy wore her traditional tribal regalia, a buckskin dress she researched, designed, and created. This, combined with her flowered beadwork belt, beaded headband and moccasins, completed her prize-winning outfit. As the Red Leaf Takoja drum group performed its honor song for the graduates, I thought back over the many steps that led us to this graduation platform in Santa Fe.

Cindy joined our family when she was three and a half. She had been placed with a foster family right after birth and was then adopted by another family at age three. When that family fell apart, Cindy resided briefly in another foster home before she came to us. Adoption was a first choice for my husband and me, and having said that we wanted to be there for an older (and probably minority) child who needed us, we were delighted when the social worker called nearly a year before we expected to become parents, saying, "We have a little Indian girl for you."

In reviewing what she knew of the health history of Cindy's birth family, the social worker mentioned that one sibling had a hearing loss, another had kidney problems, and the mother had had tuberculosis. She explained that the mother had been involved with several different men and the identity of Cindy's father was uncertain. It appeared that Cindy was placed in foster care because her mother was overwhelmed with the responsibility of caring for her eight other children. The social worker could not explain why the birth mother decided to release Cindy for adoption after three years, but when we learned (much later) that Cindy has a sibling about three years younger, we guessed that the new baby eliminated any thought of reclaiming Cindy. We knew Cindy had received excellent physical care during her first three years, her APGAR (Appearance, Pulse, Grimace, Activity, Respiratory effort) score was ten on a scale of ten, and we had no reason to assume that any of the family health problems mentioned would present difficulties. The social worker may have mentioned or we may have intuited from her description of the lifestyle that Cindy's birth mother was alcoholic, but we did not give it any thought. After all, it was 1972, and we had never heard of FAS or FAE.

I lost almost ten pounds trying to keep up with Cindy when she first arrived. We teasingly called her "Zoomer" and "The Black Jet," delighting in her lively interest in the world. "Use your words" became a frequent request as we noticed Cindy's difficulty with language. She had difficulty remembering the names of even her closest friends and often would say things like "when we have toast and cereal in the morning" because she could not think of the word "breakfast." It was usually easier for her to grab what she wanted than ask for something. Driven by what I can now identify as impulsivity, she stuck her finger into the middle of nearly every cake and pie I baked. In her more quiet moments she would hum the same three toneless notes or click a ballpoint pen top again and again and again—perseveration I later learned to call it. Although momentarily annoying, this perseveration, a quality common among FAE or FAS children, developed into one of Cindy's most valuable qualities—tenacity.

Because Cindy was our first child, we had no timetable of expectations for her to achieve certain skills. We noticed that it took her a very long time to learn to tie her shoes and that distinguishing right from left and telling time on a dial clock seemed nearly impossible for her, but we assumed that the trauma of her early life was simply taking its toll. Our pediatrician, in response to my concern about her continued bedwetting, assured me that he had never known of any bedwetters enrolling in college. Her Montessori teacher suggested that she have an extra year in kindergarten because she was "not very motivated toward academic learning." Accordingly, when we moved to Seattle, we enrolled Cindy for a second year of kindergarten.

That was the year we began to suspect that something was seriously wrong. Even with the maturity of the extra year and a very supportive teacher, Cindy was not learning to read; she was not even exhibiting prereading skills. Had I known then what I know now, I would have removed her from the school's Distar Program for reading. Even though I was a professor of English at the University of Washington and knew quite a bit about reading, I hesitated to question the teacher or principal about the curriculum. They clearly cared about Cindy, and I did not want to seem ungrateful for their support by questioning their decisions. Still, I knew from reading aloud to Cindy that her strongest skill was contextual prediction, and decoding was her weakest. The Distar Program's emphasis on phonics made reading very difficult for Cindy, and sentences such as "The dog dug the mug" confused her with their nonsense. But she kept at it, and we kept searching for the right teacher, the right school, the key that would unlock everything.

Despite everyone's best efforts, Cindy kept slipping farther and farther behind her age-mates. While they were reading fluently, she still struggled with long and short vowels. Math was worse. Learning the basic facts of addition and subtraction took years, and she could never be sure that what she struggled to memorize on Monday would be hers on Wednesday. She continued to have difficulty retrieving words for what she wanted to say, and she would often try an opening line such as "When I . . . " four, five, six, and seven times before she could find the language to continue.

By the time Cindy was in the second grade, we began saying to ourselves and to Cindy's teachers that she had a learning disability. This label gave us a way to acknowledge Cindy's spiked learning patterns and her obvious difficulties with many school tasks and at the same time affirm her many abilities. "After all," we told ourselves, "smart people can have learning disabilities." Consigned to the "resource room," Cindy began the first of the never-ending series of tests, each of them, in her word, humiliating. Somehow, though, she kept on trying, impressing and pleasing her teachers even when she had her own way of proceeding. The teacher who asked her class to illustrate the word "bash" received a stack of drawings featuring blunt objects and crumpled bodies, but Cindy's paper showed a party in full swing. In 1977, our pediatrician suggested that we take Cindy to see Dr. David Smith, a pioneer in research on fetal alcohol syndrome, at the University of Washington Medical School. Our pediatrician suspected that Cindy might have this syndrome, one about which we knew nothing.

Dr. Smith confirmed our pediatrician's suspicions, but he was not able to give us a great deal of information. At that time the FAS or FAE distinction did not exist, and he simply said that she had a moderately severe case of FAS. Today Cindy would be described as FAE because she lacks the marked physical features of FAS but has the family history and neurological damage characteristic of FAE. With Dr. Smith's diagnosis we had another name for Cindy's difficulties, but we still could not get much useful advice on how to help her, so we followed our own instincts. After three years in public school, where a child had to be two grade levels behind before she could qualify for special help, Cindy switched to a small private school specializing in children with learning disabilities. We felt that the social costs of being in the resource room were too high for Cindy, especially because the public school grouped emotionally disturbed, learning disabled, and physically handicapped children in the same room. The private school provided a healthier social environment, and Cindy learned to control some of her fidgeting and impulsive behavior, but she made slow progress academically. Reading remained an excruciatingly difficult process for her, and addition and subtraction facts continued to elude her.

After a couple of years, Cindy outgrew being in a school with fewer than twelve children, and she was able to enter a regular class in a public school with the help of its principal, our friend and neighbor. A Chapter One teacher worked with her an hour or so each day, but the rest of the time Cindy functioned with a heterogeneous group in a self-contained classroom. Although she felt awkward about being a couple of years older than the other kids, she made friends and fit in fairly well.

A life-defining moment for Cindy occurred when a police officer conducted a three-day school assembly series on substance abuse. He appeared the first day dressed like a pimp, the second like a drug lord, and the third day in uniform. I do not know what he said, but he persuaded Cindy to avoid drugs and alcohol, a stance she maintains to this day. We had begun explaining to Cindy that she was especially vulnerable to alcoholism and modeled responsible alcohol use at home, but this police officer made our task easy. Meanwhile, the academic scene did not improve. The homework sessions got worse and worse, with a frustrated Cindy in tears and her parents desperately trying to help her learn the multiplication tables or the five spelling words she had been assigned. We wrestled with the double grief of knowing that Cindy could not keep up with her peers and that we, her strongest advocates, could not make it possible for her to learn the answer to 7 x 8. We hired a tutor to relieve the pressure on our family life. Cindy switched to a private school for junior high. ("I have to wear a uniform, but I don't have to pray Catholic," she explained.) By this time my husband and I had become much more assertive about Cindy's education. We made an appointment with each of her teachers and explained how she would learn best. We prepared a list of things that they could do to help Cindy and implored them to call us when they saw her having difficulties. Even at a private school, even with our impassioned pleas, we could not always get teachers to do simple things such as assign her to a seat in the front of the room, reorient her when she became distracted, and write assignments on the board in addition to giving them orally. Some teachers, however, were very receptive. A few teachers accepted Cindy's invented spelling without a punitive response, and one included her in the school play. Still, relationships with her peers were not easy, and one day Cindy found the word "squaw" written on her locker.

We had always tried to reinforce Cindy's American Indian heritage. We pointed to handsome Native Americans and tried to shield her from the broken alcoholic Indians on First Avenue in Seattle. I bought records of Indian music and books of Indian stories. We sought Indian friends and took Cindy to a powwow and Indian art exhibits. One evening, though, when James Welch, the Native American author, was coming to dinner, an adolescent Cindy announced that she did not want to see him. "I don't like being an Indian," she said.

My heart sank at this declaration because I knew that Cindy could never develop a fully integrated personality without accepting herself as an Indian. Far from wanting to transform Cindy into a little white girl, my husband and I wanted her to claim her Indian heritage. Rather than despairing completely, however, I told myself that Cindy's assertion reflected the normal adolescent need to be just like everyone else and hoped that as she matured Cindy would grow to value being an Indian.

We had always intended to adopt a second Native American child but moved slowly because we felt that any younger sibling was likely to crowd Cindy. When Cindy was eight and seemed secure enough to handle competition, we discovered that changes in Washington state law would make it impossible for us to adopt another Indian. Accordingly, Sam arrived from Korea when he was sixteen months old. We felt that Cindy and Sam would see an ancient kinship as they looked at one another across the dinner table. Our assumption that seven years and the gender difference would protect Cindy from intellectual upstaging was quickly dispelled, however. When Sam was about six, he began reading to Cindy, and we realized that a sibling of any age would quickly outstrip her academically. Still, both of them seemed comfortable with this arrangement, and, thanks to an enduring mutual respect, they maintain a good relationship.

Resigned to the fact that school would probably always be a trial for Cindy, we tried to find other areas where she could succeed. Gymnastics and modern dance worked well, but ballet did not. We tried Suzuki violin and gave up after a few painful sessions. Determined that my daughter not be the athletic failure I was, I insisted that we organize a soccer team. Cindy enjoyed looking at the sky and playing in the mud puddles, but she never seemed very interested in kicking the ball. Girl Scouts failed, but art courses at the local recreation center succeeded. Finally, when Cindy was about fourteen, we asked her what she would really like to do. "Three things," she said, "I want to take voice lessons, learn karate, and join the Police Explorers." We made all the arrangements, and Cindy unleashed her lilting soprano voice, earned a brown belt and received numerous awards for police work. She does not exactly read music, but she learned, memorized, and performed songs well enough to win local competitions. Karate gave her a sense of control over her body and, I think, helped her make further progress with her physical impulsivity. Police work made her feel powerful. "I feel," she said, "as if I'm right at the center of things when I'm with the Explorers." Led by a Seattle police officer, the Police Explorers, a branch of Explorer Scouts, taught Cindy about investigating crimes, fingerprinting children, directing traffic, and managing crowds. Ultimately she decided that she did not want a career in law enforcement, but Police Explorers helped her see employment opportunities beyond the confines of school.

It took us two tries to find the right high school for Cindy. The first, a very structured girls' school, made her feel inadequate and, despite our efforts to intervene, few teachers responded to her special needs. They saw her messy writing as carelessness, chided her for not trying hard enough, and assumed that more drill would enable her to "catch up." Once again we felt frustrated by teachers who could not or would not respond to Cindy's special needs. Then we found the perfect school where learning disabilities were not unusual and where students, teachers, and administrators created a genuine community that excluded no one. On school trips, for example, kids would switch seats halfway so cliques did not develop. For the first time Cindy kept a journal and began to enjoy writing. One day she came home and announced, "I am going to write a book." She took an art class and discovered that she had a gift not widely distributed among her peers. Cindy made her first long-term friend at this school and, with the exception of the math course which she dropped after one semester, had a very successful year. But that summer we moved to Michigan.

No adolescent finds it easy to move at the beginning of the junior year in high school, and Cindy found it especially difficult. The public high school she attended was large, and the mainly white, affluent, and academically ambitious student body marginalized Cindy. In basic classes Cindy was often shunned because she did her homework and did not join the "burn-out" crowd, and in regular classes peers frequently dismissed her as stupid because she needed help from the resource room. Outside of her good friend Lisa, the others in the resource room were a sinister lot. One young man, whom Cindy found fascinating but never dated, murdered his former girlfriend during their senior year. A sensitive and caring teacher in the resource room worked with us and with Cindy's teachers to be sure she kept up with assignments. When she had a lengthy reading task I would often read it with her, helping her draw out the main points. Knowing that more drills and skills in English would only demoralize Cindy, I insisted that she avoid basic English and take courses in drama instead.

Free from the constraints of the college prep track, Cindy took courses such as health, American government, and consumer math. She sang in the school chorus and competed successfully in vocal competitions. For a few hours each day she went to the local vocational school for a course in visual merchandising. Her artistic skills and flair for fashion shone as she designed store windows and earned the "best student" award. With a calculator and an untimed test, Cindy staggered through the graduation requirement in math. During our first summer in Michigan, Cindy worked as an attendant at a swimming pool where she was responsible for cleaning and monitoring the pool area. In her senior year she enrolled in a program designed to help students move into the work force, and she became a client of Michigan's Department of Rehabilitation. Through this agency, Cindy took driving lessons and studied the rules of the road. Thanks to a patient instructor who worked with her one-on-one, Cindy became a careful driver and received her license. Filling out application forms reduced her to tears, because she found all the blanks confusing, and I went into a frenzy when we had to retrieve the originals of her birth and naturalization certificates after we had waited in line for an hour. Yet it all seemed worth it when she was able to say, "I'm going to drive over to Lisa's now."

Thinking back to the grim days of struggling with spelling words and math facts, I found Cindy's graduation from high school both exhilarating and amazing. There had certainly been moments when I wondered if Cindy would be able to obtain a high school diploma, but she earned one—with honors. Her conscientious work in chorus, visual merchandising, and art counterbalanced the difficulties she experienced in other courses, and she finished high school with a GPA slightly over 3.0, enough to merit a special gold rope on her graduation gown. There were many proud parents in Ford Auditorium on June 8, 1989, but no one smiled more broadly than we did.

The social highlight of Cindy's graduation season was senior prom. During her junior year she took an American history course and became fascinated with clothing of the Civil War period. After we traveled to New Orleans during her senior year and visited several plantations on the Mississippi, she was even more intrigued. She began sketching and soon had a picture of *the* dress she wanted to wear. What Cindy drew looked remarkably similar to the dress I had worn to my senior prom twenty-seven years earlier, but when she tried mine on, the difference in our sizes dictated that we construct a new prom dress for Cindy. Combining patterns, locating fabric, cutting, and fitting the dress consumed weeks that spring. Cindy needed help interpreting the sewing directions, but she stitched the whole dress herself. On prom day she was still sewing, but when her escort (a family friend whom she had been dating) arrived, she floated down the stairs in yards and yards of pink lace, looking even better than the picture she had drawn.

The summer after graduation Cindy continued her work in child care at a place called First Step and, at my insistence, took a couple of art courses. Getting through high school had been such a feat that she had not had enough time to prepare for the next step. Even though I worried about being too intrusive, I felt that Cindy needed extra guidance, and besides, I *knew* she had artistic talent. When she first arrived, at age three, she would ask me to draw her a horse and after I had sketched some unrecognizable beast, she would exclaim, "No, Mom, a HORSE!" and then proceed to draw one herself. When we decorated for Halloween, she cut witches and cats freehand out of black construction paper. She scored very high on the performance section of the Wechsler Intelligence Scale for Children (WISC), a test that emphasizes visual knowledge, and she had always been a whiz at completing mazes. When we were moving furniture or packing, Cindy always provided the best advice on how to arrange things. Although she had taken a few courses, she had not done enough work to create a portfolio for an art school's consideration.

During the spring of Cindy's senior year she had applied to the Center for Creative Studies (CCS), an art school in Detroit, and had been told that if she completed a portfolio by August she could be admitted for fall term. Probably because she had received so many negative messages from school, Cindy did not seem to have a great deal of confidence in her abilities as an artist or in her capacities to do college work. But I kept telling her that the worst was over, that college would allow her to concentrate more on the things she could do well, and besides she knew she did not want to work at First Step the rest of her life. By August she had produced enough work for a portfolio and received a document, complete with gold seal, certifying her admission to CCS.

Like many colleges, CCS employs a standardized diagnostic measure of English skills. Given my background in English, I know how limited these measures are, and given my years of Cindy-watching, I knew how badly she does on such tests. Once again I decided to intervene. I explained to the admissions officer that the diagnostic measure would undoubtedly indicate that Cindy needed to enroll in a remedial English course, but that she had already had more than enough of that kind of work. What she really needed, I argued, was to take a composition course where she would actually write. Fortunately CCS had a composition-art history combination course, and Cindy enrolled in that. With the help of a tutor and an instructor who did not mind invented spelling and unusual syntax, Cindy received B's in both semesters the year-long course. Had I not intervened, I am sure she would never have escaped the remedial course.

Housing at CCS was limited, so Cindy commuted during her first year of college. She drove to a nearby park-and-ride station where she could catch the bus to Detroit, and thus began her first move toward greater independence. At the same time she began to reclaim her Indian heritage more actively. Far from the teenager who said "I don't like being an Indian," she became almost obsessively interested in everything connected with Native American life. She had attended the Ann Arbor Pow Wow in March of 1989, and as she explained it, the visual effect of being in a space with hundreds of other Indians was both overwhelming and tremendously exciting. Through an acquaintance at CCS she met a few members of the local Native American community, while I was able to put her in touch with some others through my contacts at the University of Michigan. She and I began attending a beadwork class at a nearby Indian Center, and she went to other powwows.

We discovered the Institute of American Indian Art (IAIA) by accident. One day as I read a newspaper article about Native American artists in Michigan, I noticed that all of them had attended IAIA, a college I had never heard of. After learning more about the school, I decided to intervene again by suggesting that Cindy and I visit Santa Fe. It was immediately clear that Cindy would thrive at IAIA. In addition to the standard introductory art curriculum, this two-year college also offered courses in Native American psychology, spirituality, and crafts. Here Cindy could continue her work in art and reclaim more of her Indian heritage. She applied and was accepted immediately.

Sometime earlier, Cindy had written for information about her birth family. In March of 1990, she received a letter from a social worker in Whitehorse, Yukon Territory, where she was born. The pictures enclosed with the letter showed people who looked like Cindy, and the letter offered a welcoming response. Using the addresses, telephone numbers, and information about her birth mother and her eight birth siblings, Cindy began making plans to visit this part of her family. Although I worried about what might await her because I suspected (rightly) that her birth mother was still drinking heavily, we arranged for Cindy and a friend to visit this family in the spring. I also had to come to terms with the fact that although Cindy is my only daughter, I am not her only mother. Despite my concerns, the visit went well, and Cindy returned serene, with many questions answered.

It was not easy to put Cindy on the plane when it was time for her to leave for Santa Fe in the fall. Even though I knew that it was important—even essential—for Cindy to attend IAIA, I worried about whether she could handle this degree of independence. We bought traveler's checks so she would not have to manage a checking account (she had one when she started working during high school, but it was a constant struggle to keep it straight). I reassured myself that there would be resident assistants in her dorm, and I prayed a lot. Almost as soon as she arrived at IAIA, Cindy underwent another battery of humiliating tests. When the results came back, she was told she needed to take remedial courses in both English and math. I spent most of the next two years protesting the remedial English course (since she had already taken and received a *B* in its sequel), and a waiver was finally granted about a month before graduation. The math was even more difficult. It was never clear to me why an art school with no math courses in its curriculum would use a diagnostic test as a graduation requirement, but administrators insisted. Cindy took the remedial math course twice and still could not score high enough on the test to satisfy the graduation requirement. Finally, about two weeks before graduation, she took the test one more time and received a passing score.

Cindy did very well in her art courses, and she developed a new confidence in her own abilities. During the summer between her first and second years at IAIA, we went out for lunch one day, and I asked Cindy about a painting on the wall. She looked at it for a moment and then explained its composition, use of color, and strengths and weaknesses. In a voice very different from the hesitating one that repeats an introductory phrase several times, she concluded, "If I were doing a class critique I would tell the artist to develop that left corner, and I'd give it a *B*." Courses that required written papers presented more of a challenge, but technology made things easier. When Cindy had a paper due, she would write it out, complete with bibliography, and express mail or fax it to me so that I could print it on the computer, eliminating spelling problems along the way.

Like most college students, Cindy had a variety of experiences during her two years in Santa Fe. She fell in and out of love a few times. She joined protests and embraced causes. She took risks and came to know herself better. She enjoyed many opportunities to learn about and participate in Native American traditions. She discovered that Indians—like all other people—can be unkind as well as kind, and she continued to develop as an artist. There were moments, such as when she hurt her ankle and had to miss several weeks of classes, when she felt like quitting, but she kept at it and arrived at that glorious day in May of 1992.

During the spring of her second year at IAIA, Cindy announced that she would like to get her bachelor of fine arts at the University of Alaska at Fairbanks (UAF). Even though I cringed at the thought of her being 4,000 miles from home, I knew that it made sense because UAF would put her in much closer proximity to her Athabascan roots. She could study Native Alaskan art there and be exposed to the language of her Kaska people. Knowing that UAF's core curriculum includes a math requirement, I also worried about Cindy setting herself up for failure and began investigating what support services would be available to her. Because she is Indian and her test scores qualify her, she is eligible for tutoring and counseling from the Office of Rural Student Services. That allayed some of my concerns, but the real sense of relief came when Cindy, unprompted by me, observed "If things don't work out at UAF, I can always get my BFA from an art school." I also took comfort in the fact that I know how colleges work and have lost any feelings of hesitation about intervening on Cindy's behalf.

As a featured speaker at a recent conference on FAS/FAE, Cindy talked about both the successes and difficulties she has encountered. "It hasn't always been easy," she said, "but I've been able to keep on going." In so saying she identified an important fact of her life. Although Cindy's lifetime sentence of FAE imposes many burdens, the perseveration that sometimes made her an annoying child makes her an unusually tenacious young woman. The story that leads to her graduation in Santa Fe is studded with moments when she kept going in the face of obstacles that would have stopped most people. Cindy has always wanted to help her people, and her current dream is to become an art therapist. I do not know how that goal will figure in her narrative, but Cindy's story continues. As Leslie Marmon Silko says, stories have healing powers:

> There is life here
> for the people.[2]

2. Ibid.

# Portfolio
# Cindy Gere

Memories, *acrylic, 1992*

Transformation, *acrylic, 1992*

Turmoil, *acrylic, 1992*

Santa Fe Sunrise, *acrylic, 1992*

New Beginnings, *acrylic, 1993*

Four Directions, *acrylic, 1993*

# PART II

---

# PARENTS' KNOW-HOW

# Parental Advocacy for Alcohol-Affected Children

JAN LUTKE

*Jan Lutke, the mother of eight adopted children with FAS/FAE, is a director of the British Columbia FAS Resource Group and of the Society of Special Needs Adoptive Parents (SNAP).*

MY TWELVE-YEAR-OLD SON DAVID, who has a diagnosis of fetal alcohol effects (FAE), was accidentally allowed to walk home from school unescorted. He followed two other boys who were tracking the daughter of one of our neighbors. The other boys started teasing the girl, calling out, "I want to f—— you." David joined in. The girl protested and finally smacked one of the boys with her school bag. The other boys got the point and left. Not my son!

David continued to follow this girl all the way home, gleefully saying "I want to f—— you" over and over again and dancing out of the way of her flailing book bag. Not only did he never get the message, he actually followed her right through the door, into her own home. He said "I want to f—— you" right in front of her father, and even tried to push past her father to follow the girl up the stairs to her bedroom. David still does not understand what was wrong with his behavior. He says he was "just teasing her," and she never told him to stop. Her father's anger bewildered David.

What am I to make of David's behavior? How can I interpret his behavior to myself, to him, and to the girl and her father? What does such behavior imply for the school David attends?

David, age 13,
with Katie, age 9

I have adopted eight children who are alcohol-affected and two other children who may have learning disabilities due to prenatal alcohol abuse. A pediatrician with training in dysmorphology can immediately spot my four children with the full fetal alcohol syndrome. It will take the doctor only slightly longer to identify my four children with fetal alcohol effects.

But the other people involved in my children's lives—teachers, counselors, neighbors, relatives, employers—cannot, unfortunately, see anything different enough about these eight children to warrant what they judgmentally call "special treatment." Like David, all my children are seriously learning disabled. But they do not look out of the ordinary. After all, the world is full of short people, and the FAS phenotype is not disfiguring.

Prenatal alcohol abuse for my children and for thousands upon thousands of other children has created profoundly life-altering neurological handicaps. But most of the damage is invisible.

Without special help, my children do not have the ability to follow society's rules, especially the unwritten ones. They do not have the ability to conceptualize, comprehend, generalize, sort out, retain, and apply abstract information.

But the more profound tragedy for all these children, and certainly for mine, is that their neurologically dictated social behavior appears to be—in the eye of the beholder—deliberate and willful misbehavior. People do not see David's offensive behavior as a sign of his perseveration, as evidence of his problems with cause and effect thinking, as proof of his terrible difficulty in understanding his own experience and learning from it. They see his behavior as under his control, as actions that should, can, and will be changed if we but try hard enough and long enough, using the right techniques. This view of alcohol-affected children sets us up—both the children and ourselves as parents—for long-term frustration, low self-esteem, social isolation, and ultimate failure as we try to accomplish the impossible.

What I finally understood was that, if my children could not change, then I would have to change, and that meant learning to work not harder but smarter. I would have to acquire the skills of advocacy. I would have to acquire the skills of interpretation to make their behavior, while not always acceptable, at least understandable and logical to other people. I would have to acquire a thorough knowledge of alcohol-related birth defects. To have a rough knowledge of FAS or FAE was not enough.

Once I truly understood what was meant by such ideas as "generalization," "cause and effect reasoning," "inferential thinking," and "concept formation," I began to look at my children and their behavior in an entirely new light. I began to see why my children had so much trouble telling time—why they could not understand that 9:45 was close to 9:50. I could see why they could not handle money, remember where they put things, and perceive social signals; I began to understand such behavior as lying and stealing accompanied by a total lack of fear. I stopped seeing my children as noncompliant and started seeing them as noncompetent.

This crucial shift in my own thinking marked a turning point in my view of how to handle the problems of FAS/FAE. I now knew that if solutions were to be found, I would have to find them myself and seek out others who had done likewise. I would have to educate everyone in my children's lives on a continuing and even daily basis. I would have to be able to interpret, sort out, protect, and run interference for my children for many years to come, perhaps forever.

I see parents and caregivers of alcohol-affected children as having three primary roles. First, they must love, value and accept without reservation the child they are parenting. Second, they must devise and provide the clear structure, intense supervision, and alternative teaching methods these children need. Third, they must become the child's advocate, interpreter, and protector in the school and community at large, willing and able to take a lot of heat and to be seen as intrusive and controlling. These are not easy things to do.

At the time the child is diagnosed, the family is often at a pivotal point in their lives. Diagnosis is usually greeted with relief ("I'm not a bad parent," "I knew something was wrong"), followed by depression, desperation, and finally, determination. Parents must be given back the power that time has taken from them, the years spent trying to slay the wrong dragon. They must address their own issues, vent anger, grieve losses, and move on to the acceptance of the reality of FAS/FAE. This change will best occur in the company of other parents in a support group. This time of healing is also a time for self-assessment, reflection, and education.

Advocacy begins in the home. No family is ready to advocate for its child in the community until it has successfully changed the home. Unlike parents of children with conventional visible handicaps, like Down's syndrome or spina bifida, parents of alcohol-affected children have to fight for social support and face having their parenting skills called into question. Success at home empowers parents by rebuilding their self-esteem and reaffirming their parenting skills.

The parent then must become the reference library, program coordinator, and advisory board with respect to the child in the larger community. This is the function of advocacy. The parent is the expert on his child, and, in the end, the parent is the one who must live with the decisions that are made. Everyone else gets to go home at the end of the day.

## ADVOCACY IN THE HOME: CREATING GOOD BEHAVIOR RATHER THAN REACTING TO BAD BEHAVIOR

### Structure and Routine in Daily Life

Our family lives a highly structured life. We have found structure to be the key to living in harmony with FAS/FAE. Usually structure is invisible. But structure creates the form that holds us together, like the pail around a bucket of sand. Alcohol-affected children do not have internal structures to hold themselves together. In effect, they are the sand, and we must attempt to be the pail.

Above all, these children need structure, order, and routine. They require clearly stated and defined areas for specific activities. In my home, food must be eaten only in the kitchen space and at the table. Space needs to be visibly defined. I use masking tape on the floor to show visually which part of the bedroom belongs to each child or where his bike goes in the garage.

Only a limited number of toys should be in the bedroom or play area. Toys should be stored elsewhere and rotated in and out. A toy must be returned to its place before another is taken out. The more toys are out and in use, the more distracted these children become. We store toys and clothes together by type—all blocks together, all dolls together, all cars together, all pants in one drawer and shirts in another. If the child cannot figure out how to get his clothes together for dressing, you can group clothes in complete outfits and hang them together on a hanger. Put a color-coded tag on the hanger coded to the color of the day of the week the clothes should be worn. Feature this daily color code on a wall chart.

Grooming and hygiene aids can be grouped together by color in a container, labeled with the child's name. Keep all the items (comb, toothbrush, soap) the same color as the container and place the container in the same spot all the time. Use a loud alarm clock to limit shower time or to show the child how long the water can run in the bathtub. An indelible ink line at the right water level in the tub can also alert the child to turn off the taps when the water and line match.

Label shelves, storage boxes, and drawers with either words or pictures. Children who share a bedroom need to have all areas of space defined—a line of tape down the middle of the dresser or the shelves. Alcohol-affected children have a hard time figuring out where one area stops and another begins, and a visual cue helps prevent problems. Rooms need to be kept neat and orderly. The children need predictability with possessions—clothing, toys, schoolbooks—always remaining in the same place. They become less confused when mess is kept to a minimum.

Establish a routine around meal times. Eat at the same times every day, and use the same dishes for the same child. Have the child make his school lunch the night before, and, if he has exactly the same thing five days a week, all to the good. Always sit an alcohol-affected child at the end of the table with a large space around him. Expect that the child will take longer to eat because of the distracting conversations at meal time. For the same reason, the television and radio should not be on during meals.

Family rules should be spelled out in simple language and posted in a conspicuous place, usually the refrigerator. Regular assigned chores should be posted. A large white board calendar can help a child keep track of coming events. A daily journal listing school work and school events is also essential. Parents should help the child establish a routine in which he checks the lists and calendars at regular times each day.

My older alcohol-affected children have found it quite helpful to carry lists in their pockets, which they make the night before, of the things they have to do the next day, listed in chronological order. Making a daily schedule originally was a time-consuming process. To think ahead and then place events in sequential order was very, very difficult, especially for David, who, at the age of eleven, still did not know the days of the week or months of the year. But list making soon became a part of their regular routine. As with all the things my children do consistently and persistently, they have become much better at making lists and following the activities.

*April, age 6*

Making such lists also permits the child to experience success in managing his own affairs. When it is obvious that the children have forgotten what they are supposed to be doing or what comes next, I can just ask them to refer to the list. Much of the time they can then solve the problem for themselves. We use posted charts to show the correct order for doing things in different areas of the house. We post bathroom routines in the mirror over the sink, bedtime routines in the bedroom, and school preparation routines at the back door. Lists and charts provide alcohol-affected children with a valuable visual reference point so they can remember things they are constantly forgetting. The parent need no longer be a constant nag.

### Reducing Stimulation

Hyperactivity with FAS/FAE children, especially the younger ones, is almost universal. All but one of ours has been affected, and it is exhausting to live with twenty-four hours a day. I wonder if we would better understand what is happening to the children if we substituted the words "overwhelmed," "frightened," and "frantic" for "hyperactive." The child is becoming overactive and losing control largely because he is overstimulated.

We found we could control hyperactivity if we reduced at home the amount of stimulation our children are exposed to. We strictly limit television, both in amount and type of programming. We allow such programs as gentle nature documentaries, which the children love, or Walt Disney films. We use music of a classical or popular variety. We use soft table lighting instead of harsh overhead lights, and we keep furnishings in the same place all the time. We strictly limit the number of people outside our immediate family who can be in our house during the time the children are home. We find a substantial increase in activity levels when extra people are around, especially if our children do not know these people. We also try to keep noise and confusion to a minimum, to create a sense of calm.

My aim is to help the child eventually monitor himself so that he can slow down his own activity without adult intervention. To that end, we have created a "quiet corner" in the laundry room, where a child can go on his own or be removed to if necessary when he is becoming overstimulated. Such a corner should be friendly and comfortable and not seen as a punishment. This technique has been very successful with our children. The older ones can now manage in public reasonably well in confusing situations and are able to remove themselves to a safe area when an adult gives them a hand signal.

Younger children should never be in a situation involving a lot of stimulation, such as a child's birthday party or a class field trip, without an adult to provide direct one-to-one assistance and supervision. Stimulating activities in general should be limited to no more than one activity every few days. These children need time to reorganize themselves. The child who is in school all day and is then expected to go to swimming lessons on Monday, the dentist on Tuesday, Scouts on Wednesday, and so forth turns into an over-wound spring. The more hyperactive the child, the fewer outside activities he should have, and these should be one-to-one activities with an adult.

Most alcohol-affected children cannot handle change. The more activities you add, the more changes the child must cope with. An activity means a new event with new expectations, people, places, things, language, rules, dress, and relationships. With the best of intentions, parents can sabotage their own best efforts on behalf of the child. Parents should also break up activities that demand concentration with activities that allow for physical expression. When I can go outside with my children, I emphasize activities like running, jumping, tree climbing, and bike riding up and down the front street. Inside the house, I use dancing, exercise, and tumbling. I have found it important to avoid activities that hook the child into undesirable behavior, like pillow fights and wrestling.

### Teaching Life Skills

Teaching alcohol-affected children the skills they need for survival and self-care must begin early and continue throughout childhood. Every activity, whether getting dressed in the morning or taking the bus to school, needs to be taught in a routine, concrete manner which gives the child the best chance of learning and retaining the skill. Parents and teachers need to analyze exactly what is involved in doing a task, break the activities down into small pieces, and then teach each step in exactly the same order, time after time, until the child masters the task. If I want my five-year-old to dress herself in the mornings without assistance, she will learn and remember much more easily if I teach her to put her clothes on in the following fashion, day after day. I put my hand over her hand and teach her step-by-step directions through a sing-song: "Socks, left foot, right foot; undies, left leg, right leg; pants, left leg, right leg; shirt, left arm, right arm, shirt over the head," and so on. Keep buttons to a minimum and always go in order, from head to toe or toe to head. Teach children to take off their clothes in the same way.

I handle bath time with similar step-by-step songs of routines. What does my child need to take into the bathroom with him and what does he need in the bath? I sing, "Undies, pajamas, soap," and so on over and over again. I use the same technique to teach washing, always telling the child to go in the same order, from top to bottom and left to right. I use the same order for brushing teeth, from top to bottom and left to right. In fact, just about any physical self-care skill can be taught this way. In our family, we made an arbitrary decision to teach skills left to right, simply because reading is done left to right.

The left-right technique is useful in teaching other skills. Children learn to set the table from the left side to the right side, after the plates are down. Here you can give a child with left-right confusion easy success. If a child stands in front of a plate at the table, with the forks in his left hand and knives in his right, the natural position of his arms and hands in relation to the plate on the table will automatically put them in the right place. My children make sandwiches from left to right; butter on the left side, tuna on the right, ham on the left side, cheese on the right. We use a sequence of left-right because it keeps the process shorter and simpler. Similarly, when cleaning up, we start on the left side of the kitchen and work to the right as we put things away. This approach helps the child to see his accomplishment. A piecemeal approach to tidying creates more confusion and disorganization for the child.

We teach all chores and skills in a step-by-step approach using demonstration, simple language, and instant tactile and visual rewards for accomplishing the step being taught. We never move on to a second step until the child does the first by rote. We want our children to experience success. Self-esteem is critical for alcohol-affected children, and you cannot ask the child for more than he can deliver. In the home, make sure that the child can be successful in what he is asked to do. When a child is consistently successful at what we ask, which can take anywhere from five minutes to five months, we move up to the next step. We continue until we reach the place where the child cannot go any farther, and then we back off to the last level where he can have that consistent success.

Remember that alcohol-affected children are primarily visual learners. When teaching a skill, demonstration and hand-over-hand instruction are far more successful than telling the child what to do.

Indeed, too much talking during a demonstration will cause children to tune out. Consider that what seems obvious to you may not seem obvious to alcohol-affected children. A child who has trouble with what is the beginning, middle, and end, for instance, may know how to sweep the floor but not where to start or when to stop.

With our older alcohol-affected children, we teach life skills through cue cards. These cards give step-by-step instruction on how to do something—like how to use the washing machine, how to take the bus, what to do if your ride from school fails to show up. The cards with their concrete directions give form to situations, especially unforeseen situations.

These kinds of comprehension difficulties can turn school into a nightmare for many children. Since children spend much of their day in school and school offers them little success, it becomes even more important that their learning experience at home be made positive.

## Telling Time

Alcohol-affected children have great difficulty telling time and understanding how much time has passed. Time is an abstract concept that has little meaning to any of my children. While one of my children may be able to read a digital watch and tell me the time, he does not understand that 9:55 is the same as five minutes before 10 P.M., that it is approximately 10 P.M., and, therefore, bedtime. If you do not understand these problems with time, you can very easily view the child as deliberately misbehaving. That is exactly what happened to David in school. His teacher asked us to buy him another digital watch (he had lost his two previous ones) so that he could go from his regular class to his special class on his own. Their theory was that, even though they had given up teaching him to tell time, he should be able to be given a single number by which to know he should go to the other classroom. They told him to go to the other classroom at 9:45. He never got there, because he did not happen to be looking at his watch when 9:45 came around. As far as he was concerned, 9:47 or 9:55 or even 10:30, for that matter, was not 9:45. He just kept wandering around waiting for 9:45 to happen. Had he not been discovered at 10:40, I am quite sure that he could easily have spent the rest of the day waiting for 9:45.

We have discovered two strategies to help with this type of problem. The first is to become a verbal early warning device, announcing a five- to ten-minute count down or whatever the case may be: "Joanne, ten minutes to bath time. Joanne, five minutes to bath time. Joanne, bath time, now." The second approach is to provide a visual method of showing the passage of time. For example, when our children are doing an activity at the kitchen table, I will put concrete objects in front of them, each object representing a length of time, from as little as one minute to as many as ten minutes. I will remove one object as each time interval passes and periodically remind them to look at the time. In this way, they can see time passing and understand how much time remains to them. Both these methods succeed in giving the child a basic sense of time and its passing.

## Supervision

Alcohol-affected children need direct supervision long past the time when other children can safely be allowed increased freedom. Adolescents especially need careful supervision because their poor judgment, lack of impulse control, and illogical thinking put them at risk for all kinds of problems and victimization. Children with FAS/FAE of all ages cannot seem to appreciate or even recognize danger and can get themselves in life-threatening situations in the blink of an eye. The family home should be child-proofed regardless of the age of the child. Medications, even aspirin, should be locked up, not just put on a high shelf. Never assume that a twelve-year-old can tell the difference between two kinds of pills just because the bottles are different—he probably cannot. Household cleaners and chemicals should also be under lock and key along with anything else that could be a poison. Knives, scissors, and other sharp objects should be stored safely and their use monitored. My teenagers have left scissors with the pointed end up stuck between sofa cushions. Matches should never be anywhere except under the control of an adult, and the same goes for lighters. Children

*Karen, age 13 (right),
with a friend*

cooking should always have an adult right at hand—it takes only a moment for a protruding pot handle to be overturned or a shirt to brush a burner.

Children with FAS/FAE need to be supervised going to and from various activities and places. It is not reasonable to expect a child who has no sense of time or appreciation of strangers to get to and from school on time consistently and without problems. Especially with teenagers, the trick is to provide needed supervision without being obvious. Sometimes a child seems to be doing so well that your natural reaction is to discontinue supervision.

We recently had reason to remember why alcohol-affected teenagers continue to need supervision. Our fifteen-year-old son Ken was allowed to walk to a friend's house by himself after dinner. He had been doing so well that we just took a chance and let him go. Everything seemed to go just fine. The following morning we got a telephone call from the school principal. While going to the friend's house, Ken cut through the school yard and met a couple of boys who were throwing rocks. Soon all the windows in one side of the school were broken. How did Ken get caught? Simple. The next morning, before school and in his first class, he told every person who would listen to him that he had done it. What he could not understand was how the principal found out. To quote Ken directly, "But I didn't tell Mr. Smith, just the other kids." He added as an afterthought, "Why did he phone you?"

Parents also need a signal that immediately communicates to the child, "Stop, get out of danger." I use a change in voice tone—making my voice one notch louder and one notch deeper and saying, "Sit down now!" When my daughter was running in front of a school bus, for example, I called "Sit down now" and she dropped like a shot in the middle of our driveway. I tried to teach this signal to my daughter's teacher. But the signal, the teacher complained, made her feel she was talking to a dog. The teacher finally agreed and now uses the signal to calm my daughter down rather than sending her out of the classroom a dozen times a day. My daughter's self-esteem has increased enormously. She does not mind being told to sit down but she hated being banished to the hall.

### Talking to Children and Giving Directions

With most people, the more you explain something the better they understand. With alcohol-affected children, the opposite is true. The more you talk, the less likely they are to grasp the point. Their brains become overwhelmed by an abundance of verbal information that they cannot sort out.

Similarly, just because alcohol-affected children can repeat a direction you just gave them does not mean that they understand what you said or can act on it. They may be able to parrot back what you said without being able to interpret it. The neural links between the language and the response are defective. The information may not be stored at all or may be stored only in pieces, or may be stored at a place where the child cannot get it.

We have found a number of ways to help alcohol-affected children understand what we say. Sentences should be short and the language precise. Keep in mind that children with FAS/FAE are literal and concrete. Avoid idiomatic expressions like "put a lid on it" or "step on it." Tell alcohol-affected children what you want them to do instead of confusing them by telling them what you do not want them to do. Saying "put your feet on the floor" works much better than saying "get your feet off the wall."

When we give a negative direction to a child, we tend to use far too much language around the specific instruction. What we want gets lost in a barrage of words, such as "How many times do I have to tell you to get your feet off the wall? Look at the marks there! Now I have to clean them off—better yet, maybe YOU should clean them off?" The parent lectures, the child does not respond appropriately, and the parent gets angry and bombards the child with more words. It is much better to resist the lure of the mini-lecture and deal with a problem simply by telling the child what behavior you want him to do now.

Since so much of the conversation that goes on around an alcohol-affected child is incomprehensible to him, he will not pick out the messages you mean for him. When you speak to a child with FAS/FAE, it is important to make eye contact. Many children simply do not "hear" you unless they are looking right at you. Eye contact, along with a hand on the shoulder, ensures that the child knows you are talking to him specifically and not to someone else. I try to avoid group directions. A child with FAS/FAE may not understand that information given to the group at large is also directed to him personally. The child thus looks disobedient. I always give the child's directions to him separately in a consistent way—first the child's name, then the word "now," and then some visual aid to comprehension.

Using very expressive body language and sign language is extremely helpful with younger children and a good fall-back strategy for older children who are having a bad day. To help the children hear with their eyes, we routinely use sign language to communicate the core words in conversations when speaking to them. Speaking expressively with physical demonstrations of what you are talking about, whether making a sandwich or showing an emotion, also enables a child to "see" what you are saying. Exaggerating your body language, facial expressions, and arm positions are very useful in helping a child understand anger, pain, fear, frustration, surprise, sorrow, and happiness.

When you have to give the same direction over and over again, you should seek to use the same words. Say "Hang your coat on the hook" every time rather than "Put your coat away" one time and "Take your coat to the closet" the next time. Use language as specific and concrete as possible. The direction "Put your coat away" does not tell the child where to put the coat or how to put it away. Many alcohol-affected children will forget a direction right in the middle of trying to accomplish the task. Sometimes all the parent needs to do is to point to the object—the coat—and jog the child's memory with one word: hook. Reminders given with a smile tell the child that everything is all right and lowers everyone's level of stress and frustration.

The key to effective communication, in short, is to make it as visual and precise as possible, while keeping excess language to a minimum. This does not mean that you do not talk to an alcohol-affected child as you would to any other child. Of course you do. What you have to remember is that the child will have considerably more difficulty than usual understanding what you say unless you give him aids to comprehension.

## ADVOCACY OUTSIDE THE HOME: FINDING ALLIES AND CHANGING THE SYSTEM

When my daughter Karen was seven years old, she was assessed through the child diagnostic program at our children's hospital. We were concerned about her hyperactivity, attention deficit, and developmental delay. She was having behavior problems at school. Karen had repeated the first grade but still refused to mind the teacher. We attended the team conference with the expectation that we would get some help. At the end of the twenty-minute session, we emerged knowing no more than we did when we went in. One member of the team smelled of alcohol. Another had a conflict in appointments and had to leave in ten minutes. Another did nothing but fiddle and glance at his watch. The classroom teacher, of all things, kept nodding off. On top of that, Karen's FAS diagnosis, made when she was about three years old, was mentioned only briefly and not at all in the written reports. But her behavior certainly was a subject of discussion.

If I can pinpoint my decision to take control of my children's lives out of the hands of other people, I would have to put it down to this event. Nothing before or since has had such a profound effect on me.

When I got over my shock and anger, I became determined to change how my daughter was handled. The necessity for advocacy on behalf of my alcohol-affected children has been self-evident to me for many years now. The system as it currently functions does not meet the needs of my children, and I have come to the conclusion that it is up to individual parents to see that it changes. I have met many other families doing the same thing, and we have found strength and support in our common experience. We have found a vast body of information in the heads of parents as to what works and how to do it. We know that individual parents can and must advocate so that schools will design and establish programs which will work for an individual child. Parents need to argue, cajole, convince, and insist.

At no point is advocacy on behalf of the child more necessary than at adolescence. Improper programming combined with the expectation that a chronological adolescent should be able to manage on his own is a prescription for disaster. Alcohol-affected adolescents need an individualized program that addresses their social behaviors and life skills in context, no matter what their IQ level. The higher the level of functioning of the child, I have found, the greater the need for specific programming. The alternative is frustration, failure, and social isolation culminating in a cycle of alcohol and drug abuse.

The changes we made over the years for Karen have paid off. Today she is seventeen years old and enrolled in a grade ten program tailor-made to suit her needs. She attends a very small school where all the staff understand her needs and our requirements. We

*Katie, age 8½ (left),
and April, age 5 (right)*

require, for example, that she have access to the office telephone whenever she needs to call home. Other children must use the pay telephone—which means having a quarter and remembering where you put it. Karen is still very active but no longer hyperactive and can pay attention for a reasonable amount of time. She still cannot make change but she has mastered telling time. Most important, she is able to follow a structured sequence of events to get through her day, like getting up, making the bed, washing, dressing, eating, brushing her teeth and hair, and so forth. We do not have to supervise her as long as the routine remains the same. We have and will continue to assume responsibility for reminding her of all those things in her life that do not occur on a regular fixed schedule, like changing the bed linen or going to the hairdresser.

But what is most important is that Karen has developed sufficient social skills to be at least marginally acceptable to her peers.

She has two friends who are regular kids. She still has trouble generalizing from one social situation to another. She still has problems understanding the effects of her behavior. Picking up someone else's money which they have left unattended on the assumption that they have lost it, for example, and then forgetting whose money it is and where you got it would usually be seen as stealing. But by and large Karen manages and can participate in school activities in some fashion.

How did we get there with Karen? We got there by working harder and longer than I have ever worked before; by doing one thing at a time, thousands of times, hand over hand; by providing a safe and structured environment in which Karen could be herself; by providing the very close supervision Karen needs to prevent negative experiences; by providing as many successful experiences for her as possible to build her self-esteem; by interpreting and explaining her behavior in light of her neurological functioning but without excusing it; and by seeking out and finding other parents whose suggestions worked.

## Organizing Advocacy Groups

In British Columbia, we have formed the Society of Special Needs Adoptive Parents (SNAP). SNAP is a registered nonprofit organization that started when a group of adoptive parents became concerned about the lack of information, support, and post-placement services for families adopting older children. All had suffered severe and prolonged problems with their adoptive children and came together initially as a support network for themselves. Our initial group of about six families sought funding from a local provincial government program, set up an office, and began to provide information, referral, and advocacy services for adoptive families. The organization got minimal funding and ran on largely volunteer services and donated equipment with everyone pitching in what they could.

Like a snowball rolling downhill, SNAP has picked up size, force, and speed. A fifteen-member board of directors now runs the organization with an advisory board made up of professionals in the fields of adoption, mental health, and medicine. We have an executive director and secretarial staff. SNAP provides such services as support groups, buddy parents, resource parents, a quarterly newsletter, an extensive library of books and audiovisual materials, and a 1-800 line. We hold monthly workshops for parents, evening professional seminars at local community colleges, and major conferences about twice a year for the professional community, bringing in nationally recognized experts.

We also formed a second organization, the British Columbia FAS Resource Group, a multidisciplinary group of professionals involved in research, pregnancy outreach programs, education, and child assessment. A staffed FAS clinic is now functioning at a children's hospital. In addition, SNAP produced a fourteen-page newsletter entirely on FAS/FAE, which has been circulated to every social service office in the province, to public schools, public health officials, mental health professionals, and to hundreds of adoptive parents.

All of this came about because people put their heads together and started comparing notes. While individual parents had only bits and pieces of information, every family knew another family, who knew another family, and so on. When you put it all together, you suddenly find that you have a foot in a lot of doors. You find out who is good at doing what and get them to do it. Fund raising, public speaking, getting to the media, writing articles, organizing an office, tackling the government bureaucracy, or selling an idea—all need doing. You collect resources and take it one step at a time. You operate out of someone's basement and pass the hat to pay the telephone bill. The only thing you cannot make do without is commitment.

A group does not have to be big and powerful to be successful. A small, coordinated and committed special-interest group can work and lobby very effectively precisely because it is small. Sometimes all that is necessary for one family dealing with a reluctant school is to take along another unrelated third party to the meeting to be an observer and note taker. The third party can often provide needed emotional balance for the parents.

When a support group grows to a significant size, it may choose to organize officially under its own banner. This happened with SNAP. But no matter how large or politically active the society becomes, it must never forget its roots and what it exists to do. Service to the individual must never get lost in the rush to become a political force or to provide generic services to the masses. The net result would be to leave the family and alcohol-affected child isolated and alone.

### Getting What You Need from the School System

I have eight children diagnosed as FAS/FAE in kindergarten through tenth grade. Over the years that I have sought to obtain appropriate services for my children in the school, I have come to the conclusion that parents of alcohol-affected children are up against two things. First, they must face the barriers in the individual, usually the teacher or the administrator, who does not understand the nature of the child's problems. Second, they must deal with the structure of an educational system that is designed to meet the needs of the average student.

At the individual level, the barriers are the toughest. Many people believe that FAS, and especially FAE, do not exist and that these diagnoses are excuses for bad behavior. They see the child's behavior as deliberate and make the child responsible without in any way holding the adult accountable for his own reactions. Some teachers blame and shame the child. Others refuse to read the files on a problem child because they want to give the child a fresh start in the classroom. Some teachers are not able to implement what they see as complex and time-consuming changes in their classrooms and resent being asked to do too much for one child. They then find themselves in escalating control battles where they insist that "this kid is going to learn" and get more resentful when he does not.

At the system level, the main problems are lack of funds and lack of services specific to alcohol-affected children. Most services are based on a child's IQ level, and a child with an IQ above that magic number is supposed to be able to follow the regular curriculum. What happens to the child who cannot understand cause and effect or solve problems, no matter how high his IQ? Frustration and failure are the gifts of the school to the child. How much better it would be to provide him with an individualized education plan that eliminates such subjects as social studies and science, focuses on those subjects vital to his survival as an adult, and gives him a sense of worth and purpose.

I have not gotten all I want for my alcohol-affected children, but I have made what I want very plain to their teachers and I have gotten a variety of educational programs and services:

- April (age six) is in a regular grade 1 class with speech and language therapy. Her expressive language is significantly delayed and she has problems articulating and finding words.
- Katie (age eight and one-half) is in a regular grade 2 placement. She has pronounced visual perceptual problems and finds it hard to do anything that requires small motor skills, like printing letters or numbers. She is able to read if you allow her to wiggle and squirm. She needs access to a computer for school work. The expectation for written language should be dropped, and a full-time aide should be supplied.
- Joanne (age nine and one-half) is in a behavior-management class for children with serious problems in the regular classroom. She is in the slow learner range of intelligence and has a severe language disorder and learning disabilities.
- Patsy (age ten) is in a special learning assistance class for mentally handicapped children.
- David (age thirteen) is in a regular class placement with three hours minimum daily placement in a class for children with severe learning difficulties.
- Mandy (age fifteen) is in a highly structured and supervised alternative school program for children with severe learning disorders and behavior problems.
- Ken (age sixteen) is in a learning disabilities program at the junior-high-school level with an emphasis on life skills.
- Karen (age seventeen) is in an individualized education program designed to teach life skills and give her vocational

training but within the regular high-school programming which will include supervised work placement.

Advocacy for my children has gotten them services but not nearly enough services. What we need are changes in the system that make children eligible for special programming based on the diagnosis of FAS or FAE and not on IQ. We need small, highly structured classes geared specifically to alcohol-affected children. These classes should emphasize social skills and life skills, appropriate behavior management techniques, and intensive supervision of students, including times like recess and lunch hour. These classes should use the particular teaching techniques that work with alcohol-affected children, like visual approaches, clear and concise directions, exaggerated body language and sign language, and teaching a skill in context. After grade seven, alcohol-affected children need alternative school programming that emphasizes life and vocational skills. At every age, programs must emphasize the development of self-esteem and close communication between the home and school. Nothing should start, stop, or change without parental involvement. Alcohol-affected children need continuity of action and response.

At this point, we do not have such special school programs for alcohol-affected children. So where does that leave me and every other parent who had a child with FAS/FAE? It leaves us on the front lines with this manifesto (see next page.)

CONCLUSION

The decision to become an advocate for your child arises out of the love you feel for your child and the pain you experience as you watch your child struggle every day in a world he does not understand, with expectations he cannot meet, and which turns him into a "bad" person when he fails. Advocacy gives the parent some measure of control over his child's life as well as the knowledge that a situation is not hopeless and the parent and child is not helpless.

An advocate provides a safe and structured place where the child can be himself, accepted and valued as he is. An advocate knows the difference between deliberate action and random

---

### A MANIFESTO FOR PARENTS OF CHILDREN WITH FAS/FAE

- It is the educational system's job to educate my child. My job is to make sure the schools do their job.
- I am in the best position to know what is working.
- School has a limited investment in my child. My investment is for life and I will be there long after the school is nothing more than a memory.
- Education must be useful to be valuable.
- Figure out what programming you want, design it to fit what the school already has, get inventive, and do it all in stages.
- Educate, advocate, and insist with every teacher in every class in every school in every year.

- Help in any and every way you can. Indicate you are available and visit in person often.
- Learn to work with people and not against them. Use their own arguments to prove your points. Do whatever you can to make their jobs easier.
- Deal with issues immediately and do not let them accumulate.
- Always follow through and always thank those who help you even minimally. Remember to thank in writing the people who have been especially helpful, effective, or taken a chance for you. Write to their superiors.

---

impulse, and strives to keep the child in controlled environments where people know how to respond to such impulses. An advocate strives to capitalize on his child's strengths, to provide successful experience, and build his child's self-esteem. An advocate knows the value of relationships outside the immediate family and exposes the child to other children and adults who have been taught to understand him. An advocate does not allow the child to be isolated from beneficial human contact while at the same time refusing to expose the child to social situations negative to healthy ego development.

An advocate teaches a child those social and behavioral skills the child needs to survive and function in a social world in small, incremental steps in the context in which the skills will be used. An advocate knows well that it is these skills that are vital to self-esteem and that make the difference between rejection and the acceptance that ultimately determine the place these children fill in society. An advocate not only gives his child hope but belief in his future, the promise of belonging in some meaningful way.

If we can do these things, we will have done our very best. We will have fulfilled our role as parent and succeeded in raising a child who can contribute in some way that gives meaning, joy, and validation to his life.

# Nurturing the Delicate Rose

SALLY CALDWELL

*Sally Caldwell is the mother of an adopted son with FAS. She has completed graduate work in special education, has assisted in special education programs, and brings both a professional and a parental perspective to fetal alcohol syndrome. She has also written several articles on parenting children with special needs. The events and impressions in her chapter are written with the permission and encouragement of Antone's birth mother. She hopes many who read it will understand what a serious mistake it is for a woman to drink while she is pregnant.*

SINCE HIS BIRTH, I HAVE BEEN ENGAGED, with my son, in a fight for his life.

Before my adopted son was born, I considered whether I would keep him if he were damaged by his birth mother's alcoholism. After his birth, I saw his first smile and dreamed that one day he would be distinguished among men for the warmth and integrity of his character.

Would I keep him if he were damaged? It seemed a faded question months later when the doctors first discussed the possibility of fetal alcohol syndrome.

## PURPOSE

My hope is to invite an alliance between educators and parents and to encourage sensitivity and innovation as we explore options in education for children with fetal alcohol syndrome and fetal

97

alcohol effects (FAS/FAE). The support I receive from teachers helps me look on daily incidents with detachment and humor.

I remember what brought me to the first teacher's door. We fondly call it "The Honey Incident." Home from a weekend camping trip, my husband and I decided to nap before we finished unloading the car of camping gear and leftover food. I was the first to wake to an unnerving silence, the kind of silence that screams out: Children are into something. I searched outside and heard muffled snickering coming from behind our car. There was my four-year-old son, Antone. He and his little friend had taken a five-pound container of honey and poured it all over themselves.

I recounted this story to my son's special education preschool teacher; we both enjoyed a hearty laugh. She then explained that my son is very sensitive to kinesthetic stimuli. She said he probably loved the sensation of the honey running over his skin.

With a little innovation on my part, I am now able to provide structured and supervised sensually stimulating experiences to quiet Antone's creative demands for touch. For his birthday, I gave him two cans of shaving cream and ten pounds of kidney beans. He played with the shaving cream in the bathroom sink. He enjoyed squishing it in his hands.

His favorite, however, is the beans. I poured them into a large, stainless steel bowl. He likes to stand in them and wiggle his toes, and he often sits on the floor and sinks his hands and arms in up to his elbows.

One teacher's observation and encouragement caused a burst of ideas that helped ease the stress between my son and me. But teachers offer me more than a few ploys to keep my eight-year-old out of trouble. We are partners in unleashing my son's unknown potential. Despite the irreparable damage my son suffered in the womb from alcohol, I believe that through education, he can acquire a strong and noble character.

But only some kinds of education have helped my son. He has been a student in four different classrooms: two brought setbacks and strain, while the other two seemed to set the stage for tremendous growth. I am humbled by the responsibility of nurturing such a delicate child. Figuring out what kind of education helped and why also helped me as a parent.

## CLASSROOMS THAT DID NOT WORK

At age three, Antone entered school for the first time. I was sure he would respond to the Head Start program with teachers who were Alaska Native, as he is. However, that year was trying for him. Two years later, he attended a traditional preschool. That time his response was even more pronounced and he only attended for two weeks.

At both the Head Start school and the traditional preschool, my son's behavior deteriorated when in the classroom. Though he shared readily at home, he would not share with his classmates. He was unwilling to leave playtime and join group activities. If he did join the group, he would not stay with the activity. At one point, he refused to enter the school building at all. He slumped down in the snow outside, crying miserably.

Now that I better understand my son's needs, I can see where things went wrong. The classroom dynamics—the teacher/child relationship, the classroom set-up, and the daily routine—left my son confused and frustrated. He did not understand the curriculum or even simple instructions. The following section outlines the specific characteristics of these two classrooms and why they were troublesome to my son and probably to any child with fetal alcohol syndrome or fetal alcohol effects.

### Mixed Messages: Why the Teacher and Child Do Not Connect

Dynamics in the teacher/child relationship seem to have a critical influence on my son's ability to function in the classroom. Communication between teachers and my son broke down for the following reasons:

1. *Teacher communications relying heavily on verbal mode backed up by elusive nonverbal cues.* Characteristically, the teachers in unsuccessful classrooms were subtle in facial expression and

body language. While most children could appreciate these signals, they did not register in my son's brain.

Group commands were given verbally with modest to no accompanying body language cues. Personal feedback, imperative to my son's success, was often communicated with soft looks that did not always catch his attention.

Visual cues can enable my son to understand communication better, but only if they are overt. For example, eye contact and a broad smile to indicate approval, or an obvious cue from the environment like blinking the classroom lights to signal a change in activity.

2. *Teacher inconsistency in responding to the student.* In both schools, teachers sometimes ignored and sometimes intervened with inappropriate behavior.

For example, when the teacher called students to one of the activity areas, my son usually did not respond. The teacher would repeat the command, then at times she would escort him to the activity area, while at other times she would leave him to play.

As the weeks passed, the teacher more often tried to escort my son to the group activity. However, the more she insisted, the more intense his refusals became. My son was confused. He needs highly predictable situations in order to flow with the school routine.

3. *Teacher passively involved with the school day.* Teachers in these schools seemed to function parallel to the students instead of interactively. For example, instructional time was minimal to introduce the craft activity, and the project was explained in the broadest terms. The teacher sat at the craft table with the children but worked in silence on the same project. Students watched the teacher for a while, and then began using the materials themselves. Students asked few questions and teachers seldom intervened with students' work.

Also, teachers did not join students during free play and did not supervise them closely during transitional times. When students stood in line after lunch, waiting to brush their teeth, teachers busied themselves setting up the next activity in the main classroom. They intervened only if there was a serious problem.

My son needs close supervision. He can forget why he is waiting in line or become distracted by other children moving about. Waiting to wash up can be made easier for him if teachers help him prepare for the event by discussing clean habits with him in the hall.

4. *Methods for teaching appropriate behavior.* The teachers seemed to rely exclusively on three methods of teaching appropriate behavior. Though challenged with the same difficult behaviors at home, 1 was never asked what worked.

One classroom method used to teach appropriate behavior was to capitalize on the children's natural inclination to model other children. This is not effective with my son. He does not isolate events in his surroundings such as other children's behavior. The teacher must direct his attention specifically to the model.

A second method, used for extremely inappropriate behavior, was a time out offering the child time to reflect on what was done wrong. Difficulty generalizing makes it hard for my son to predict "what will happen if . . . ," which is the premise for this form of time out.

A third method of teaching appropriate behavior was somewhat successful. Teachers would highlight one child to illustrate the appropriate action to take. Statements like, "I see this girl sitting at the table ready to begin" touched upon my son's eagerness to please and directed his attention to a visual representation of the desired behavior.

5. *Teacher impatience and withdrawal of attention.* Though sincerely caring people, the teachers became impatient with my son's repeated noncompliance with program routines and school rules. Their interactions with him grew less frequent, and their tone of voice became strained.

My son needs both much reteaching and frequent encouragement. In fact, positive feedback may be the most critical dynamic in Antone's ability to function. The communication barriers between these teachers and my son, based mainly on misunderstandings, left everyone feeling unsuccessful and frustrated.

## Jumbled Classroom Settings

Another difference between these unsuccessful early school experiences and ones in which my son excelled appeared in the physical set-up of the classroom:

1. *Casually organized classroom space.* At one school, toys and materials were stored on open shelves in the one large classroom. Craft activities were usually done at a small table in the main room; yet posters of cultural handicrafts were displayed across the room, near the back door. Storytelling was usually held in the main room, although books were stored in a small office off the hallway. Posters of children playing were displayed in the hallways and in the bathroom, yet the children were not allowed to play in either place.

At the other school, rooms were small and closed. Teaching materials were laid out on office desks, folders were piled on top of file cabinets. The day's projects were set up on the floor.

My son depends on environmental cues and is easily distracted by visual stimuli that are not related to the activity or event at hand. Visual cues purposefully placed and organized around an activity can help him concentrate his otherwise scattered thoughts around the event.

2. *Inconsistency in use of classroom space.* Teachers at both schools often experimented with holding activities in different places in the building. Storage rooms became libraries one day, and on another the same room might be used for a craft activity.

Changing activity areas in my son's classroom is like moving furniture around in the house of a blind person. My son relies on environmental cues to orient himself in a setting and then to draw from memory appropriate behaviors and skills that are required to perform in that setting.

## Unpredictability of Routine

A third major classroom dynamic that can have profound effects on my son's school success is program routine.

1. *Regular activities lacked consistency in schedule.* In both programs regular activities were unhesitatingly rescheduled in length and order in the day, and, at times, were simply canceled.

A period of free play in the morning was used to give the teachers time to set up the table activity. Free play, then, would be interrupted once the teachers were ready to begin the first group activity or when the children tired of each other. The first activity of the day varied with no regular pattern.

2. *Special activities were haphazardly scheduled.* There were interruptions in the day's program for community health and safety presentations. These were sometimes scheduled, though rarely prompt and often of varying length. Such community-based programs occasionally arrived unannounced.

If my son is playing with manipulatives, it is hard for him to be interrupted to sit and listen to a presentation by a dentist. This would require him to move from a self-initiated visual or kinesthetic activity to a speaker presentation, an abstract talk through primarily the auditory modality.

Preplanning the flow of the day's activities can help my son move from one activity to another. Antone needs predictability, and I have found it difficult to be spontaneous with him. When there is to be a change in routine, he needs much preparation, and still it can be difficult for him to adjust.

## THE CLASSROOMS THAT WORKED

My son has done especially well with teachers who are visually expressive and impeccably consistent. He does well in classrooms that are structured and interesting.

### Preschool

At the age of five, Antone was enrolled in the district's preschool classroom for children with communication disorders. Antone excelled in this school. He adjusted quickly and looked forward to attending.

1. *The teacher was explicit and consistent when addressing the children.* She used visually descriptive language, accompanied by gestures with her hands and arms. She often pointed to appropriate posters and illustrations around the room as she referred to school

rules and during instruction. This teacher was always with the students; she interacted with them during free play and transition time.

Discipline at the preschool was primarily preventative. Stickers and stamps were used as reinforcers. An engrossing puppet crew delivered lessons daily. General social skills were taught as an integral part of the curriculum, and the teacher interacted so frequently with the students that many incidents were prevented or caught in time to use as extended learning experiences.

2. *Visual aids and classroom arrangement reinforced classroom rules and program activities.* Signs around the room defined various areas and illustrated the proper use of school furniture, such as illustrated signs for how to use the coat room. Simple drawings illustrating the classroom rules were on the board where all students could see them.

There were posters associated with various activities and these were displayed in the area where the activity occurred. Additional posters with the day's lesson were hung on the wall. Those things not in use were hidden from view. For example, a cozy corner of the room was the puppet's home, with the puppet's mysterious bag of tricks tucked away under a table.

Classroom rules were illustrated on the board and reviewed daily during the opening activity. The calendar was hung on a bulletin board next to the blackboard, and was also a part of the opening.

3. *Program routine varied only slightly.* Music, library, and gym classes were offered on the same day each week and at the same time. Always, a basic group of activities were repeated daily at the same time and in the same sequence. For example, each day offered free play, opening and calendar review, a lesson, and a snack.

My son excelled in this preschool. I called the teacher several times during that year. She was eager to help and always hopeful. In the spring, she contacted my son's new kindergarten teacher, and to this day, they share news of my son's progress.

### Elementary School

In first grade my son entered a full-day public school program. He worked independently, attended to the program and participated in large group activities. Walking by his class, I often peeked inside and found him sitting with his back straight and hands folded on his desk.

Both the teacher and the program gave plenty of encouragement and positive feedback. Worksheets were not assigned grades and all efforts received a happy face. The teacher used language that was simple and explicit. His use of kinesthetic references, e.g., "Class, give yourselves a pat on the back," and "Class, answer by snapping if she [student] is correct," played on my son's strengths.

The teacher was highly consistent, understanding and personable. He spoke softly and whispered in my son's ear to redirect him to the task. Many of his techniques worked to empower, not intimidate, my son.

In first grade, classroom decorations changed gradually, and themes were not overemphasized. Centers around the periphery of the room were left in the same position all year. At midterm, my son sat in the same seat he sat in on the first day. The students around him, generally, were the same group all year.

Second grade offered my son an opportunity to adapt to a different, more challenging environment. The teacher was boisterous. The classroom decorations and seating arrangement changed often throughout the year.

Structure and consistency at school assured my son's continued strong performance in second grade. Both the first and second grade offered activities presented at the same time each day, in the same format.

Special activities, such as a fire and safety presentation, were scheduled neatly into a time slot with regular activities remaining at their same time. The students were well prepared for these special events with supportive stories and craft activities integrated into the daily program a week or more in advance of the event.

### THE BUILD-UP TO A FRIDAY SHUTDOWN: A WEEK OF SCHOOL

My son's report cards consistently show satisfactory except for fine motor skills of coloring and working neatly. The teachers' comments note how well he adjusts to classroom routine. "I enjoy having your son in our class," teachers often write.

But, even in a friendly environment at school, my son still gets frustrated, and his memory still fails him. He still misses much of the information that is presented verbally. Worksheets and writing assignments continue to make demands beyond his capabilities. He is still alcohol affected.

Though my son's classes follow the description of the ideal classroom situation, each year between second and third quarter my husband and I observe a deterioration in his after-school behavior.

It manifests itself in a weekly pattern. On Mondays, he comes home from school and is willing, focused, responsive, affectionate, sympathetic, able to work, and complete tasks independently. He is experiencing success.

On Tuesdays these qualities are dimmed. By Friday, he is resistive, scattered, inattentive, unable to follow even simple, single command instructions independently, and is failing at any attempt to use techniques that ordinarily help him focus and regain some control and integrity.

Sharp, repetitive sounds erupt from him at inappropriate times. These are purely self-stimulating, totally unproductive, and clearly unfulfilling. He frequently grabs and squeezes family members nearby in an awkward, irritating attempt to show affection or to express discontent.

Conversation with him is laborious. Like a stuck record he repeats phrases and loses his train of thought, effectively ending any meaningful communication.

With this continual barrage of activity, sounds, and words he erects a great wall between himself and his family and friends. It is his FAS perseveration, which often leads to shutdown. He is confused, disappointed, and alone.

This weekly pattern worsens as the year progresses. Only weekends and holiday breaks bring relief. Sundays become wonderful days when our son is back to normal and a delight to be with.

Each year I approach the teacher with concerns about the build-up of frustration and the subsequent erosion of his interpersonal skills at home. It is difficult, though, for the teachers to notice the shutdown or that it might be related to school. My son's behavior during the school day appears unchanged.

Only when I review his schoolwork more closely do I find hints at the conflicts he deals with daily in the classroom. Signs of perseveration appear in his journal where he writes, "I want to go home" and other sentences and phrases, often page after page. As language, math, and reading assignments become more complex, he drops from above average to low average.

I recommend that teachers modify one or two of the assignments that seem to cause my son particular distress. His teachers, however, consider the drop at mid year only slight and encourage me to accept his low average scores.

But as he becomes more articulate and states, "Jeremy finishes his math ahead of me and Alinda has started getting all 100% on her papers," I hear the voice of his own frustration. I know his potential and share his personal dreams. He is not satisfied with his performance or the intensifying struggle.

The structured classroom and the gentle, consistent teacher help my son maintain appropriate behavior at school and help him develop many new skills. But I find the rigid curriculum demands and classrooms with twenty to thirty students make it difficult, at best, for the teacher to respond in an innovative way to my son as an individual.

The loss of the integrity of his character after school, his slip in academic performance each year, and the signs of perseveration in daily assignments are warning signs to me that the present system is still failing to provide conditions which enhance the unfolding of my son's true potential.

### Dealing With These After-School Blues

I try to encourage understanding within the family and make efforts to create a forgiving and accommodating environment at home. I teach him to be aware of signs of the tension.

I teach him deep breathing and point out other activities that seem to help him relax, such as sitting in my lap for a look through the family photo albums. We also move the trampoline into the family room, and my son is allowed to forward roll into the kitchen for meals. This helps him release energy in a constructive manner.

Each year I request the new classroom teacher to consider my son's specific learning style. This year his third grade teacher is prepared to shorten the timed math worksheets if he has difficulty with timed activities, a difficulty common to alcohol-affected students.

My husband and I also teach our son at home. We reinforce basic skills with strategies effective with alcohol-affected students. Last year we introduced our son to new math concepts a week before they were introduced in his class. This seemed to give him a concrete reference for material the teacher presented in the abstract.

## ON THE HOME FRONT

Though frightened by the everyday challenges and the dismal future much of the professional literature presents of children with FAS or FAE, I remain hopeful. I believe the most critical environment for my son is the home and relationships in the family and the community close to the family. During these first three grades of school, I have had no academic goals for my son. At home, I focus on strengthening his self-esteem and establishing social skills.

My son constantly surprises me with his abilities. After studying compound words at school, he recognized the word "cookbook" at home in the kitchen library and said, "that's a compound word." He counts his pennies by twos. He consistently uses the words "left" and "right" instead of pointing. Yet he has many challenges that require the family to help him overcome.

One challenge is my son's activity level. It can easily escalate and become disruptive to others and unfulfilling for him. I have discovered two useful techniques in my efforts to help him calm himself and focus his energy.

*Antone, age 9*

Photograph by Calvin P. White

## Technique One: Time Out

I use this technique when my son is out of control and other approaches are not working. I speak close to his ear. I tell him that his behavior is disruptive to me, or that he seems out of control. If it seems necessary, I give him an example of what he is doing that is against house or relationship rules.

I remind him that he can usually get back into control by sitting on his bed for a while, and I make a point to assure him he is not being punished. At first, I escorted him into his room. Now, he goes willingly. I believe he is not comfortable being out of control and sees this as effective in helping him regain his composure.

During this time out, he must stay on his bed. He must choose a single toy or game which he can play with. The time-out period must be twenty to thirty minutes. I set the stove timer for myself, and I explain to him how he can read the time on his own clock.

Occasionally, I join my son in time out. He treasures that time, just as I do. After a brief gearing-down talk, he usually rests in my lap while he and I read a story.

When he emerges from his room, he is calm, focused, and pleasant. I ask if he feels the time in his room has helped him become more courteous toward others and purposeful with his energy. He is eager to tell me that it works for him.

This technique introduces two useful basic concepts: it is not acceptable to impose inappropriate behavior on others, and quiet time alone is an option that might help regain composure.

Also, I suspect that for a child who relies heavily on environmental cues, the bedroom is an ideal place for my son to regain control. It is filled with memories of positive feedback and peaceful, focused moments.

In our family, the bedroom has always been the scene for prayers and bedtime stories. At the end of the day, it is often here that we bring ourselves to account for the day's happenings. Apologies are made, if needed, extra hugs are given, if missed earlier. And, on request, I still sing my children to sleep.

**Technique Two: Metaphors for Developing Insight and Inner Dialogue**

My son's impulsiveness is the most troublesome of his characteristics. Though his impulses are not necessarily inappropriate, the problem is that he fails to use any judgment before acting. He does not stop to think.

The purpose of teaching my son an inner dialogue is to teach him to think things through before he acts. As I work with my son, I try to help him understand his behavior, because with self-knowledge comes empowerment. And I try to help him accept his behavior, because with self-acceptance comes a willingness to change.

The foundation of this technique is to translate abstract concepts into concrete ones through animals. Within one or two sessions, I helped my son identify two seemingly conflicting aspects of his personality and symbolize them with animals.

I chose a quiet time with my son on his bed, the bed acting as an environmental cue for reflective behavior. First, I had him choose any animal. He chose the cheetah. He related to the animal's speed. I noted how like the cheetah he is.

I told him to choose a second animal, the opposite of the cheetah. He chose the elephant. He described the elephant as slow. We then acknowledged the qualities of the cheetah's speed as bringing him success in hunting and the elephant's slowness in making him cautious.

In a second session, I asked my son to describe a turtle. When he said that a turtle can pull himself inside his shell, I explained that people can do the same thing. I explained that one of the things he would find inside is that he is both creative and fun-loving, like the cheetah, and also quiet and cautious, like the elephant.

We use these animals to develop an inner dialogue. We find comfortable time for him to go inside himself. He has the cheetah talk about his actions. These moments are opportunities to express both his enchantment and his frustration with the cheetah's behavior. At this point, I enter the dialogue to express the elephant's love and admiration for the cheetah and to offer the hand of friendship on behalf of the elephant.

At this early stage, he views their relationship in conflict, feeling the cheetah is bad and the elephant is boring. We have begun working on his appreciation of both aspects of his personality and on establishing the cheetah and the elephant as loving and unified co-workers.

During a recent major clean-up at our house, my son displayed some measure of progress in acceptance of the cheetah. He was assigned to wash out three large paint buckets with the garden hose.

When I checked his progress, I found the sidewalk soaked, his jeans up to the knees soaked, and my son standing tall and straight watching the sunshine twinkle in the fine spray of water misting out over the front lawn. "Are the buckets clean?" I asked.

I was delighted by the integrity of his response. He shut off the spray and said, "No," and explained that he loves to play with water and he got distracted.

He pulled the hose over to the buckets and stated, "I'll clean the buckets now." And he did.

I was pleased with his response because (1) he took responsibility for his inappropriate behavior; (2) he acknowledged the creative playfulness of his behavior with an air of acceptance; and (3) he took action to adjust to the appropriate behavior. As my son matures, we drop some techniques and add new ones. The magic is not in the technique but rather in the process of problem solving, with solutions coming from my son.

## THE SOCIAL WORLD

Though I feel we are approaching the end of my son's honeymoon with academia, my gravest concern centers around social issues. Relationships with others and within themselves are serious trouble areas for children and adults with FAS or FAE. I believe that his success and self-fulfillment as an adult will depend on whether my son can function in relationships with compassion, honesty, respect, and equality.

### Courtesies

Developing human relationship skills at home began with instilling routine good manners. My son excuses himself before leaving the table, and he asks permission before taking food. He says "please" and "thank you" even in casual conversations with his friends.

I suspect he learns such simple courtesies because they are taught in context, with consistent environmental cues, an abundance of meaningful reward, and much re-teaching.

For example, asking permission before taking food is taught when he has the impulse to snack; it is taught primarily in the kitchen; it is taught more than once a day, seven days a week; there is the immediate gratification, as I have usually said "yes"; and it has been reinforced over the years.

But simple courtesies are only a beginning in the development of social skills. As my son has matured, the complexity of human relationships has increased.

Touching

The first real challenge to me in the area of human relations was my son's tactile defensiveness. When he feels a touch to his skin, my son has an involuntary reaction to push against that touch. When he was a toddler, he had a habit of hunching his shoulders. As he became more articulate, he explained that the material from his shirt bothered him around his neck.

By the time he was five years old, my son's sensitivity to touch was having serious social repercussions. One incident illustrates this problem clearly. My son was sitting on the floor with his long-time best friend. In a moment of tender affection, his friend moved closer and rested his leg against my son's. Unconsciously, my son pushed against his friend's leg. His friend perceived that as an aggressive action and hit him back. Both boys were shocked and hurt by the incident.

Perhaps related to this kinesthetic hypersensitivity is my son's overwhelming need to touch others. He greets me with a tackle around the knees and expresses affection with death-grip hugs.

At first, I addressed these inappropriate touch behaviors with behavior modification. I worked closely with the school counselor, and began with an immediate reward/consequences system. The only immediate, meaningful reward for my son was my approval. Loss of my approval, then, was the consequence of undesirable behaviors.

The problem came with my son's reaction to my disapproval. However emotionally controlled I was, my son reacted with mild to intense denial, anger, and shame. This is still true today. As much as I involve him in identifying the problem and setting up a program of rewards and consequences, when his behavior fails to meet what is expected, he breaks down.

Persistence with behavior modification only brought mounting frustration for my son. He became more tense and aggressive. He lost his cheerfulness.

Now that he is eight years old, I notice a decrease in my son's physical roughness and in his age-inappropriate touching. What may

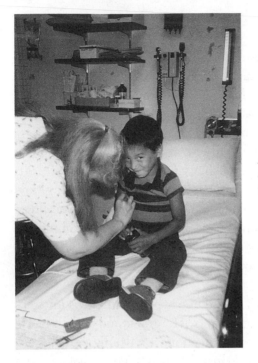

*Antone, age 5, at the emergency room for the third time in his life*

be working is my own perseverance with a variety of techniques. My techniques are primarily to (1) avoid situations that aggravate his tactile sensitivity, and (2) teach him to exercise control at a conscious level.

Siblings and close friends discourage inappropriate touching by avoiding physical contact with my son when they can. When my son does tackle them in play, they have learned to relax. Trying to pry him loose only causes the tactile defensiveness to come into play, and he clinches down even harder.

I teach the children to express their displeasure at his attack in a gentle, forgiving tone. As an alternative, older children offer appropriate wrestling or piggyback rides. Weekly sparring in Tae Kwon Do class also offers appropriate body contact.

I help my son acknowledge the treasure of his affectionate nature, while we explore alternatives for expressing it to others. Today, when he wants to connect with a parent or a friend, he will often initiate a board game, or suggest a wrestling match, using the form and rules he has learned from wrestling clinics.

Though we have progressed, instances of inappropriate touch still occur. Currently, we are working on a new technique using the metaphor of force fields.

My son enjoys requesting my permission to enter my force field. He approaches me and makes eye contact. He prefers to make his request with nonverbal language. When I give him permission to enter my force field, he gives me his gentlest squeeze around the waist. The wrinkle-face smile I get says "I got it right!" This quality in our relationship is what was missing when we used behavior modification.

Another thing that seems to help my son is to meet his increased kinesthetic needs. The bowl of kidney beans mentioned earlier is one of his favorites, but there are many other opportunities I can provide that require little effort on my part.

For a whole body sensual experience, I offer him a swim in the bathtub. He can wear his swimsuit and not wash his hair. Sometimes he swims every day for an hour or more, sliding back and forth across the bottom of the tub, pouring buckets of water over the top of his head. There was a new thrill when he discovered the pulsating massager.

As my son has gotten older, he has learned to provide some of these kinds of experiences for himself in appropriate ways. At the beach, he sits cross-legged and slings warm pellets of sand over his bare chest and legs. He has learned that his need and desire for creative kinesthetic activity is okay and that there are appropriate ways to meet that need.

### The Question of Conscience and Empathy

Social relationships are a major focus for us, and I am most concerned about the development of empathy and conscience. These qualities draw the devotion of friends and offer protection from violating serious rules in relationships.

The literature suggests that children with FAS or FAE have no conscience and are unable to empathize. When my son was very young, though, I was moved by his displays of empathy and conscience. One evening my son found me resting on the sofa. He quietly disappeared and returned with his quilt. While he tenderly covered me from head to toe, he said, "I thought you were cold."

Though tenderhearted acts distinguished my son when he was young, at eight years old, his displays of empathy are more rare. Still, though, he shows empathy.

Antone and a small three-year-old were playing on a friend's snow-covered deck. My son was playing, crouched down inside a small homemade igloo. Alerted by the cries of his younger playmate, my son peered over the three-foot wall of ice that separated the two boys. The boy had fallen through the bottom slat of the deck fencing and was dangling over the edge, holding on to the fence. When my son saw this, he climbed over the ice wall and pulled the little boy back onto the deck.

At a dinner party not so long ago, I went to check on my son and his playmates after hearing a cry. I watched while my son helped lift a rather heavy, awkward child with cerebral palsy and then stay beside him until he was walking steadily again. Seeing the child was all right, my son returned to his play with the other boys. Neither boy ever saw me.

Children with FAS or FAE tend to be attentive toward younger children. I often wonder if this is acting out of conscience to behave in a guiding and protecting way toward someone younger or less able? Touched deeply by my son's actions, I am compelled to rethink the statement from the literature that these children have no conscience.

When my son perceives a need and when he imagines that he can fill it, he takes action that many call highly mature and conscientious. Although these qualities may fail him when he is approached by a peer, he is showing an increased ability to maintain his personal integrity and commitment to family values in socially intense situations.

When he and his sister come to a crosswalk, he puts out his arm and cautions her to wait and look for cars. When he was younger, if she had suggested they dash across the street to beat the oncoming car, he might have run across with her. Today, however, he is more likely to become insistent that they be cautious.

Recently Antone was playing in the woods with a neighborhood friend who is two years older. They came across a bicycle that belonged to another neighborhood boy, one the older boy was feuding with. The older boy picked up a nail and began to puncture the tires of the bicycle. My son counseled the older boy three times to put the nail down, explaining that it was wrong to destroy the other boy's bicycle. How my son reacts seems to depend on how well he has been prepared for the specific situation. In this example, previous incidents with the older boy were catalysts to prepare my son for the incident in the woods.

I do feel my son has a conscience and can empathize. My task is to take the germ of these qualities and work with my son to develop them into character.

My efforts focus on acknowledging and emphasizing his accomplishments, giving him opportunities that draw out the qualities he is strengthening, and showing tender understanding toward his failings. As I do this I believe he begins to develop an image of himself that evolves out of his own successes.

When I hold up a mirror to my son at just the right moment, he can see that he is empathic, conscientious, quiet, or whatever qualities he needs strengthened. This works. On several occasions, I acknowledged his quiet nature and discussed it with him: how he felt, how I felt, etc. One day, out of the blue, he told me that he is a quiet person sometimes. Later that day, he requested a quiet meal. I encouraged the family to comply, and we sat through dinner in almost complete silence. With this atmosphere at the table, my son was able to be less agitated.

He had requested the support of the family to help him achieve that image he had of himself as a quiet person. I saw this as a beginning for him in making decisions based on an ideal self-image.

### SELF-ESTEEM: THE ANCHOR IN THE STORM OF LIFE

Though we have discovered a variety of techniques which help with specific behavior, what often seems to make or break my son is

*The three Caldwell children creating with straws: Evelyna, age 3 (left), Antone, age 5 (center), and Micah, age 7 (right). Antone made Eskimo dance fans and Indian leg feathers with his*

whether his emotional needs are met. It seems that there are, indeed, a certain number of hugs that are required each day, and a certain number of affirmations must be given for him to be calm and focused or, if not that, then to be able to use the techniques that help him function.

Self-esteem is a critical factor in his ability to function, and my son's self-esteem seems to be very connected to the feedback he receives. Even on days when he is focused and calm, there is a reservoir of frustration inside. He has difficulty with so many routine communications. His unreliable memory leaves him stumbling through ordinary childhood experiences. His impulsiveness is an obvious irritant to others and can easily result in some kind of disaster.

An article on attention deficit disorder brought to my attention the critical role personal relationships can play in building self-esteem. The author suggests we listen instead of lecture, sympathize instead of preach, and "try to understand the youngster's plight."[1]

---

1. M. D. Levine and R. D. Melmed, "The unhappy wanderers: Children with attention deficits," *Pediatric Clinics of North America* 29, 1 (February 1982): 105–119.

It has fascinated me to find how almost desperately my son clings to our relationship. As I was preparing this paper, I spent a lot of time in my office area, away from the family. After about one month, though my other two children were exasperated with the new situation, it was my son with FAS who was not able to cope.

His purposeless activity accelerated, his interactions with others became rough, there was a decrease in his creative problem solving, and he resorted to hitting, poking, and tantrums.

I slowed down on the paper and turned my attention to my son. Within two days he began to calm down. His behavior became focused; he was relaxed and cheerful. It seemed clear to me that, to weather the storm of his life, his threatened self-esteem needs constant nurturing from others.

## THE QUESTION OF LABELING

When I first considered the possibility of fetal alcohol syndrome, I read pamphlets with lists of debilitating characteristics, and I studied the illustrations of deformed babies. I suspected that my infant son had FAS and suggested it to the pediatricians. However, the doctors seemed to avoid the issue, and this left me feeling anxious.

At five weeks, a specialist diagnosed a ventricle septal defect, and there was emergency pyloric stenosis surgery at six weeks. My baby had chronic diarrhea and five bouts of pneumonia by the time he was eleven months old. When my son was about one year old, the doctors finally confirmed my suspicions.

I felt so alone. My son would smile at me and touch my face yet I felt he was far away. In my mind, he had become the baby in those pamphlets, afflicted with the birth defect the doctors did not want to talk about.

Today, I accept the diagnosis without letting it dampen my enthusiasm for caring for my son. Thinking about his future, I am encouraged by remembering a dear adult friend who had FAE. In his twenties, he had tremors and learning difficulties. To me, his family, and neighbors, he was a devoted and capable husband and father, a responsible businessman of high moral standards, and a caring, giving member of his community. He was gentle and trusting. For these qualities he was a powerful influence on the people in his life.

My son continually defies the limitations the FAS label imposes. Poor coordination has not stopped him from riding his bike with his feet on the handle bars. A language processing disorder has not stopped him from getting where he wants to go, and reading remains one of his favorite pastimes.

He is popular in school. He was elected student council representative of his third-grade class, and has had the same best friend for over five years. He can tell me that it feels empty when I am not there. He can say "I love you," and I know he understands love as the force behind commitment, because it is mutual hard work and self-sacrifice that characterize our relationship.

When children with FAS or FAE do well, people question the diagnosis. But my son, tragically, has fetal alcohol syndrome. That diagnosis is based on two crucial elements: maternal history and physical manifestations.

My son's birth mother has been an alcoholic since childhood. She was an active drinker during the pregnancy, including the night she delivered.

My son has the characteristic small head circumference and both the usual and even the less frequent facial anomalies, e.g., the short nose, flat midface, and extra bone in his ear.

Many nights I have looked down at him, sleeping soundly, his bloated belly and bony legs sprawled out in the bed. There is nothing that can make the reality of FAS disappear from his life.

I do not like a label. However, in the context of a medical diagnosis, identifying the FAS has helped me acquire the technical information I needed to understand my son. For example, I began to understand his acting out behavior and shutdown at home as an expression of the personal frustration he experiences at school. I understood more clearly how school demands continually challenge my son in areas of his deficits and fail to draw on his characteristic strengths. And I now understand the erosion of his self-esteem.

Though I want the cooperation of teachers to help me deal with my son's challenges, still I fear a label. My people-pleaser son is dependent on the feedback he gets from those around him. I fear that prejudice and misinformation, as they color perceptions, can estrange him from the people he aims to please.

I wanted to help my son understand his situation to ease his frustration. How to tell him about the FAS became a major issue when he was eight years old. Immediately I was struck by the rigidness of his burning desire to achieve a high standard in everything he attempted.

This was the first roadblock, even though, in many ways, this indomitable spirit had propelled him through early childhood's stages with distinctive success.

When my son was about four years old, he graduated from a tricycle to a two-wheeled bike with training wheels. One week after his first ride on the Huffy, he asked me to remove the training wheels. I resisted. I imagined that his poor coordination would undermine his efforts.

The next week, I conceded. His little tennis shoes pedaled around as fast as his legs could move. His hands gave the handlebars a white-knuckled grip, and his constant wobbling defied the laws of physics. But he stayed up.

His older brother was incredulous, remembering how it had taken him two summers to get off the training wheels. "How can he do that?" he demanded. My husband and I shrugged our shoulders, a bit amazed ourselves. "Because he believes he can," seemed the only plausible explanation.

The FAS label, as with so many labels, describes children in terms of what they cannot do. As my son draws an image of himself, I want it to be a full picture of himself as a vulnerable human being colored with self-confidence.

The telling has to be a process. We enhance the process by acknowledging the times when he is having difficulty. We clarify just what it is about the task that is difficult and then note, with him, when the same difficulties repeat themselves. In this part of the process, we emphasize acceptance of his personal frailties.

For example, when I say, "Take this trash outside," and he carries it into the kitchen, we briefly talk about how he has lost one of the details of my instructions. Yes, he took the trash but he did not take it outside. Then I ask if this has happened to him before and if it happens often.

Quickly, acceptance became a stronger impulse because, I suspect, it just feels so good to be accepted as you are.

Though a problem-solving style of parent/child interaction has characterized our relationship with our children, Antone had always had difficulty problem-solving. The work we did on self-acceptance tore down that once impenetrable wall between my son and this valuable technique. All of those years of problem-solving then began to click.

When he was forgetting to bring his textbooks home to do his homework, we instituted a reminder note system at his desk at school. It was his participation in problem-solving and his eagerness to use the device that developed out of that process and led to the reminder note and his use of it.

In class, when he was not getting his work done due to excessive visiting, the teacher drew up a bingo card to help. It listed behaviors which contributed to completing classwork and behaviors that interfered.

Each time my son leaves his seat to sharpen his pencil, get a drink, or visit, he crosses off the corresponding square on his card. Each time he is prepared for the next subject, is following directions or participating in the discussion, he marks off a square on his card.

Within only a few days he saw that when his marks were on squares like visiting or sharpening his pencil four or five times a day, he had a lot more homework. By the end of the first week, using this problem-solving device, he was coming home with no homework at all.

When the teacher first instituted the bingo card, she used it as a disciplinary measure. When Antone had used up all of his squares for pencil sharpening, getting drinks, etc., there was a consequence. He had to put his head on his desk for five minutes of recess.

At home my son exhibited intensive perseveration and shut-down behavior. Once the teacher turned the card into a problem-solving device, using it to organize his behaviors into some meaningful pattern, Antone turned his own behavior around.

He used the strength of his creativity to figure out how to get out of having homework and ensured the appropriate squares were marked. Also characteristic of the FAS/FAE child, my son uses his strong determination to maintain classroom behavior that results in meeting his personal goal of no homework.

Once I asked my son how he feels about his situation. "Happy and sad," he answered. "Sad because I have problems. Happy because I'm doing so good."

After much thought and worry, I decided to tell him about fetal alcohol syndrome. Sensing his boredom with my long explanation, I asked, "What does *F A S* mean?"

Antone's clever response was: "Fantastic Antone!" "And what about the *S*—it's FAS," I said. We agreed on "FAS—Fantastic Antone Succeeds!"

## THE UNDAMAGED SOUL

Having responsibility for raising my son is like finding a rose in a patch of marigolds. It catches me off guard. It calls on knowledge I do not have. Yet, I know the sweet fragrance it offers and the delicate, velvet beauty it can become, and it beckons me to the task.

Though he loves animals, I am anxious about his constant handling of his pet rat, thinking it is not clean. He gives away his toys and money to his best friend without hesitation. I want to hold onto them. My value is in the material item; his is in the generosity of the act.

His creative urges compel him to fill the sandbox with water and make elaborate underground water systems. I am driven to keep things orderly and to use things the way they were designed to be used.

He believes he can and perches his bike at the very top of the hill for a thrilling ride down a sixty-degree incline. I stand at the bottom, afraid of a broken arm and the disappointment of a failed attempt.

Sometimes, it seems easier to simplify my relationship with my son. I get the most out of him and he gets the most of me when I love him selflessly. Although my son's brain has been irreversibly damaged by alcohol, his soul has not. My efforts at home are to reach that undamaged part of him and draw out its qualities.

A nurse once commented, "if more people in the world were like your son, the world would be a nicer place to live." What she saw in him were the qualities of his soul—his kindheartedness, his generous spirit, his joyfulness, his radiant acquiescence.

At times I talk to my son about his birth mother's drinking during her pregnancy and about the FAS. I ask him how he feels about this. He says, "I love both my moms. I love my birth mother because she born me. I love you because you raise me." Like a little mirror turned to the brilliant sun, Antone's actions continue to reflect a spirituality that is profound.

Native elders have advised me to work with the soul through the subconscious. Traditionally, the elders advised young mothers to talk to their children while they slept. So, I approach my son as he sleeps and whisper affirmations in his ear. I encourage him to drift off to sleep with a cassette tape on, one that tells stories of the indomitable spirit of man to win out over obstacles thrown in his path.

I crawl into bed with him in the early morning hours and hold him gently, hoping to give him a sense of family strength and safety. I teach him moral values through family activities, games, and stories. And constant memorization works to engrave the love and protection of prayers and scriptural verses on the tablet of his heart.

As I tucked my son into bed one evening, I considered his disabilities. I remembered a recent school assignment. My son's response was exceptional among his first-grade peers, in that it related so precisely to the content of the lesson. After reading a simple story about Martin Luther King, Jr., the teacher instructed each student to express his or her dream for the world. The figure on the following page shows the class response.

THOUGHTS ON DR. MARTIN LUTHER KING, JR.'S
"I HAVE A DREAM . . ." SPEECH:

I Have a Dream . . .
that there was no fighting.
that there was no such thing as war.
that we could go into the new system where no one dies and no one gets sick and everyone could do everything they want to.
that everyone could live for a very long time.
that there was no killing.
that everyone lives in peace.
that no one gets hurt anywhere.
that everyone could live in peace.
that nobody would die and we could go through anything.

that nobody will litter.
that there is no polluting.
that no one would litter the sea.
that no one would take drugs.
*that the bad rules about black people will be changed.*
[emphasis added]
that everyone will be friends and hold hands together.
that everyone is friends with no fighting.
that no one will kill anyone else.
that Saddam Hussein will get out of Kuwait.
that nobody will get in jail.
that everyone will live in peace.
that all people grow up safe.
that no one dies in the war.

To this day, I am moved by my son's answer to the question. "If I had a dream," he wrote, "it would be that the bad rules about black people will be changed."

Tucking Antone in bed, I was moved by his conviction when he told me he was keeping that dream alive, he and another person—"the woman who refused to get off the bus." Though characteristically confused by the complexity of social situations, his sensitivity to King's cause of the injustice of racial prejudice and his own commitment to action on behalf of his oppressed fellow man is evidence again of a healthy and radiant soul within.

The first years' struggles for my son's survival are behind us, and he is now fulfilling his mother's dream, that he become known for the warmth and integrity of his character.

*Antone, age 9*

Photograph by Calvin P. White

## EPILOGUE

### Psychologist's Report and School Test Results

At eight and one-half years old, Antone was evaluated by a psychologist who specializes in FAS/FAE. The evaluation combined performance on seven standardized tests with behavioral observations from his parents, classroom teacher, and the psychologist.

The psychologist noted that Antone was diagnosed by a dysmorphologist as having "facial features and birth anomalies typical of a moderate to severe expression of the effects of prenatal exposure to alcohol."

When brought for psychological testing, "he appeared thin and had the distinct facial features of FAS."

Despite a classic FAS physical profile, Antone's behavior and test results did not indicate the serious learning and social problems common among children with FAS. While his problems had by no means disappeared, Antone performed far above what many people expect from children showing serious effects of prenatal alcohol exposure.

The psychologist noted his excellent behavior in the testing situation:

> During testing, Antone was sometimes restless, rolling his pencil and moving his feet, but he never required re-focusing. He displayed impeccable manners and good social skills. He was candid about his dislike of drawing and writing, but he was consistently cooperative, fully engaged, and motivated in these and all other tasks.
>
> Probably the most notable aspect of Antone's overall performance was his economical use of time, especially on non-verbal tasks. In addition to earning several time bonus points, Antone completed basic testing in almost an hour less than expected.

On the Wechsler Intelligence Scale for Children-Revised (WISC-R), Antone received a full IQ score of one hundred and six, within the average range. His strongest scores were on tests like block design and object assembly, which draw on visualization skills. His weakest performance were on tests like digit span which requires attention and sustained concentration.

The attention-deficit problems common among children with FAS/FAE were apparent on the WISC-R. Problems with concentration and memory as well as with fine motor skills also showed up on the draw-a-person test, where Antone showed a two-year delay in performance.

While many alcohol-affected children have special problems with social skills, Antone's adaptive behavior, as measured by the Vineland Adaptive Behavior Scales, ranged from the fifty-third to the fifty-eighth percentile. These scores are slightly higher than average. His greatest strengths were on the "performance of domestic chores such as food preparation, household cleaning, and neatness (tidying his bedroom)."

The teacher's rating on the child behavior checklist put Antone in the normal range, and his parents' ratings did as well. Some indications of low self-esteem and sadness in Antone's emotional life were evident in his responses to the sentence completion test and other measures—suggesting the difficulty he has in coping with daily demands.

In a concluding letter to his mother, the psychologist stated that Antone's "general competency is a testimony to the consistency and structure you have provided for him."

> Sally Caldwell began to spot problems soon after Antone was born. She realized that Antone's birth mother was in treatment for alcohol two or three times in the last six months of pregnancy, that she deteriorated again in the eighth month, and was drunk when she delivered him at thirty-seven weeks gestation.
> We do not know what Antone's development would have been without the excellent home environment the Caldwells provided for him. But Antone's remarkable achievements strongly suggest how much an alcohol-affected child can achieve with early diagnosis, early intervention, a nurturant family extraordinarily sensitive to his problems, and the careful choice of schooling that provided the structure and external cues that Antone needs.

In addition to the psychologist's report, Antone received standardized test scores on the Iowa Tests of Basic Skills administered by the school district. On this objective test as well, Antone's scores in many areas reached the average level or above. On the reading test, he scored at the fifty-fourth percentile and in mathematics he scored at the seventieth percentile. His weakest area was vocabulary where he scored at the twenty-seventh percentile. Two sets of test results, both individual tests administered by a psychologist, and a standardized group test administered in the classroom, have put Antone at the average level or above despite his severe alcohol-related birth defects.

## Sally Caldwell's Observations

Though the psychological evaluation was reassuring, what pleases me about my son's achievements is his success in the basics of life.

He has sustained a long-term friendship with a same-age peer. In that friendship, they run for help when the other gets hurt, and they get angry and make up. They figure out how to solve problems and encourage each other to do the right thing.

They are vulnerable with each other, sharing what scares them in movies and dreams and what makes them sad, like losing a pet or when one of them goes on vacation. Most of all they laugh belly laughs until tears roll down their cheeks.

To see my son enjoy a friendship of this depth gives me great hope, hope that one day he will experience the fulfillment of the trials and comforts of marriage and the demands and rewards of parenthood.

My son is a yellow belt in Tae Kwon Do. He tells me his hope is to be a black belt instructor when he is an adult. His immediate goal is to become a green belt, and he believes he can achieve that by the time he is eleven.

He also tells me he wants to be a doctor because he wants to save people and help them get well. Whether he becomes a doctor or an emergency medical technician, a forest ranger or a mechanic, that he has the audacity to dream and the confidence to pursue personal goals encourages me to believe his life will continue to be rich in relationships and successes.

# Early Intervention for Alcohol-Affected Children
## Birth to Age Three
### Jan Hinde

*Ms. Hinde has worked with alcohol-affected children for over ten years both in Alaska villages and in the urban community of Fairbanks, Alaska. She served as coordinator of the McGrath Infant Learning Program, which also provided itinerant early intervention services to nine villages along the Yukon, Innoko, and Kuskokwim Rivers. From 1988 to 1992, she provided early intervention services at Project Teach in Fairbanks and was program coordinator. Currently, she is executive director of Fairbanks Head Start.*

## THE CASE OF JEFFREY

When Jeffrey was born, the doctor diagnosed him as having fetal alcohol syndrome. His mother had a history of alcohol abuse. Jeffrey was small for his gestational age and had several identifying physical characteristics, such as a thin upper lip. His mother gave him up at four weeks, and two school teachers adopted him at two months. Jeffrey was their first child.

I met Jeffrey when he was five months old, and his parents sought help through an early intervention program for special needs children. Jeffrey had serious motor delays, such as lack of head control. A physical therapist addressed his motor needs, and Jeffrey showed great improvement. At sixteen months, his parents and I began to work on his speech and language development and

131

especially his attention span. Jeffrey flitted from one activity to another, hardly able to concentrate on anything at all. Since he could not focus his attention, he found it hard to learn. I showed his parents how to develop his ability to pay attention through intriguing games like "Find the Object." At twenty-eight months, Jeffrey was still unable to sit still long enough to do anything, even to eat. He also started repetitive behavior like head-banging.

But Jeffrey gradually did better. At thirty months, he had learned to play with toys, and he used a richer vocabulary when he talked. But his fundamental problem remained—a difficulty in focusing and paying attention. I worked on expanding his attention span by gradually increasing the time he could focus on a task even in the presence of distractors. At thirty months, he could stay at the table for only about five minutes. When anything distracted him, like a passing car outside, he would zoom to the window. By thirty-three months, he was able to stay at the table for forty-five minutes and ignore the car.

When Jeffrey left the program at three years, he tested so close to age level that he no longer qualified for special services. But his parents continue to use our strategies with him. They also let his teachers know how to work with him. He learns best through visual channels, and he finds it easier to pay attention if his teachers use the same cue at school that his parents use at home. Jeffrey's parents are his greatest asset.

Early educational intervention can make a dramatic difference to the success of alcohol-affected children. I have seen many other children like Jeffrey. Even though they have classic FAS or FAE patterns, they thrive in their early years, overcome their medical crises, and leave our early intervention program with developmental test scores hovering right about the average level.

Other alcohol-affected children do not make such progress. In part, the nature of the biological damage explains these poor results. The impact of the alcohol on the developing infant's system varies; therefore, the injury varies. These physical differences need to be kept in mind when developing educational goals for alcohol-affected children and their families.

But the character of the home also has enormous impact on what happens to young children with FAS/FAE. Children who remain in their natural homes vary the most in their progress. Some families are able to make changes, but others, deep into denial and the disease of alcohol, do not have the power to give the children care and intelligent attention. Alcohol-affected children placed in temporary foster homes or foster-adoptive homes also have problematic outcomes. Moving children from one home to another harms all children but especially hurts alcohol-affected children who need, even more than other children, predictable routines.

My own experience supports Judith Kleinfeld's conclusion, "Children with prenatal alcohol damage do best in stable, predictable, nurturing home environments where they receive intense attention."[1] In such homes, I can show parents specific educational techniques they can adapt to their own family situation.

First, I make sure that we have ruled out any physical problems that may be limiting the child's development. Heart problems, visual problems, auditory problems, treatable attention deficit disorders (ADD) and attention deficit hyperactivity disorders (ADHD) are common examples. Once we have addressed these problems, we can attend to the educational issues.

Alcohol-affected children do not pick up the knowledge and skills that other children seem to learn on their own—understanding the difference between familiar people and strangers, for example, or knowing that they should hang up their coats when they come into the house. I want parents to realize that the child is not simply being bad when he throws his coat on the floor. The child must be taught—in small and careful steps—the skills necessary to hanging up a coat on a peg.

## TASK ANALYSIS

I teach parents the basic principles of task analysis. In a nutshell, you need to identify a desired outcome and then break down

1. J. S. Kleinfeld, "Fetal alcohol syndrome in Alaska. What the schools can do," University of Alaska Fairbanks, Northern Studies Program, Fairbanks, Alaska, 1991. Prepared for the Alaska Department of Education.

the task into small steps. An adult must teach the child each step of the task, reward him for success, and then reward him intermittently so he will continue to accomplish the task without prompting.

Always start teaching tasks and skills at the child's developmental level, beginning with what the child can already accomplish. If you want your child to learn how to set the table and you know he can get spoons and forks to the table, do not ask him to take the napkins first. Napkins tear, require gentler handling, and may not make it to the table in good condition. Give your child several days of success with spoons and forks and then add the napkins. Give specific directions in how you handle napkins to avoid tearing.

I encourage parents to choose their battles and to avoid setting up children for failure. If you know Jeffrey has difficulty sitting still, then why would you take him to some place where you know he must sit quietly? If you know a child cannot act appropriately or within an acceptable range in a certain type of situation, why choose to humiliate him? This is not to say that you cannot challenge the child—but you need to do so in small, easily accomplished steps.

### Envisioning the Future

I try to give parents perspective by helping them think about what their child will be like when older. In providing early intervention services, the focus tends to be on the here and now. Families are often in crisis with an alcohol-affected child. Focusing on what skills the child needs at a later age can help diminish the current crisis. Often parents will see that the current problem will have little meaning for their child at age twenty-one or thirty.

Even though I provide services for children from birth to age three, I ask parents to write down long-term goals for each age level. What are your hopes for this child at twenty-one? At thirty? At forty? What skills do we need to foster in the early years that will ease his or her way in the adult world? Encouraging a family to look beyond the current frustration often leads to less discouragement and more hope.

## Honest Communication and Alliances with Professionals

Parents need open, honest communication with the professionals who work with their children and they need to create mutually supportive alliances. I communicate with parents the way I want professionals to communicate with me. I want honesty and I expect honesty from those who work with my children. Parents need information. As professionals, we often need to make judgments about timing when we deliver information. But I believe that parents are entitled to all the information we can gather so they can advocate for their child.

Parents should be straightforward with professionals. Inform your doctor that you want specific information about your child's medical condition. If you do not get cooperation, find a doctor who will work with you as a team member.

Share the knowledge that you have about your child with the professionals. If you have trouble remembering, take notes. Identifying patterns in behavior often helps you figure out successful strategies. Keep a developmental journal. Track your child's growth on a developmental chart. Note what is easy and what is difficult. Identify the types of activities that spark your child's interest.

Parents should tell professionals, especially teachers, how to work with their particular child. In both home and school, for example, children will pay attention better if they get a specific, consistent cue. Use the same phrase, like "Now, Jeffrey" when you want the child to pay attention rather than different phrases like "Jeffrey . . . " or "Come, Jeffrey." If your child is in child care or a preschool setting, make sure that the people working with him know what cues you use. It is not too much to ask them to use the same cues. Using mixed signals makes life especially difficult for alcohol-affected children who have trouble sorting out the message from the noise in their environment.

Make teachers aware of what you consider to be your child's strengths as well as problems. Too often professionals focus on the problems and forget the strengths, which are the foundation for self-esteem. If your preschool teacher talks about Jeffrey's inability to attend during story time, tell the teacher about Jeffrey's interest in Legos at home and what he has created. Do not hesitate to point out the positives to professionals.

### Strategies for Social-Emotional and Cognitive Development

I use a three-step approach in providing early intervention services: (1) find out where the child is, (2) figure out where the parent wants the child to go, and (3) identify the steps we are going to use in getting there.

While I suggest below a cookbook of educational strategies, parents need to keep in mind that no one approach works for every child. I tell each parent, "We'll try it and see if it works." I have often been pleasantly surprised when something worked that I did not anticipate and equally frustrated when something I really believed would work did not. Each child is an individual and the impact of alcohol exposure is specific to each one. Especially with alcohol-affected children, the same strategy does not work all the time. Key #1 works some days and key #2 works on other days. You need to have a lot of keys to get places.

### Bonding and Hypersensitivity to Touch

For alcohol-affected children, bonding is not always a natural, flowing developmental process. They need assistance and lots of affection, even if they jerk away when you try to hug and kiss them.

One of your goals should be to develop in the child the habit of making good eye contact, since people expect eye contact when communicating with others. Another critical goal is to decrease the child's hypersensitivity to being touched. You want the child to respond positively to pleasurable touching and to develop appropriate behaviors in response to physical contact. Teaching these responses now when your child is an infant or toddler is far easier than trying to break bad habits later on.

With a very small child, start by directing his focus to your face through touching the child's nose and then touching your nose. Early morning wake-up time is often a good time for this activity. Keep the time periods short. Do not force the child. This play should be comforting, not stressful.

Whenever you speak to your child, establish good eye contact first. Touch Jeffrey lightly on the shoulder, kneel down eye-to-eye and say, "Jeffrey, look at Mom." When Jeffrey looks at you, then give him your message.

Help an infant or a young toddler to cuddle in with you. Support the child strongly by rounding your shoulders and bringing your hands together.

For a toddler who is sensitive to touch, never touch or grab him without telling him first. Say in a quiet, calm voice, "Jeffrey, I'm going to touch your arm to help you off the chair." If your toddler reacts sharply to touch, let him initiate the touching at your verbal request, "Jeffrey, take my hand now."

Playing games like "So Big," "Peek-a-Boo," tickling and finding body parts also teach the pleasures of human contact. Bath time offers especially good possibilities. You can use the bath to briskly, but gently, rub a child's arms and legs and talk about what you are doing. Rub lotion on the child's body after the bath and allow him to rub lotion on himself and on you. Talk about how it feels so the child will learn to become aware of touching and will associate being touched with warm and pleasant times.

If your child reacts negatively to hugs and kisses, keep them short and brief. But keep them frequent and use them as rewards for listening, good behavior, and "just being you." You want your child to link hugs and kisses with positive feelings.

### Hypersensitivity to Sensory Input: Vision, Sound, Taste, Texture

Parents usually have little trouble identifying the problem of hypersensitivity to touch. But they may be slow to recognize that alcohol-affected children can have temper tantrums because they are hypersensitive to other kinds of sensory input, like loud sounds.

If you suspect your child is hypersensitive to certain kinds of sensations, first observe his behavior carefully and keep records of how your child reacts to specific sensory inputs. Then slowly introduce changes and monitor his reactions.

If your child is losing his temper, running around, or hiding when he hears loud sounds, then think about how to make daily life more comfortable. You can remove your doorbell, turn down the phone ring, and encourage siblings not to scream. Talk about sounds that are going to happen so the child can prepare for them. If you are riding in the car, for example, you can talk about the sounds of cars, diesel trucks, and train crossings. Point out ambulance, police, and fire sirens. If you can, avoid noisy environments.

Some alcohol-affected children are sensitive to light. If you are going to the store, talk about the lights. Try out a special pair of sunglasses just for shopping.

Specialists can help you with these problems. If your child has visual sensitivity, consult an opthamologist to rule out any other visual problems. See an audiologist for a hearing examination. If food texture and taste are hypersensitive areas, consult a nutritionist to be sure your child is getting good nutrition and to get suggestions about introducing foods. An occupational therapist specifically trained in sensory integration can be particularly helpful.

**Identifying and Communicating Feelings**

Alcohol-affected children often have a hard time expressing and identifying their emotions. It is hard for them to identify internal feelings, just as it is hard for them to identify events in the external environment. If you teach them to label these emotions early, they are much better able to express their emotions appropriately in later years.

When your child appears to be expressing an emotion, or an incident has occurred that should elicit an emotion, help the child in recognizing and labeling the internal feeling. Suppose Jeffrey has just fallen down the front steps. You can say "Jeffrey, that hurts. It hurts when we fall down." If Jeffrey is fighting with another child and the child has taken away his toy, you can say, "I know you're mad, Jeffrey. When someone takes something away, we feel angry."

When your child is acting out due to anger or frustration, acknowledge the feeling but also tell the child what behaviors should accompany this feeling. Hitting, pushing, breaking, and so forth are not appropriate actions, but the emotion the child is feeling is appropriate for the incident.

## Recognizing Familiar People Versus Strangers

Parents are often disturbed to see alcohol-affected children approach strangers and even leave with them. You need to teach children early to separate familiar people from strangers and you should show them explicitly how to act with strangers.

First, teach children to name and identify family members and talk about the role each person plays in the family—mom, dad, brother, sister, and so on. Stress to the child that these are people in our family and people that we know.

When you go to the grocery store, talk to your child about all the people who go to the store that you do not know and who live in their own houses. If you meet a friend at the store whom your child often sees at your home or a place like the doctor's office, talk about the friend with the child. "Jeffrey, that's Mrs. Mack, you see her at Dr. Wilson's office." Say to your friend, "Hi, Mrs. Mack, I was telling Jeffrey that he sees you at Dr. Wilson's."

If your child approaches a stranger inappropriately, do not get upset. Talk to your child with the stranger present and identify the person as a stranger, not someone that the child knows. Let the stranger know that you are teaching your child that some people are familiar and others are not. Show the child exactly how you want him to deal with a stranger.

When a stranger comes to your house, talk about not knowing the person. Your child will model many of your own words and attitudes toward the stranger. Teaching a child at a very young age who is familiar and who is a stranger will help the child expand this discrimination skill as he matures.

## Developing Social Judgment

Alcohol-affected children often have a hard time figuring out what is going on in social life and how they should behave in different social situations. Just as in teaching them how to deal with strangers, you need to teach them how to interpret and respond in particular social settings.

Talk with your child at a very young age about what is going on around him or her in a social context: "That baby is crying." "The boy is talking loudly." "The lady is screaming." The more you can talk about what you see, the more aware the child will become of what is happening in the social world.

Use these observations as a basis for learning how to act in different circumstances. Suppose you are at the library with Jeffrey and another child is talking very loudly. You say to Jeffrey, "That boy on the chair is being too loud for the library." Help Jeffrey to see the boy and listen to his voice. Kneel down next to Jeffrey and say in a quiet voice, "Mom likes you to be quiet at the library. Let's see how quiet you can be."

Be careful to model what you consider to be appropriate social behavior. Keep in mind that alcohol-affected children have a hard time discriminating between appropriate and inappropriate contexts. If you swear at home but not in public, more than likely your child will swear both at home and in public.

### Keeping Children Safe

Alcohol-affected children need to be taught explicitly about the dangers in their environment. They will not necessarily learn on their own that dogs will bite, cats will scratch, doors will close on them if they are not held open, papers will rip if pulled—the list goes on and on. You need to provide your child with information about dangerous objects. You cannot assume they will learn just by watching what happens to other people.

If your child cannot reason about safety, then child-proof your home just as you would for a toddler. Put locks on the doors, get rid of slippery rugs, and latch the cupboards. Think about what might happen if, for example, your child opens the front door. What are the options? Is the road accessible? Is there a gate he can open? Think about how to handle the problem. Could you put a bell on the door to let you know it has been opened?

Give your child explicit messages about what is safe, what is not safe, and why. Climbing on a rocking chair is not safe. Show your child how it falls over when tipped too far. Assist your child in getting in and out of the rocking chair and demonstrate how far you can rock without the chair tipping over.

Be sure to give accurate information to teachers about safety issues. If your child thinks all straight items are for stabbing and climbs everything, let the teacher know what to expect. The teacher will then be able to cope much more easily and be less judgmental.

## Teaching Your Child How to Play

For young children, play is a means of learning. Alcohol-affected children, however, may not know how to play. They often scatter their attention over too many toys and hurry from one activity to another. Parents typically need to teach children with FAS/FAE how to use toys. They can also use play time to teach language and concepts that alcohol-affected children have trouble acquiring on their own, like cause and effect sequences.

Since children with FAS/FAE often learn better when they gain information from as many senses as possible, parents need to provide learning opportunities in as many modalities as possible. Mirror activities, which provide visual information, are especially valuable. You can start working with your child in the mirror at three or four months of age. The child sees his image and your image in the mirror. He hears you talk about what he sees in the mirror. He touches the mirror, himself, and you. You can help the child find and label body parts through mirror games. You say "eye," help the child see the eye in the mirror, and then help the child touch his eye. The next developmental step is to find the parent's eye. The child can go on to identify eyes and other body parts on dolls, pets, and stuffed animals.

To teach cause and effect, use toys with clear cause and effect sequences, like pop-up toys. The child needs to learn that if you push $A$ then $O$ pops up, that this sequence is dependable, and a result of purposeful action.

You may need to show alcohol-affected children how to play with a toy. Especially valuable are toys that require children to perform a sequence of activities, like dressing a doll. Show the child, putting your hand over his, how to use the toy. Reward the child for every step mastered. If your child cannot handle the toy, put it away until he has more skill. You want your child to have successes with toys and to use them appropriately.

Creative play situations, such as a garage or airport with little people and equipment, also offer unusual difficulties and opportunities. Alcohol-affected children will often continue to do the same thing with a toy. They will push a car on the floor, for example, and repeat "Zoom." They need someone to show them that the car can carry people, go home, and park in the garage. The people riding in the car can go in and eat dinner and then take another ride. Begin with what the child can do well—push the car—and expand the activity.

Play needs to be purposeful. If your child empties toy containers, spreads them around, and moves on to another activity, the play has had no developmental effect. Dividing toys into small containers is helpful: blocks in one, Legos in another; magnetic blocks in another, and so on. These bins should be out of the child's reach. Then you can offer a choice for the activity. The child can play, put everything back in the container, and then choose another container.

Stressing to the child that play and other activities have a start and an end is an important concept to develop. Ask if Jeffrey is all done with the blocks. If he is done, then say, "Put all the blocks in the container, and you can have the cars." You are trying to build the concept that activities have a clear start and stop.

Games like "What happens next?" also develop the concept of a sequence as well as teaching children important daily routines. Get Jeffrey interested in learning a routine by turning it into a song. Mom sings, for example, "I get up in the morning." Jeff sings, "I get up in the morning." Mom sings, "I kiss my son." Jeff sings, "I kiss my mom." Mom sings, "I go to the potty." Jeff sings, "I go to the potty." Mom sings, "I wash my hands." Jeff sings, "I wash my hands," and so forth.

With an older child, you can teach sequences of activities by asking questions like, "First we get the bowl and what happens next?" If the child does not respond, you give the answer, "We choose our cereal . . . .We get the Cheerios and then we . . . ?" The child answers,

"Pour it in the bowl." Providing alcohol-affected children with both the action and the language for the action helps them learn the sequence of the activities.

### Teaching Children to Pay Attention

Parents can use play time to develop alcohol-affected children's ability to pay attention, one of their most common difficulties. You are trying to intrigue children with a task and gradually develop their abilities to stay focused on the task, even when tempted with distractors.

The game of finding objects, for example, develops the skill of focusing on a task. You can use a container full of lentils or rice and an assortment of small toys like cars or rings. With your child watching, hide the toys in the lentils. If your child messes around with the lentils and makes no attempt to find the toys, gently place your hand over the child's hand and guide the child in digging and finding the toys. "Oh, Jeffrey, you found the car. Find more cars." Continue to guide Jeffrey in finding the objects until he locates objects on his own.

If you are having trouble getting your child to pay attention, try using a specific and consistent cue such as "Look." This word lets the child know you want his visual attention for a specific period of time. Use this word only when you have a message to communicate. Suppose you want to teach Jeffrey the word "clock." Start the sequence by saying "Look." When you have his attention, point visually to the clock, and pick Jeffrey up physically, saying, "Look, the clock." When Jeffrey looks at the clock, reward him with a hug, a pat on the shoulder, a kiss, or a smile. Even if you do not get the complete response that you want, reward Jeffrey for any indication that he knew you were requesting something of him. Jeffrey thus gets stimulation through many channels and learns that he gets a reward for interacting with other people.

### Providing a Definite Place for Learning Activities

Providing a defined space for learning activities is especially helpful for alcohol-affected children, who find it hard to focus on a task. You establish visual and physical cues which tell the child "it's time to learn."

Choose an area that is visually accessible to the main activity area in your home, like a family room or kitchen. Ask yourself where your family spends the bulk of time. Your purpose is to provide a space for learning, not to isolate the child from everyday life.

Choose furniture for your child that is size-appropriate. Your child's feet should rest on the floor and his elbows should just clear the table top. You can use a cardboard box as a footrest and make it more permanent by pushing the front legs of the chair through the box. You can adjust the height of the table by taping small wooden blocks to the bottom.

When you put your child at the table, always give him the same verbal cues, like: "Let's learn"; or "Time for work"; or "School time." Use a positive term and make the time fun. From the beginning, be consistent about the behavior that you expect during this time. How much wiggling is acceptable? How many activities does the child need to complete, or just try? Are you going to take telephone calls during this time or does your child get your full attention? The more consistency you can provide, the better your child will do. Start out with short periods at the learning table and then build up to longer periods.

### Dealing with Hyperactivity and Impulsive Behaviors

Alcohol-affected children often find it hard to focus on a task because of constant restless physical energy. You are asking Jeffrey to sit and attend to a task and all his body wants to do is move. This physical energy needs to be directed, not capped off. The trick is to link the physical movements to the task you are trying to get the child to accomplish.

Suppose you want to teach Jeffrey the names and functions of objects. Put these objects into small blocks that snap open. The child must choose a block, shake the block, open the block, find the object, and make the object work. ("The bunny hops." "The truck zooms." "The watch ticks.") Then the child must place the object back into the block, close the block, stack the block, and choose another one. With this enjoyable game, I have watched children increase their ability to sit at a small table from two minutes to thirty minutes. The children are not perfectly still. That physical energy is still flowing—they swing their feet, wiggle on their chairs, turn around on their chairs, pick up what they have dropped, and so on. But the main goals are accomplished: the child learns vocabulary and also improves attention and memory.

Giving the child a focused physical activity helps control hyperactive behavior. Place your toddler's favorite toys around the room and encourage the child to get them. When you see a three-year-old becoming scattered, provide a specific physical activity. Offer the child a trampoline, punching bag, or stationary bicycle. Put a mattress on the floor to jump and roll on. Tape a circle on the floor and ask the child to run around the circle. Draining off energy often improves the child's ability to attend.

Whenever your child displays an uncontrolled, impulsive behavior, make the child aware of it. Be matter-of-fact, not critical or judgmental. But the child needs to have a verbal label for the behavior. If you start such labeling at an early age (twenty-eight to thirty months), you will find it much easier to address similar impulsive behavior later on.

Structure and consistency are critical in extinguishing impulsive behaviors. Give the child the same message ("No, Jeffrey. No screaming.") in the same manner (calm and without anger), and the behavior will gradually stop.

In short, to control impulsive behavior:
1. Start at a young age, twelve to fourteen months, to model appropriate behavior.
2. Do not discipline inappropriately—"time-out" may or may not work.
3. Provide appropriate outlets for the child's physical needs, like running, jumping, and bouncing.
4. Keep it positive—anger and frustration will not build attending skills.

### Providing Structure, Routine, and Consistency

Alcohol-affected children are far more successful if parents and teachers provide them with structured, consistent routines. Such repetitive sequences reduce cognitive demands on their brains. The children can depend on consistent cues in the setting to tell them what to do. Structure and routine turns their environment from a place that is confusing and upsetting to a place that is understandable and predictable.

Develop a sequenced progression of activities for the child's daily life. Use the same early morning routines, for example, such as eating breakfast, getting dressed, getting ready to leave the house, and arriving at the child-care facility. Do the same activities in the same order each day.

Bedtime is a priority time for consistency and routine. Often children with FAS/FAE have trouble winding down and cannot settle in for the night. Talk about bedtime coming soon and develop a routine like reading a story, having a drink of juice, taking a bath, rubbing on lotion, getting into pajamas, talking quietly on the bed, and then settling into the bed to go to sleep. Talk the child through the steps and use the same steps every night.

Changes in activities, even stopping at the grocery on the way home, can cause an alcohol-affected child great stress. If you must change a routine, prepare the child. If you know that you usually spend the morning at home with Jeffrey but you have to go shopping the next day, then start talking at bedtime about what you will be doing the next morning. When you wake up Jeffrey in the morning, remind him that today is the day we are going shopping. Even if your child is young and nonverbal, hearing your words and tone of voice will help him understand that something different is happening.

If your child is having difficulty during a nonroutine activity or a transition to a new activity, stop what you are doing and pay attention to the child. Calm the child by talking in a quiet, smooth voice and assure the child that everything is fine. Talk to the child again about the steps and what needs to happen next. Keep in mind that this process may take a long time, but your consistency and patience will eventually help the child deal with change much more easily.

Since discipline creates strong, disruptive emotion, consistency is especially important for alcohol-affected children. Parents, teachers, and child care providers should be in agreement about what type of discipline will be used, what behavior limits will be set, and what practical consequences will occur if the child does not comply.

## The Prognosis

Over the last ten years, I have worked with about thirty to thirty-five children who were diagnosed as FAS or FAE. Time and again I have noticed two factors that make an enormous difference to the child's development at age three. The first is whether the parents are willing to make the changes in their lifestyles that the child needs to succeed. I have seen vast differences between children raised in families able to alter their daily routines and children who come from families too disrupted to focus attention on the children.

The second factor is the family's ability to provide a positive atmosphere and focus on what the child does best. You work from strengths and success to weaknesses and problems. The children are hungry for success and for strategies and structure that enable them to learn. Even though Jeffrey had spent all day in a child-care center, when he came to our early intervention program, he would zip into his chair and wait to learn. But if I changed this routine he fell apart.

When parents follow through at home with the strategies we teach them, we have seen great improvement in the children. With such families, children leave the program at age three close to their developmental age level in language, large and small muscle activities, and other skills. Serious problems remain—especially attention deficits. But many children are so improved that they no longer qualify for special services. Their test results show that they are quite close to their developmental age.

Alcohol-affected children who do not get home support or who come to us very late look very different from those who have experienced the benefits of early intervention. When we see these children, they tend to be six to twelve months behind in developmental level at age three. Early intervention cannot overcome the damage of alcohol. But early intervention can dramatically improve the child's life skills and can lay the foundation for later development.

# Getting Jeffrey Ready for School
## Kindergarten at Home
### MICHELE SAIZ

*Michele Saiz is an experienced junior high school science teacher. She and her husband adopted a baby with FAS. When her son was four years old, Ms. Saiz decided to take leave from science teaching in order to help him develop the language skills he would need for kindergarten. When Jeffrey was five years old, she decided to stay home another year to home-school him for kindergarten. The Saizes have organized a support group in Alaska for children with FAS/FAE, which publishes the FAS/FAE Newsletter. [See Appendix II for more information about the newsletter.]*

"LOOK, MOM, I ATE ALL MY CEREAL. ZERO CHEERIOS," *says my five-year-old Jeffrey.*

My heart fills with joy every time Jeffrey says something so intelligent. Grasping that concept that "nothing equals zero" after just one lesson is amazing. Many children with FAS have trouble with arithmetic and abstract concepts; Jeffrey does not.

*"I sat in my seat the whole time," says Jeffrey so proudly.*

Teaching him to sit still took years, and it remains a constant struggle. We bring his distractibility to his attention—he needs to learn to sit still. "Jeffrey," we say, "Remember the rule. You need to finish eating before you can be excused. . . . You have to ask to be excused before you can get down." At five, he can do it. Before, we had to pick him up and put him back in his seat. You have to be consistent.

*"Mom, Mom, B for boots," he says with excitement, holding up his winter boots.*

I am thrilled he can transfer a phonics lesson on the sound of B to the actual boots he and his sister are playing with. I thought he would never catch on that the letters of the alphabet make special sounds. When we first started when Jeffrey was age five, it took him a full month to connect the B sound with words that start with B. Now he has grasped the basic concept and can make connections between letters and the sounds they make in words. That is the beauty of home-schooling—easy real-life connections. My husband and I can work the lesson of the moment into whatever we are doing with Jeffrey.

*"I can write my name all by myself," he announces.*

When I started to teach him to write letters at age five, he would sit and cry. Then he taught me something important—to guide him. I take his hand and make the letter. Then I encourage him to try it on his own, one letter at a time. He started fooling around with his pencil, and one day he wrote his name.

*"Mom, I want to eat up here so I can watch Reading Rainbow."*

That was a sentence with thirteen words, AND he is reasoning. It is lunch time and he knows the rule is to eat at the kitchen counter. Jeffrey is giving me a reason for eating in the living room. We call, "That's great, Jeffrey! Good talking!" For more than a year, we have been trying to get Jeffrey to speak in sentences longer than six words. Now he has got it.

"I feed the hungry," Jeffrey says, as he walks into the Food Bank and hands over the groceries he bought. He has earned the money from recycling aluminum cans. We help Jeffrey collect aluminum cans, and he crushes them with a can crusher he purchased with money from his see-through bank.

We have started a yearlong and maybe a lifelong project—thinking of others and recycling. Jeffrey has empathy for others, despite what is said about children with FAS not having a conscience. It is a delight to see him want to feed the hungry.

## ADOPTING JEFFREY—WHAT THE PSYCHOLOGIST PREDICTED

At birth, our adopted son Jeffrey was diagnosed as borderline FAS. He had the characteristic thin upper lip, lack of a defined philtrum, a heart murmur, extreme sensitivity to touch, and a rigid body. Jeffrey's birth mother had two other children with alcohol-related birth defects. While we do not know the diagnosis for her first child, her second has severe FAS.

When Jeffrey was three months old, the adoption agency requested a psychological consultation so a long-term placement plan could be made for him. After giving him a battery of tests, the psychologist found his overall development to be "half to two-thirds of what is expected of an infant his age." She frankly stated that his delays were due to "intellectual limitations and predicted an IQ range of fifty to sixty-five."

Special education would be required throughout his school career. She recommended that Jeffrey promptly be enrolled in an Infant Learning Program to begin physical therapy. As an infant, for example, Jeffrey would not turn over in his crib. He would require parents who would carefully follow through on all the expected medical and therapy exercises and advocate for him with schools and institutions.

When we first heard about the possibility of adopting Jeffrey, we knew nothing of this devastating report. My husband and I had just gotten a letter from the adoption agency with wonderful news. It looked likely that Jeffrey would be available as our son. His birth mother had chosen us above several other families who wanted to adopt her child. She chose us because she wanted parents who were of the same religion, who could provide for him educationally, and who were not fat. Because of the Indian Child Welfare Act, the adoption agency had been pleased that my husband is Native American as is Jeffrey.

Then we got the psychologist's report about FAS. I sat on the sofa for a long time with the paper in my hand. My husband and I said to each other, "What should we do?"

That evening the adoption agency called and asked, "About adopting Jeffrey, have you changed your mind?"

Because we had thought of Jeffrey as our son ever since we heard of the possibility of adopting him and because my husband and I wanted a child so very much and because both of us are educators, we felt we could give the little guy a good home with lots of love and a nurturing, consistent environment. We said "yes" to Jeffrey.

We also began an all-out campaign to learn about fetal alcohol syndrome.

### The Infant Learning Program: Progress Disrupted by Seizures

When we got Jeffrey, he was four and a half months old. We had another set of test results from the Infant Learning Program that his foster parents had enrolled him in. These new results were inconsistent with the psychologist's report. Tested at three months, Jeffrey scored about average in language, gross and fine motor skills, and adaptive behavior.

But these results underscored for me a lesson I was to learn again and again. Such early testing results are inconsistent, unreliable, and terribly misleading. At fourteen weeks, he scored "sixteen weeks" on language development. But this score was based entirely on his foster mother's subjective observations. She said he "chuckles, coos, and has an alert expression." We found that Jeffrey, quite the contrary, was a quiet baby who seldom made sounds. As he grew older, it became all too obvious that he was language delayed.

Jeffrey needed an early intervention program. We knew that he had serious problems on the basis of our everyday experience with him. His body was rigid and he could not move his head from right to left. He could move his head only from right to midline and then he would stop. He made few sounds. What was positive about the negative testing results was that he qualified for help. Jeffrey needed help throughout his preschool years. We knew it. But he did not always get it. Ironically, only when Jeffrey got poor testing results did he qualify for the help he needed.

Through the expertise of the Infant Learning Program therapists, we taught Jeffrey to roll over, sit up, drink from a straw, crawl, walk, build towers, play with balls and blocks, use words like "more" in place of whining, and speak in short sentences. As parents, we had to teach Jeffrey skills that most babies pick up on their own. We learned how.

We began by working on the basic skill of rolling over. Jeffrey would lie in one position for hours, hardly moving. The therapists showed us how to teach him to move from his back over to his side. "Try to keep his bottom hip and legs straight," they directed. "Place his hand on the top side of his pelvis, giving him a downward push. Push him from the left and then the right. This strengthens neck and stomach muscles." First, we turned him over. Then he learned to turn over on his own.

This has been our fundamental experience with Jeffrey. What he is taught, he will learn. But he needs to be taught things that most children learn on their own. And it may take a long time. But sometimes it does not.

With Jeffrey, we have also learned to focus on one developmental area at a time. During his first two years, we focused on gross motor skills. When he reached average level, we moved on to fine motor skills. At age two, when both gross and fine motor skills were at average levels, we started to work on expressive speech. You cannot do everything at once.

At age three, Jeffrey was too old for the Infant Learning Program. Since he had made so much progress, he did not qualify for special school district assistance, even though my husband and I knew his language skills were far from where they should be. Before he left the program he received tests that did not reveal his need for further language assistance.

The next fall, Jeffrey suffered a seizure that lasted for one and a half hours. I was at school when the sitter called to say, "Jeffrey is sick. Please come and pick him up." It took more than thirty minutes to find someone to take my place in the classroom. I had no idea he was having a seizure and that this was an emergency. When I arrived at the sitter's house, Jeffrey was lying on the floor; his eyes were rolling in his head; he was making animal-like moaning sounds; his body was jerking. My husband had gotten there two minutes before I had and called an ambulance.

We thought he would never stop convulsing and agonized over the possible damage caused by such a lengthy brain seizure. The numerous tests he underwent were inconclusive as to the cause. Seizures are a symptom of FAS, so that was one possibility. Jeffrey's sugar count was very low following his seizure so that was another possibility. His doctor recommended a daily dosage of phenobarbital for one year to prevent further seizures and recommended frequent, small meals to alleviate the hypoglycemia.

Jeffrey did not have another seizure again, so at the end of twelve months we started weaning him from the drug. At the end of fourteen months, he was completely finished with it. But the drug had its side effects. He became sluggish during the day. At night he became hyperactive and had trouble sleeping. He did not advance with his expressive language skills or with his fine motor skills during that entire year. He was further behind, but he had suffered no further seizures with their risk of brain damage.

### Jeffrey Goes to Preschool and His Parents Back Up the Program at Home

When Jeffrey reached age four, we asked the local school district to test his language skills. He scored below normal levels in verbal ability. According to the report, he "could not repeat six to eight syllable sentences and he did not know opposites like 'boy/girl.'" Nor could he reason about events outside of his immediate personal experience like, "What do you do if you have lost something?" Jeffrey qualified for the district's preschool language program for two and one-half hours each day, five days each week.

Jeffrey started to advance. He began to speak in six- to eight-word sentences. He started to learn alphabet sounds, developed coloring skills, and extended his attention span. At home, we reviewed each day what he had learned in school and praised his progress. We looked at the papers he brought home, emphasized the letters he was learning, and reviewed them again on the weekend. He especially liked the special yellow school bus that came to pick him up and he learned quickly in this special program.

When Jeffrey was almost five, we adopted a baby daughter. Her birth mother also abused alcohol and we were on the alert for FAS/FAE. If she was severely affected by alcohol, we decided, we would not accept her because we felt we would not be able to do well by both of them. But Susan was absolutely normal. She constantly verbalized, and we were amazed and pleased to see how much she helped Jeffrey's speech develop. He imitated all her cooing and gurgling noises and babbling sounds. He had rarely made these sounds as a baby himself, and Susan was helping him go through this developmental phase. His sister became a major factor in his speech development.

Jeffrey developed big brother responsibilities. He fetched diapers, held her bottle, and read baby books to her.

## DECIDING TO HOME-SCHOOL JEFFREY

When Jeffrey turned five, we decided he was ready for school—that is, home-school. We decided to give our son an extra year of kindergarten through a home-school correspondence program before enrolling him in a regular kindergarten. I decided to take the year off to teach him.

We began with one main goal: enabling Jeffrey to express himself verbally on an average level by age six. After beginning home-schooling, we saw the importance of two additional goals: developing his fine motor skills and lengthening his attention span.

### Language Development

At home, we capitalized on Jeffrey's ability to learn visually. We made signs with his first and last name and placed them in the kitchen and his bedroom, the rooms he was in the most. We hung up all his schoolwork and talked about the papers and expanded what he had covered. We bought a see-through bank so Jeffrey could learn the names of his coins and actually see his savings grow. We used drawings on charts to remind him to hang up his coat or brush his teeth. He liked putting the star on his chart himself when he did these tasks. Three weeks later he did not need the star any more, only the chart.

We also worked constantly on Jeffrey's speech development. We read him more and more books, pausing to ask for his ideas. We emphasized books with repetitive words like Eric Carle's/Bill Martin, Jr.'s *Brown bear, brown bear, what do you see?* to encourage him to talk. We gave him hand puppets. He took the puppets to bed and had conversations with them before he fell asleep.

Picture books without words have been a tremendous help. The *Carl* books by Alexandra Day, for example, use pictures, not words, to depict the adventures of a dog named Carl and his owners' child, known as Baby. The first few times we asked Jeffrey to tell the story in words, he said absolutely nothing. After we modeled telling a story for him, he learned to do it, too.

We also expanded his sentences to teach him cause and effect. At first he would say only short sentences like, "Can I have a drink of water?" I would ask him, "Why?" At first he would say "I don't know." Now he says, "Because I am thirsty." We rarely have to prod him to tell us "why," and he uses other causal connections like "because" or "so" on his own.

Sounding out letters to read words has become contagious. Jeffrey sounds out the words he sees in books, road signs, newspapers, and the grocery store. Computer programs like Reader Rabbit and The Playroom have helped with reading as well because they focus Jeffrey's attention. We also play games, like a card game based on the "at" word family. He places the beginning consonant on the "at" game pieces and matches the word he is sounding out to its picture. Jeffrey thoroughly enjoys playing this game so we have expanded it to include other word families. He is thrilled to be reading.

## Lengthening Attention Span

The computer has become invaluable in developing Jeffrey's ability to concentrate. At first, when he was so distractible, we could use the computer to focus his attention on one thing at a time. My husband put Jeffrey on his lap and enclosed him with his arms to focus Jeffrey's attention on the screen. They would play games, like Kids Pix, where Jeffrey chose pictures from two columns and used the pictures to draw a scene on the screen. This game intrigued Jeffrey and was compatible with his visual learning style. It also developed his language abilities, since we talked about the pictures he drew.

I noticed Jeffrey could not sit still for an assignment for more than three seconds. His feet were constantly moving or he was always getting up and moving about. He could not stay on task. Whenever he moved around, I brought it to his attention. I was surprised to find he was not conscious of his constant moving. I told him to tell his brain, "Be still." I gave him a reward for focusing, like something delicious to eat whenever he wrote a letter across a line, something he hated to do. When he finished an activity, he could have a break if he wanted one.

These strategies are working.

*"Mom, the chair is too hard for me," Jeffrey says and goes to get a pillow. He kneels on his pillow and remains focused on his task.*

Clearly, Jeffrey has a long way to go but he is improving. When he likes what he is doing, he can sit still for ten or fifteen minutes.

## Developing Fine Motor Skills

Coloring, drawing, and cutting with scissors were not Jeffrey's strengths. He disliked any activity involving them. His advisory teacher from the correspondence study program suggested daily fine motor activities to overcome his hesitancy. We started gradually because he found these tasks very difficult and demanding. First, Jeffrey was allowed to tear up colored papers and make a book of colors. He tore out pictures of toys from catalogs to tell Santa what he wanted for Christmas. Next, he scribbled on a large piece of paper following a direction like, "Make a wavy line from one end of the paper to another." With a needle and thread, he sewed paper scraps together. He liked sewing so much he helped me sew buttons on clothing.

Finally we got to writing the letters of the alphabet. We started with sky writing where he made letters in the air. He wrote with his finger in cornmeal. He would write out letters with glue and put glitter on them. He made letters with colored chalk on black paper and then made them on the chalkboard.

All these activities he now enjoys. When he colors, writes, draws, or uses scissors I no longer guide his hand. "I can do it myself, Mom," says Jeffrey.

### Math Skills—Jeffrey's High Point

Jeffrey has not had to struggle with his math work. He grasps concepts easily and quickly. He enjoys the lessons, and his easy mastery of the material boosts his confidence. I line up animal crackers and show him how to ask for the second one, then the third. Computer programs like Turbomath and Math Shop, Jr. reinforce the math lessons I present in a visual way.

## VALUE OF HOME-SCHOOLING FOR CHILDREN LIKE JEFFREY

For a child like Jeffrey, home-schooling offers a number of exceptional advantages. Other parents of alcohol-affected children have turned to home-schooling for similar reasons.

First, home-schooling has given Jeffrey the time and attention a regular classroom teacher may not be able to give. One of his assignments, for example, asked him to draw grass for some animals to walk in. He cried and refused to do it. After calming him down, I asked what was wrong. He shrugged his shoulder and said, "I don't know." I insisted that he complete the grass and he cried again. Finally, it occurred to me that he might not know how to draw grass at all. I asked if I could help him do it. He agreed so I modeled for him what he was to do. This lesson was illuminating for me as well as for Jeffrey, and the importance of modeling is now in all my lesson plans. A busy classroom teacher might not have the time to figure out what was behind Jeffrey's classroom behavior and might have labeled him obstinate for refusing to do the work.

Another advantage of home-schooling is the easy transitions from school lessons to real-life experiences. For example, Jeffrey sometimes confuses his right with his left. Whenever we drive together in the car, I put on the blinker and say, "The car will make a right turn." After a few verbal samples of left and right turning, I will point the way the car will turn and ask him whether it is left or right. Such practice reinforces the concept and the review is fun.

Home-schooling is also teaching Jeffrey socially acceptable behavior. When we first started, Jeffrey would throw objects in frustration if he did not understand or was asked to do something he did not want to do at that time. A teacher with twenty children in a classroom would find it difficult to cope with such episodes—other children could get hurt. A mother can lovingly insist that he perform the task without throwing anything. These episodes occur rarely now and just require a reminder that he must sit and complete the task before he can go on to something else.

## CONCLUSION

The amount of time, energy, patience, and commitment required from us to teach Jeffrey is staggering. But it is essential and we have learned not to give up. With loving insistence, a structured routine, and explanations for changes in schedule ahead of time, experience shows he will understand. Experience shows he will learn what he is taught. We think at this point he is about average in kindergarten skills. He can blend words but he cannot yet read.* He can write letters but he cannot use invented spelling to write his own stories.

We do not really know where Jeffrey is developmentally. We have seen too many predictions that do not come true, such as— fortunately—the psychologist's original prediction that he would

---

*Note [added in proof]: Jeffrey reads simple books now, books with two or three lines per page. He started in January 1993 at age five and one-half.

have an IQ of fifty to sixty-five. We have seen too many test results that do not tell the story.

Perhaps his arithmetic skills will continue to be strong or perhaps when mathematics becomes less concrete he will fall behind. Perhaps he will learn to read easily or perhaps he will not.

But Jeffrey has excellent self-esteem. This is a crucial advantage of home-schooling. Jeffrey is not constantly comparing himself with others. He is developing confidence, which is what he needs to conquer what comes.

# Raising Alcohol-Affected Twins

CHRISTINE KING

*Christine King from Surrey, British Columbia, is the adoptive mother of identical twin girls, later found to have fetal alcohol syndrome.*

*"Writing this paper is one of the most difficult things that I have ever had to do, because I can talk to my heart's content about what it is like to live with Whitney and Haley, but trying to write it all down on paper is a very difficult task."*

WHITNEY AND HALEY ENTERED OUR LIVES AND OUR HEARTS when they were born on March 28, 1987. They came into our family by way of a private adoption arranged by my doctor. I never would have dreamed in a million years that I would ever get to be a mother to twins. People have since said to me that sometimes things are just meant to be, and that we are the best parents that Whitney and Haley could have. Most of the time that is far from the truth, but I know when they curl up in my arms at night, they were meant to be a part of our lives, no matter what the cost. They are my world and my everything.

My husband and I spent over five years trying to conceive a baby. This process included several major operations and two cycles on the *in vitro* fertilization program. Unfortunately, all of this effort was to no avail, and I had a hysterectomy at age twenty-seven.

About three months later my doctor called me to say that she had a young woman in her office who was giving up twin girls for adoption. She did not even bother to ask if I was interested; she knew that I would jump at the chance. She asked me to write a letter to the birth mother telling her about us. This I did with great difficulty, and subsequently after two more letters and many sleepless nights, we were chosen from six other couples to be her babies' adoptive parents. We received one letter from her. She gave us some information about herself and her family and also said that she had taken a couple of Irish coffees, which she was not proud of, but nothing more and certainly no drugs.

I learned that she and I are very much alike in personality and habits. She loves the outdoors, as I do, and is extremely sensitive, as I am. She is around my size and height, and we are similar in appearance. She also gave us information about the birth father that was interesting to have. He was not supportive during the pregnancy and did not even know that the girls had been born until many months later. I wish I had gotten the chance to meet him, too. The twins' biological grandparents have since lost seven grandchildren, three to adoption and four to abortion.

I spoke to her most nights on the telephone for about three weeks before the babies were born. She was finally admitted to the hospital because of malnutrition, and the babies were showing no gestational growth.

After it was determined by amniocentesis that the babies' lungs were developed sufficiently to live without respirators, she was given a Cesarean section and the babies were born at 4:03 and 4:10 that afternoon.

I got to see the twins on their second day of life and will never forget seeing them for the first time. Words cannot capture the emotions that were flowing through me. After I had seen the twins, I went to my doctor's office and she told me that it was her policy not to let the adoptive parents into the hospital to visit the baby (babies in our case) until the birth mother had left the hospital. I spoke to their birth mother on the telephone that night and she asked me when I was going to see them again. I told her the situation and she immediately said, "I'll fix that."

The next thing I knew my doctor was on the phone telling me to be at the hospital the next morning for the 8:00 A.M. feeding. I was ecstatic. The birth mother truly felt that I was the babies' mother and therefore I should be there bonding with them and taking care of them. I was so lucky that she felt this way. I spent all day at the hospital for the next nine days and even breast-fed Whitney during the daytime with a special breast feeding system for adoptive moms.

On the day that the papers were due to be signed, their birth mother told me that she wanted to be the one to give me the good news, so we arranged that I would wait for her call at the hospital. She was thirty minutes late calling me and I was beside myself. I looked up and saw a young woman walking towards the entrance. I looked at her, she at me, and we knew instantly who each other was. We hugged and cried until our arms ached and our tears ran dry. We then went across the street and talked and talked about lots of different things, not just the babies. After talking, we decided that we would end contact and get on with our lives. I gave her a beautiful ceramic photo album filled with pictures of the twins from their first few days of life, and we said goodbye.

After I returned home that night, I called her. I just could not say goodbye. Luckily, she had been waiting to call me to say the same thing. I guess things were just meant to turn out that way.

## EARLY CHILDHOOD

The twins were diagnosed with fetal alcohol syndrome (FAS) when they were two years old. My pediatrician and the infant development worker actually suspected FAS when the twins were one year old, and the diagnosis was confirmed a year later. I felt like my heart had been broken. It was a heavy weight to carry. I had always tried to convince myself that the twins had the developmental delays because they were so little or maybe because I had not spent enough time with them. Then when I was told they had FAS, I felt totally helpless and fearful, and above all, asked the question, "Why?"

If we had known that Whitney and Haley would have special needs when they were born, I am positive that we would still have brought them into our lives. But it would have been helpful to have been emotionally prepared for the diagnosis. One of the things that

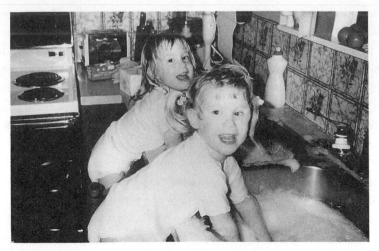

*Whitney (back) and Haley (foreground), age 3½*

bothers me most when meeting people and talking about the twins is that people say, "Well, they look fine." I always felt that I had to justify their behavior, which now I do not even think about doing.

We are lucky that, except for mildly dysmorphic features, they are cute, strawberry-blonde little munchkins. They are also very small for their age, so people do not expect as much from them as they would if they looked their age. One of the hardest things is watching their friends develop into typical children while Haley and Whitney lag behind, never appearing to catch up. We have to keep telling ourselves that they are developing (although slowly), and it is so wonderful to see something new that they have learned.

When the twins reached the age of three, they were referred to a special needs preschool program because of their developmental problems. They entered the program in September of 1990 and attend for four hours a day, five days a week.

The girls are picked up by a school bus shortly after 9:00 A.M. and arrive at school with the other dozen kids in their class at 9:30 A.M. When they get home, they usually watch television, play outside, do puzzles, or I take them to visit with friends. They are very social little people and love to visit. Also, their attention span can be excellent, if they choose; they can sit and watch a movie for an hour or so with no problems.

Their preschool program is solely for special needs children, but the special needs range widely. Some children have only speech delays, while others have various syndromes and varying degrees of behavior problems or developmental delay. One other child in the class is diagnosed with FAS. However, this child has additional medical problems and also was adopted at an older age than Whitney and Haley.

Whitney and Haley are seeing a speech language pathologist once a week. Whitney's language skills are much better than Haley's. Haley tends to let Whitney talk for her, but the result is that Haley becomes very frustrated. They are learning to take turns and sometimes even willingly give up an object that the other one really wants. The girls require specialized help right now in order to learn fine motor, language, gross motor, and social skills that kids without FAS typically learn by themselves, and they will spend another full year in the special needs preschool.

I am very grateful that the girls are as happy and healthy as they are. So many people have children with far more serious problems than our daughters, but that fact does not make our efforts any easier.

With the twins still so young, I am unsure of what lies ahead. The way things are going right now, their prognosis is not too bad, although we will have to wait a couple more years to see what learning disabilities arise. A developmental delay of approximately one year is not too far behind the norm, but if this delay increases, and it usually does, then we will encounter more challenges.

### GETTING THE TWINS UNDER CONTROL

Unfortunately, apart from teachers at school, Whitney and Haley do not respond to requests or discipline from any one other than myself. So, I have become their primary caregiver. The girls are very insecure and quite undisciplined if they are not absolutely sure that the person they are with has full control over their behavior. I am not able to leave them with anyone for more than a very short period of time as their behavior becomes uncontrollable. The twins need to be dealt with firmly and very consistently.

Any change in caregivers, routine, or even a different clerk at the video rental store can and usually does send them into a temper tantrum. I believe that the girls' need for consistency in every aspect of their life compels them to fight with their very being any changes that must occur, even accidentally.

On the whole, they are relatively calm, peaceful little girls, but anything can and will provoke a screaming fit if things are not familiar. Their school tends to ignore such behavior and the teachers let them decide when they are ready to return to their activity.

One has to be extremely patient and willing just to wait or walk away when things get out of hand. The less patient I become, however, the more they misbehave, and the longer it takes to calm them down. It is far more constructive to remain composed.

## THE DESPERATE NEED FOR TEACHER-PARENT COMMUNICATION

One day at school, a rainstorm turned their preschool schedule around a bit. When Whitney returned home from school that day, she urinated on the floor twice and was generally hysterical, cranky, and unpleasant. Much later in the evening, I talked with one of the teachers and she mentioned that their school routine that day had been very different from normal. Whitney was sent for several time-outs after she was caught biting and misbehaving. If I had been aware of the schedule change and the reason for her outbursts, I would not have become so frustrated and impatient with her after she returned home.

It is very important for the preschool or day-care to relay information about the child's day. Make arrangements with the teacher in advance to provide this information, and discuss the importance of doing so. Ask the teacher to provide information about the child's accomplishments as well. I was pleased to learn from Whitney's teacher that she is starting to let other kids share her space, which is great progress for her.

## How Problematic Discipline Is

When the children misbehave, they often know that they are at fault. Scolding is generally ineffective, however. Discipline works best if I remain calm, have eye contact with the children, speak slowly, and make sure they understand what I want them to do and why they are being disciplined.

Discipline should not only be constructive, but it often requires creativity. For example, the twins used to dawdle over their meal. So I set a timer and told them that the meal was over when the buzzer sounded. When it sounded, I did not say a word and simply removed their food. At first, they reacted with temper tantrums, but soon they learned that they must eat their meal within a reasonable period.

Making idle threats is one of the worst things that one can do. I am very careful not to say something that I cannot carry through. When they are calm and comply with my request, I feel a great sense of accomplishment.

## My Solution to Ongoing Problems

### Language Skills

Haley's language skills are quite behind Whitney's. So we started using sign language with her as much as we can. It helps her to have the visual cues. I find that she understands instructions if I sign them as well as say them. They both have problems finding words, and signing helps.

### Feeding, Sucking, and Facial Sensitivity

Whitney and Haley were very weak suckers as infants. I took them off the bottle at just over a year old. Drinking from a cup was a lot easier and they learned how to do it rather quickly, although they tend to gulp their beverages.

The girls took a long time to learn to drink from a straw, and they still have a very immature grasp with their lips around the straw.

They are extremely sensitive in the facial area, and I am the only one who can brush their teeth. The speech therapist is working on this problem, without much success.

### Gross and Fine Motor Skills

The girls are behind about twelve months in gross and fine motor skills, and we do not qualify for assisted therapy because the girls are not physically handicapped. Consequently, nothing is available to us to help improve these areas except time.

### Speech

Whitney's and Haley's language development is very slow. They knew three words at the age of two. I hope we will see improvement by taking them to the speech therapist. Together with good role modeling, there is not much else that can be done.

I have learned subtle techniques to encourage the girls' use of words. If one of them asks for juice, I hand her the container but do not remove the lid. By doing this, I am literally forcing the child to use more words to tell me what she wants. If she has trouble finding more words I might say, "Do you want juice in your cup?" If my husband is around, I suggest that she "ask Daddy for more juice." This technique helps the girls use more language. The problem is that it is often quicker and easier just to pour the juice myself.

### Dressing

Whitney and Haley are able to dress themselves, but they are slow. On those mornings when I do not have the time or energy to encourage them to get ready for school, I dress them myself. At bedtime, I have more flexibility to wait until they undress themselves and put on their own pajamas. If they do not comply within a reasonable time, however, they go to bed naked. Unfortunately, this is often what they prefer.

### Playing with Toys

In order for the girls to play constructively with their toys, we have to be sure that everything is very neat and packed away or sorted by type, such as kitchen play toys and play food. If all their toys are lumped together in a big bin, they lose focus and playtime becomes aimless. We must be sure that only one thing is out at a time. What I find most frustrating is that they seem unable to play pretend games without a substantial amount of input from me. Playing with them takes time and energy.

## CONCLUSION

Society seems to be built for kids who are flexible and who can be moved in and out of situations without many problems. It has been difficult to find a place within the system where my children can receive the strength and consistency that they so desperately need.

My husband and I take each day one step at a time and hope with all our hearts that Whitney and Haley will be able to have the kind of life all parents wish for their children.

As parents of special needs children, all we can do is love them and work as hard as we can to give them all the help, support, and understanding they need to reach their full potential. This poem I wrote says it all in a nutshell:

Sun Rise

As the sun rises on yet another new day
I thank God for the twins he sent our way.
Before they came, we seemed so alone;
The arrival of them has made our house a home.
Our lives are now full of ups, downs, and twirls
But we love so very much our precious little girls.

Whitney and Haley are our lives and we love them more than life itself. We would be lost without them, and their special needs just seem to make our lives that much more challenging, interesting, frustrating and, yes, rewarding.

## AFTERWORD

August 1992. I am now a single parent and have been for one year. The twins are now five and one-half years old and have a delay in development of eighteen to thirty-six months. This delay has increased, which is what I was told to expect. Taking care of them and

*Whitney (right) and Haley (left), age 5*

working full-time is a handful, but I would not give them up for anything in the world. Consistency and patience are still the most important aspects of dealing with their problems. Any change in routine still throws them off and the smallest thing seems to throw their minds into chaos. Such a simple thing as dropping a toy and not being able to locate it right away sends both of them into a tantrum. It is very difficult to always remain calm and try to keep them from losing control at every turn in their lives. They will be staying in their preschool for their kindergarten year, which is very important, then first grade the following September. That time will come soon enough. Slow growth is still an issue.

# On Raising Lisa

MARY WORTLEY WITH DAVID WORTLEY AND THE GRANDPARENTS

*Mary and David Wortley are the parents of an adopted daughter with FAS. Lisa was seventeen months old when she became part of the Wortley family.*

## A MOTHER'S PERSPECTIVE ON RAISING LISA

Mary Wortley

LISA WAS OUR FIRST CHILD, ADOPTED INTO OUR FAMILY at the age of seventeen months. Nothing prepared us for the onslaught of raising Lisa. The background information informed us that Lisa did not receive enough nutrients *in utero* or during early life and that "her development both physically and mentally should be closely followed." It was also noted there was probable alcohol and possible drug abuse during the pregnancy. As if this rocky start in life was not enough, Lisa was removed from her biological parents at the age of three months for failure to thrive. Apparently she was receiving only two bottles of milk a day when she should have been getting nearly seven bottles daily. Lisa was a slow feeder who initially failed to suck.

At the time of the proposal for adoption, Lisa was still below the third percentile in weight, height, and head circumference, although she had apparently reached all her developmental milestones and was progressing normally. At seventeen months, Lisa was described as a small child who was quite active and responsive to those around her.

171

We were concerned about Lisa's background and requested a developmental screening test be done before we met her. This test, preformed by a public heath nurse, stated that "Lisa's development was within normal limits." Based on this report we proceeded with the adoption of Lisa. She came home to us on July 21, 1979, amid great excitement from grandparents, friends, and neighbors. Little did we know that we were about to embark on a process that would drastically change our lives. The not knowing, the constant seeking of information, and the constant dealing with professionals, some of whom have been just great and others we could definitely have done without, combined to produce a constant source of stress until Lisa reached school age.

This is our experience of raising Lisa, an experience that has been both trying on the patience and heartwarming at the same time.

*Infant Programs*

I noticed Lisa's development was delayed within her first two months in our home, and this awareness combined with her background information rang alarm bells. I immediately enrolled Lisa in the Infant Development Program, which she attended until the age of three. That program was a life saver for both Lisa and myself.

Initially an infant development worker came to our home once a week and a program was drawn up to introduce Lisa gradually to lumpy foods in order to teach her to chew. Eating lumpy foods became the major goal for the next six months. What I learned from this experience is that once Lisa was locked into a certain routine or way of things, such as eating only smooth baby foods, she would not voluntarily learn new ways. Lisa needed to be pushed from the baby foods to lumpier foods. During this time Lisa developed severe breath-holding spells, the ultimate sign to show her displeasure with changing from what was known and comfortable. The breath-holding spells were very scary, as Lisa would arch her back, turn blue, and pass out. Again, once she locked into this behavior, drastic measures were required to break it. As Lisa was gaining consciousness, I learned to carry on with what I was doing, apparently ignoring the blackout. After a couple of sessions of responding in this manner, the breath-holding spells stopped and fortunately never returned. With perseverance Lisa gradually accepted chewable foods.

Lisa then attended an infant development play group where attention was given to fine motor development: stacking cups according to size, learning shapes, matching colors, doing puzzles, drawing circles and straight lines, recognizing big and little, and stringing beads. Gross motor development was also taught: throwing and catching a ball; walking on a balance beam; walking forwards, backwards, and sideways; standing on one foot; walking up and down stairs; walking on tiptoes, and jumping off a step. Lisa also learned to recognize simple songs (though she enjoyed them, she would not participate) and to enjoy having stories read to her.

At the age of three, Lisa was enrolled in the Children's Hospital Diagnostic Speech Center, which she attended four mornings a week, with one of these days devoted to swimming. In this program, attention was given to Lisa's expressive language skills, which appeared to be approximately one year delayed. Center staff members recommended we provide limited direct speech stimulation by allowing Lisa to attempt to name objects that she wanted and by not responding to grunts and gestures. We also provided indirect language stimulation for Lisa by making statements to her rather than asking questions or giving commands. We talked about what we did and what Lisa did in order to provide her with a language model for learning sentence patterning. They noted Lisa was very sporadic in her performance in both language skills and cognitive development. She had good social skills but could be very controlling and stubborn.

We next enrolled Lisa in Trout Lake Preschool. Here she was integrated with other children. It was a well-structured program, with special attention focused on Lisa's vocabulary and speech.

We delayed the start of Lisa's formal schooling for a year, during which she attended Berwick Preschool at the University of British Columbia. Lisa attended five days a week until 2:00 in the afternoon. One day a week her class went swimming. The concentration was again on language skills, sequencing, counting to ten, play skills, and fine and gross motor development. I found this to be an excellent program and I wished I had enrolled Lisa here after the Infant Development Program. This would have ensured a consistent program and environment which I now know is highly beneficial for her needs.

*Diagnosis and Progress*

At the Berwick Preschool we finally came to accept the fact that Lisa's developmental delay was in fact mental retardation. It was a difficult process to come to this realization. We had stated in our adoption homestudy that this was the one thing we could not handle.

We pulled together all the massive amounts of reports accumulated over the years from Children's Hospital Diagnostic Center and Lisa's various programs. We had a profile of a child with mild mental retardation, difficulty with short-term memory, poor attention span, a sequencing disorder, a severe perseveration problem, a receptive and expressive language disorder, nasal speech due to palate problems, and food allergies (wheat, milk products, soy, rice, peas, apples, and citrus). Finally, at the age of ten, Lisa was given the most likely diagnosis of fetal alcohol syndrome by the Department of Medical Genetics at Grace Hospital, where we had taken her for testing on the possibility of another genetic disease. The diagnosis of fetal alcohol syndrome was based on Lisa's phenotype and past history of possible prenatal alcohol exposure. Why it took the medical profession over ten years to arrive at this diagnosis, I will never know, given their involvement from Lisa's birth onward.

Lisa's general health, fortunately, is good. No heart, kidney, head or spine deformities were found in the diagnosis of FAS, nor is she hyperactive. Lisa was a small child with weight, height, and head circumference below the third percentile. Her clothing sizes changed very slowly over the years and this pattern of growth remained stable until the age of eleven, when all of a sudden Lisa jumped from the third percentile to the twenty-fifth percentile in height in a matter of a year and a half, astonishing us all. Her weight is increasing, though more slowly.

We have noticed Lisa's overall stamina is not great, and she appears to tire easily from physical activity and from prolonged mental activity. Lisa requires a good ten hours of sleep a night and frequent short rest stops during her day, which take the form of tuning out in front of the TV after school for about an hour, then happily going out to play, or in school, changing from a mental activity to a physical one.

Lisa's stamina also lessens considerably when she is off her allergy diet. If Lisa is off her diet for more than three days in a row, she develops a bronchial cough with resulting chest infections and high temperatures. Before we discovered the allergies, Lisa was prone to numerous chest infections throughout childhood, resulting in frequent antibiotic use. As Lisa does not tolerate wheat, I bake Lisa a bread using corn flour as a base. I allow Lisa to get off her diet for special occasions such as birthday parties, special events, school pizza days, and sports day, and she seems to manage this all right. As soon as Lisa's permanent teeth are in, she will require braces as she has massive overcrowding resulting in misaligned teeth, as is common in children with FAS.

In spite of all these difficulties, Lisa has emerged at age thirteen as a delightful young lady who is enthusiastic about life. She is happy, with good skills and a positive attitude toward school and schoolwork. Lisa has just completed her sixth year of schooling at Eastview. Her teacher noted it has been a most productive one for her. She goes on to say,

> I have witnessed a great deal of social growth in Lisa's development this year, and I am very impressed with the way she is so quickly becoming a mature, grown-up young lady. You must be very proud of her! Academically Lisa has also had a very good year and has completed all of the goals in her individual education plan. In her reading program, both her vocabulary and comprehension skills have shown much improvement. She has made significant gains in all her academic subjects. Lisa continues to put forth her best efforts at all times and to maintain her excellent work habits.

Lisa enthusiastically joins in many activities, especially those where other children are involved. We are constantly amazed with the number of children and adults she knows, from school, guides, the YMCA, or other programs she is involved in. We find Lisa is well accepted in the community, as she can be very cooperative and her behaviors are excellent amongst her peers. Lisa enjoys her pets, a cat and a dog. She is responsible for feeding them (with reminders) and walking the dog. Lisa is thrilled when she takes Lady for a walk and her cat Boots follows along for the outing. The bond Lisa has with her animals is a very special one and at times helps to take away the loneliness of being an only child.

*Eating*

Food has been a constant problem for Lisa since birth. Initially Lisa was a slow feeder who failed to suck. At no time would she take enough food to maintain a reasonable caloric intake. It was also noted during this medical investigation of failure to thrive that she really seemed completely uninterested in food. Lisa's foster mother fed her with a teaspoon in place of bottles, and sometimes it would take an hour to finish one bottle. When we first met Lisa at seventeen months, she was still on bottles and baby food and had not yet learned to chew. Today Lisa is still a slow eater and unwilling to try a variety of foods. She now prefers chewable foods and will not touch smooth-textured foods such as jello or pudding.

Lisa does not eat large meals, but she likes to snack often throughout her day. I make sure Lisa can help herself to nutritious snacks such as left-over chicken and spaghetti. Frequent snacking is what Lisa seems to need, as she will only eat so much at the dinner table whether she snacks or not. We have gone out of our way not to make an issue out of food.

Sometimes during a meal Lisa will perseverate on the dessert and absolutely refuse to finish her main course. We must figure out that this is happening; Lisa does not or cannot verbalize her wants as she is so totally focused on that dessert. We found that by allowing Lisa to eat the dessert, she will return to finish her meal quite happily. We have also found that Lisa has a craving for salt. She will eat it by the handful if we let her. On occasion we have had to throw her dinner out and start over as Lisa poured salt on her dinner before we could stop her. Consequently, we removed the salt shaker from the table. We do not know whether the salt craving is related to FAS.

GRANDMA & GRANDPA'S PERSPECTIVE

Lisa brought great joy to us all that July day, 1979. Being grand-parents, we found the relationship just clicked, and of course, we are very proud of her today.

Way back then, we babysat Lisa one day a week while Mary did volunteer work in the office of the Big Brother Program. Lisa really got to know us and all the neighborhood. The only problem we had, and it was scary, was that while playing with youngsters on our lawn, Lisa held her breath. I [Grandma] scooped her up and took her inside, and we applied ice to the back of her neck. It happened twice to us, and that in itself was enough.

It is Mary who has borne the brunt of the problems. David is a won-derful dad and a great stabilizer for Lisa, and come to think of it for Mary, too. They have performed a miracle, and with further guidance, we hope for a few more.

*—Janet and Harold Boye*

*Communication*

The development of speech was a very slow process, and at times I wondered if Lisa would ever talk. Lisa has a receptive and expressive language disorder. Often she has difficulty with word retrieval and requires a hint, a beginning sound, or the word itself. Lisa's sentence structure and excellent vocabulary are perfectly sat-isfactory but difficult to understand because of the nasality of her speech. This also has social implications, as Lisa appears to antici-pate that she may not be understood and chooses not to engage in conversation. We met with a plastic surgeon recently to explore what could be done to correct Lisa's nasal speech. Unfortunately, she refused to talk to the doctor. We later found out that this was in part because she was extremely nervous.

We managed to ease Lisa's discomfort and explore solutions with the help of Lisa's pediatrician, who is also her case manager. The pediatrician arranged an appointment at Children's Hospital with a speech pathologist along with Lisa's school speech therapist whom Lisa trusted and worked well with. This kind and dedicated lady offered to come in during her summer holidays. With all of the support and planning in place, the visit went well and Lisa cooperated beautifully. The end result is that Lisa's palate is functioning normally. The nasal speech was produced by a weakness in the controlling muscles associated with speech. Lisa's speech becomes more noticeably nasal when she is tired or stressed.

*Behavior*

If Lisa is placed in a demanding situation (as mentioned above) where the focus is on her performance or when she is unsure of the expectation, she usually refuses to cooperate by silently ignoring the instruction. If pressed, she may say "I don't want to," "I can't," or "I won't." Lisa can be persuaded, in most cases, to participate in tasks she has initially refused to perform if asked to show another child lacking similar skills how to do the task. Once started, Lisa follows through and appears very pleased with her success and the resulting praise. Lisa likes approval and is very responsive to praise.

Although Lisa is mentally handicapped, I find the most difficult issue to deal with is her perseveration. I noticed very early in Lisa's life that she would become stuck on things: a small injury, a present activity, a future event, a person, or a particular video or book. It was not until Lisa was nine that a therapist finally gave me the correct term for being stuck: perseveration. Lisa cannot stop when started or start when stopped. The inertia of moving in one direction or standing still cannot be worked against effectively. I was told Lisa must finish what she starts before being able to proceed to the next activity.

Lisa's perseveration requires the ultimate in patience on my part. For example, Lisa will perseverate when playing with a friend; she is unable to change her direction from actively playing when her friend has to go home. As Lisa does not or cannot verbalize this frustration, we have to figure out the resulting flare-up in behavior. Another example is when Lisa phones a friend to ask her over and the friend invites Lisa over to her house instead. Lisa usually hands the phone to me as she cannot switch mental gears quickly enough to make a decision about accepting the invitation to her friend's house. She is perseverating on the friend coming to her house.

Lisa needs constant repetition on everything—her morning routine of washing her face, combing her hair, hanging up her jacket, turning off the TV, where we are going, what is going to happen when we get there, and on and on. It is our job to remind her. Dave calls this our "broken record syndrome."

Lisa has extreme difficulty in adjusting to any change in her routine or environment. We try to prepare her for any changes as much as we can, by talking about them in a positive way well in advance of the change. Warnings help when an activity must end, such as "dinner is in five minutes," or "we are leaving in five minutes." Lisa at times becomes very frustrated when she must leave an activity, and flares up. Time out or quiet time allows her to change mental gears and refocus, and then she quickly rejoins the next activity quite happily.

I believe Lisa finds the world a very confusing place to live in and I know she puts out an enormous amount of energy into trying to understand the basics of it. Lisa wrote a Mother's Day poem at school last year, entitled "I Love My Mom," which sums up her need:

> I love my Mom because I see her making my breakfast,
> I love my mom because she helps me
>     with my shoe laces when I can't do them.
> I like you mother.
> I love you mother.
> I cannot live without you.
>
> —*Lisa Ann*

FAS has meant that I am the organizer of her world, and without this highly organized structure in place Lisa cannot survive to be a happy, outgoing, productive member of society. Lisa's daily routine is set in stone; she needs this type of predictability in order to function. Other children around help her to keep focused, and changes flow easier. She also knows to check the calendar every day to see if there are any special events taking place for that particular day.

Lisa will always require an organizer in her world as she progresses to adulthood. My greatest fear is, who will be there for her to take on this necessary role when we are unable to do it? In order to prevent burnout, we find we need frequent breaks in raising Lisa. We try to get a weekend away every two months, but this in itself provides stress, as Lisa does not tolerate time away from us without a lot of preparation ahead of time. She perseverates on abandonment. This is an adoption-related issue.

*Social Skills*

Lisa is a happy, outgoing teenager who is popular with other children. She is thoughtful of others and has a good sense of humor. As Lisa is an only child in our home, we must get her involved in as many activities outside the home as possible. She belongs to Guides and a church youth group, attends Sunday school, and participates in Special Olympics plus swimming, rhythmic gymnastics, and bowling. In the summers she attends day camp at the YMCA Lisa enjoys camping with us only if another child is along for company.

She has maintained friendships with other children she has met at school. She has a group of about five friends she is in close contact with. She phones them and invites them over to play on the weekends. They often go swimming, bowling, or to the movies, listen to music, play Nintendo, and occasionally they still play with their Barbie dolls. She visits her friends at their houses, stays for dinner, and sometimes will sleep overnight. To my knowledge Lisa's behavior has never been a problem when visiting her friends' homes, as she is always invited back.

Children with FAS/FAE need contact with other children, starting very early in life, to serve as role models for their behavior. As Lisa is a visual learner, she especially picks up on this type of modeled behavior. Lisa now uses the same method another child modeled for her, writing notes or drawing pictures to say she is sorry for some behavior. Given the choice, a child with FAS/FAE should never be adopted as an only child.

*Routines*

As Lisa lacks flexibility and often can be quite rigid, her world needs to be consistent and highly structured both at home and at school. Routines must be maintained or Lisa's world disintegrates. A typical school day begins with Lisa dressing for school in the bathroom, so we avoid the many distractions in her room that may cause Lisa to perseverate and throw her off course. This way the morning gets off to a good start and we do not get caught up in a power struggle about being late for school. I choose Lisa's clothes, as again she would perseverate and be thrown off track. We talk about matching colors and appropriate clothing for the day's weather as she dresses.

Once dressed, Lisa proceeds happily through breakfast and off to school. On returning from school Lisa usually gives me any school notices and checks the calendar to see what is going on for the rest of the day. Checking the calendar has become an important event for Lisa as it organizes her world, reminding her of any activities (e.g., Guides, bowling) that are happening on that day. Due to the FAS, Lisa has trouble with urinary control, so we set up times to remind Lisa to get to the bathroom.

Having Lisa do chores such as setting the table, helping with dinner, making her bed and cleaning up her room can become an endurance test in patience for me. Lisa performs these tasks more than willingly, but often perseverates on them and time becomes an issue. Some days go better than others.

In the evening Lisa sometimes watches TV if there is no activity planned for that night. Bedtime is 9:00 and we try to have pajamas on, face washed, and teeth brushed before nine. I let Lisa get herself ready for bed at night, as long as there are no time deadlines.

I know Lisa understands this routine of dressing in the bathroom as a device to keep her on track. One evening she asked to see a program on TV and I told her she could watch it if she was in her pajamas and ready for bed, but that the program started in ten minutes. I never expected her to make the program on time, but she did. I later found out she met the deadline by changing in the bathroom.

On a vacation day or weekend, we try to plan some family activity in advance so Lisa is well aware of these plans and can ask a friend along for the outing. Otherwise the structure is quite loose, with meal times having set schedules.

*School*

Our focus in education from the time Lisa entered the school system has been to encourage her to do the best of her ability without pushing her beyond her capacity, to build her self-esteem and confidence, and to encourage the building of friendships. Lisa attends the Resource Center for reading, writing, and math and is integrated into the regular classroom for homeroom, physical education, art, and music. This arrangement has worked out well for Lisa throughout the school year.

Lisa's teacher has commented that Lisa always tries hard to do her best work in the Resource Room. Lisa needs the smaller classroom size because of her many learning disabilities, her need for high structure, her perseveration, and her distractibility. She cannot function in a large classroom without becoming severely frustrated and giving up. I have found that the most important ingredient to success in school, along with a small class size, is a patient and understanding teacher who fosters self-esteem and confidence. Although Lisa is not integrated in the regular classroom, we have pursued integration in her activities outside school (e.g., Guides, bowling, church youth group, and the YMCA summer day camp).

When Lisa was younger she often used to reach learning plateaus for two to three months at a time and then jump forward with a rapid burst of knowledge. These plateaus used to worry us, but we have come to the conclusion that they give Lisa time to digest the material presented and to incorporate her new knowledge. Usually Lisa's school progress is slow but apparent. When Lisa was learning to read, her teacher commented that Lisa has a determination and persistence that is to be admired, despite severe learning difficulties. Lisa learned to read, of which she is extremely proud.

She has the greatest difficulty with math and math concepts. The use of the calculator has greatly aided Lisa in this area. Lisa is a visual learner and enjoys using the typewriter and the computer both at home and at school. As printing and writing take a great deal of thought and time and Lisa has eye-hand coordination problems, the computer helps tremendously. Lisa is just learning to play Nintendo. She likes the simpler games and challenges herself to improve over her last game.

### Conclusion

Overall Lisa is a happy girl, with good social skills and a positive attitude toward school and schoolwork. We are extremely proud of her. Our main hope in raising Lisa is that she will continue to achieve to the best of her potential and that there will be enough resources in place in the future to ensure her continued success. We know that if these resources are in place Lisa can and will make it.

## A FATHER'S PERSPECTIVE ON RAISING LISA

**David Wortley**

Lisa likes to be my helper. Whatever is happening, she likes to be actively involved. From the time she was four years old and we were renovating our home, she wanted to be part of it. When we did carpentry she had to have a saw and hammer of her own with boards to cut and pound nails into. When painting she had to help, on one occasion putting a quart of paint in one 3' x 3' area. This helper role has continued through the years. At home she likes to help with the cooking, and when camping she helps with cutting wood and building a fire.

Our time together has meant much to both of us, from reading a story to her to playing cards (usually "Fish") or a matching game. Lisa is very visually oriented, which makes her good at doing puzzles.

When we work on her Guide badges, like learning the requirements of pet care or sewing the badges she has earned on her sash, Lisa learns slowly, but she learns. Her favorite sport is swimming, which she has learned to do well. From her early days, we have had her in lessons. At first the progress was slow, but with the lessons and our swimming together she has become a good swimmer. Last fall at the age of twelve she joined the Special Olympics swimming team.

Lisa's love of books has instilled in her a great desire to read. We have used a great number of simple books. Her visual learning ability has brought us to use the computer as an aid with a color monitor to help keep her focus on the screen. Computer programs such as Concentration, a matching game, have helped her memory. Other programs she used were Tut's Typer and Buttons, Fingers, Mazes to learn the computer and keyboard, MECC's Elementary Volume 7 to help her with number and letter sequencing, and Sticky Bears Reading and Numbers, among others. But far and above the others, her favorite was Dragon's Keep, in which she read simple instructions and decided where to go to save the animals from the dragon, which she does quickly now. The addition of the Print Shop for fun and a simple word processing program to keep her writing neat has been a help.

Mathematics is too abstract for Lisa to understand without concrete aids. The calculator allows her to perform the math calculations and get a correct answer without frustration. Lisa's fine motor problems prevent her from printing neatly, and she finds the typewriter easier and less stressful.

These and other aids help Lisa to work at her own speed, help to hold her attention, and motivate her because she produces better work. As with many learning-disabled children, Lisa is highly sensitive to errors and adult intervention. Anything we can do to reduce frustration and help to build her self-esteem and confidence, we do.

The YMCA summer programs have been a great benefit to Lisa. The great support they give and the chance for interaction with other children in an integrated setting has helped her to gain a measure of independence. Her empathy for other children was evident recently when the lists were given out for each child's donation to the camp-out evening meal. One small boy was upset because

| Child with FAS Learning Problem | How a Computer Can Help |
| --- | --- |
| Unique learning speed | Computers are patient. With self-pacing and rate of presentation controlled, the computer will wait for the answer, gently correct the error, and unfailingly reward success. |
| Poor fine motor coordination | Calls for and promotes motor skills and visual motor coordination. |
| Need for step-by-step task | Consistent, sequenced instructional breakdown steps are programmable. Well-designed software proceeds along straightforward intellectual road maps to provide models to understanding. |
| Short-term and long-term memory | Easy and frequent repetition with drill and practice programs. |
| Low frustration level | Repetition without pressure, immediate feedback, and branching capabilities. |
| Short attention span | With their immediate feedback, active participation, screen graphics, variable pacing and reinforcement, computers can make learning captivating and motivating. |
| Distractability | One-on-one use, active involvement, motivation, and frequent reinforcement aid in holding attention. |
| Defensiveness | Many learning-disabled children are highly sensitive to errors and adult intervention. The computer can correct errors and branch to the appropriate area of instruction while at the same time being personal, but noninvasive and nonthreatening. |
| Inappropriate attention-getters | The child can share or show off success by demonstrating mastery of some skill. |

he felt his family could not afford his donation. Lisa assured him it was not a problem; she would bring it for him. The first thing we heard about that evening was the boy. Lisa wanted our assurances that we would look after him, which we did.

For a child with FAS, early intervention is needed from birth on. It takes a vast amount of work and dedication to keep these children on track and progressing, to prevent them from becoming stuck in one stage of development. Where standard methods do not work, other indirect methods must be used. If a child cannot add 2 + 2, but learns to balance a checkbook using a calculator, fine. If her handwriting is illegible, but she can do her work on a typewriter or computer, great. Indeed, we have found the computer an extraordinary help for a child like Lisa (see previous page).

The purpose of a parent is to help the child to learn to the best of the child's ability, so that as a young adult the child can integrate into society with pride and self-esteem in his or her own individual accomplishments, whatever they may be.

If you can do this with any child, you have succeeded as a parent.

# PART III

TEACHERS' TECHNIQUES

# Shut Up and Talk to Me

## Maureen Murphy

*Maureen Murphy is a specialist in multihandicapped educa-
tion and an itinerant special education teacher in Bethel, Alaska.
She has worked with many alcohol-affected children and their
families in the Yukon-Kuskokwim Delta in Alaska and also on
a Navajo Indian reservation.*

Eight years ago, as a wide-eyed volunteer from a city just
outside Manhattan, I traveled to a small desert mountain town in
northwest Arizona. I was going to work with Navajo people at a
special education school on the Native Nation. A vast assortment of
syndromes had come to my attention, but I was not familiar with
fetal alcohol syndrome (FAS). I was completely unprepared for my
first encounter with a child with FAS.

I saw this small individual throwing rocks at another disabled
child. When I ordered him to stop and went to assist the wounded
child, the child with FAS made a gesture, mumbled some interesting words, and went on his way as if nothing had happened. Following policy, I reported the incident to his classroom teacher. She said
something to herself and talked about what she should do to him
the next time she saw him.

The frustration in the teacher's voice shocked me as she detailed her concerns over this particular eleven-year-old who was in
her special education class. I looked up to this veteran teacher; I
thought she was fair, creative, and well liked. I could not believe
that a child that small could bring out such overwhelming feelings
of inadequacy in a professional.

She moaned about dealing with children who had FAS, and at the time the label meant nothing to me. I remember thinking, "I have lots of children with lots of syndromes. What difference does it make?"

Then I met Stan and Matthew. Stan always had the appearance of being an unreal child. He had a silly elfish grin and used to have crossed eyes. He was small, wiry, and quick. He was someone out of a fairy tale, and I was never sure who. The room was never dull when Stan was in it. Stan made me happy—even now when I think of him I am forced to grin.

Stan was, for me, wonder, joy, anguish, truth, laughter, misunderstanding, success, failure, and frustration. But above all else Stan was a child I had to educate.

No matter what knocks he took—physical blows, mental setbacks, misunderstandings or misrepresentations, he always came up smiling. This eight-year-old had the capacity to make me absolutely insane but the good sense to finish off each unacceptable act with an impish smile and a heartfelt, "I'm sorry."

Matthew left an even stronger feeling. I could never predict his reactions. Later as my skills as a teacher expanded so did my ability to hear Matt's silent cries and interpret his mixed messages.

His extremes defied human comprehension. One day he might pet and tenderly care for an animal in our 4-H camp; the next day he would throw rocks at it. He drew strong emotions in every one, even those who were usually easy going. Staff who were not very expressive became attached to him; he touched virtually everyone in an enduring manner.

Nothing seemed in balance for Matt. He was too small, too emotional, too neglected, too abused, too happy, too sad, too knowledgeable. He always seemed to know that he was just off the mark, just behind the others, just a little different, and that there was nothing he could do about it.

I have never felt for any child what I felt for Matthew. He was loyal, honest, sweet, and insightful. Yet he could wound you with his careless words and make you jump. He taught me how to be patient, feel secure, be myself.

I realized how unprepared the schools were to handle these students. Program designers could not understand their needs and therefore could not meet them. The behavior of kids with FAS/FAE is so easily misinterpreted as lazy, uncooperative, or downright malicious that often they are written off before they even begin.

Many of the children who came to the school on the Native Nation had been neglected by other schools or simply could not get the services or attention they needed. Through trial and error, a team of teachers and physical therapists found creative methods to mitigate behavioral problems and to teach the children. The program they developed spans the entire educational career of the children and aims to instill the skills they will need to survive in our complex world. We did not set out to establish a model program for other classrooms and schools; we simply were trying to reach the children enrolled in our school.

## THE BENEFITS OF EARLY INTERVENTION

Ideally, education for the child with FAS/FAE should begin soon after birth. We placed children in day-long intervention programs as early as one week of age.

Infants with FAS/FAE tend to have a high-pitched cry; they tremble often and do not wish to be held. Bonding is difficult to achieve. Infants with FAS/FAE also tend to block out or overreact to cues from their surroundings, such as voices, sounds, and light. Their ability to control their bodies seems to develop with remarkable inconsistency. Although as toddlers they are often very physically mobile, they never seem to have a sense of position in relationship to their environment. For example, a child may be able to run, jump, and hop but repeatedly falls off a chair.

The cornerstone of educating an infant with FAS/FAE is to locate activities that prevent the child from becoming over- or understimulated—mentally and physically. The need for sensory input can be adapted to the child's level of functioning with constant intervention. Here I highlight stages of the program that helps stabilize them:

### How to Increase Tolerance to Touch

- Swaddling is probably the most effective way to reduce a child's hypersensitivity to touch. Swaddling entails wrapping a child in a covering that inhibits movement and gives the body a protective cover. Swaddling is comforting, yet limits the amount of contact while being held. It helps to establish bonding, as swaddling makes the child feel secure.
- Rub the child's limbs with lotions and textured, nonabrasive materials. Use materials such as cotton, tissue paper, plastic, etc., and pair contact with a verbal cue. ("Oh, isn't this one soft?" or "Feel how rough this one is.") Use a steady, even pressure, and do not rush.
- Introduce a rocking motion. For example once the child is swaddled, rock him slowly in your arms. Later introduce this motion in a net swing. Next, swing the child around in your arms in a spinning motion. Give the child the feeling that he is in control, and be sure his body is secure. Observe the child's reactions. Introduce these motions progressively, according to the child's level of acceptance. The point is not to induce sleep but rather to develop tolerance to touch and motion.

### How to Increase Tolerance for "Noise" in the Environment

- Make the environment stimulating but not stressful. Add noises, music, beeps, and bells as the child learns to tolerate them. Pair this sound with a verbal cue, "Oh Joey, do you hear the music? Don't be afraid, it helps our ears." Introduce auditory stimuli when the child is sitting or lying in a position where he or she is secure. Do not do this randomly, but rather in a way to give the sound meaning so that the child can begin to give the environment meaning.

I have found that these techniques help children with FAS/FAE to overcome their sensory deficits. I have also observed that infants who received this training seemed to make a smoother transition to formal schooling than those infants with FAS/FAE who did not.

Achieving early intervention means cooperation with doctors, who must make a diagnosis and referral, and a delicate hand when dealing with parents—natural, foster, or adoptive. The approach that worked best at my school was to have a doctor explain the diagnosis, referring the family to the Infant Stimulation Program with an explanation of the impact it will make on the child's life. The parents appeared to appreciate straightforward advice and details.

In some areas of the U.S., doctors and schools are reluctant to recommend early intervention. Many people are uncomfortable with the possibility of a confrontation with parents; others worry about the expense or lack of infant programs. But years of frustration for the parents and the child can be lessened through early intervention and information about the distinctive needs of alcohol-affected children.

The next section identifies some of the classroom techniques I used with the older children that helped them learn. Some apply to all alcohol-affected children, such as a consistent schedule, and others are based on individual methods that have helped one child but may help others as well.

### IN THE CLASSROOM: STRUCTURE AND OPTIONS

A structured environment gives children control over their world by presenting consistent routines and clear options. I used two forms of structure by (1) presenting the children with choices between clear options, and (2) maintaining consistency in schedule without losing spontaneity. Giving options prevents the teacher from being bossy or overly punitive. A regular schedule enables the child to keep track of the day. The child is less apt to become frustrated, unproductive, or withdraw from overstimulation.

Structure should begin when the child wakes up and end when the child goes to sleep. It requires cooperation among parents, teachers, and peers. Since children with FAS/FAE cannot give themselves the appropriate amount of sensory stimulation or control, one key to constructing an ideal educational environment is to regulate their environment for them.

Our school day began in one of two ways. The first was to start the day with a sensory activity that offered the children physical or tactile stimulation they could not give themselves. We often started the day with a rub down. The occupational therapist showed us methods of deep pressure massage. I took this opportunity to teach the children about body parts or appropriate touching.

Classroom staff assisted children with FAS for intensive inter-action and allowed the other children to operate alone (they put on their own lotion while I applied lotion to the children with FAS). In this way the staff constructed a time for receiving sensory tactile input and an appropriate way to apply it. We found that this ap-proach reduced a lot of tactile inappropriateness. We emphasized this period as a time to touch and we structured the touching. We also were trying to see if overloading the child with being touched would reduce the need to touch. We believed it did.

The second way we began the school day was with physical exercise such as running or jumping hurdles. We worked on count-ing skills while we ran. The children with FAS/FAE usually enjoy concentrated physical activity, because it offered them the oppor-tunity to release energy. Physical activity may also enhance memory skills.

During either activity, we stated the purpose to make it mean-ingful. The communication was simple and direct. "We are going to run now and get rid of energy," or "Let's run to relax!"

### The Three-Option Model

Options, not rigid controls, are the building blocks of struc-ture. I developed a three-option model because it was efficient and easy for the child to follow.

*Trying to remember a schedule*

Option 1 is memory recall: "Bill, what do we do today?" If Bill does not respond, option 2 is looking at the pictures we drew the night before to depict the schedule: "Bill, what did the pictures say we would do today?" If Bill still does not answer, option 3 is remembering music: "Bill, sing to me today."

*Hands in mouth behavior*

Option 1 is simply a social reminder: "Bill, where should your hands be?" If Bill does not quickly remove his hands from his mouth or if he returns his hands to his mouth after having removed them: "Bill, your hands need help." Option 2: Place Bill's hands on vibrators taped under the desk, or near by. If his hands are still in his mouth, option 3 is: "Bill, maybe your mouth needs help." This cues him to another form of oral stimulation: apply peanut butter around his lips (which he would lick off with his tongue) or insert raisins next to his gums.

Be aware of the child's bodily needs. Hands in mouth or finger-sucking is a common behavior with children who have FAS. Since many do not seem to outgrow this behavior, I treat it as a sensory need. In my current school district, we recently encountered a child who shredded paper as a student. We discovered an effective way to stop this activity by placing underneath his desk sandpaper and a "koosh" ball (a special multicolored ball with hundreds of long, thin tentacles).

*Out-of-control behavior*

Option 1 is a social reminder: "Bill, you are getting too silly," or "Bill, take some time." Option 2 is the use of what the staff at the school called a "focus room." The child would remove himself to the room and sit quietly in the focus room until he is ready to come out. Afterward, I would say "Bill, I'll give you help." Option 3: Bill and the teacher or a peer went into the focus room and reviewed behavior goals or sat in silence. I had a lot of success with this approach. Students began to recognize when they knew they could not control their behavior and when they needed to go to the focus room. In six out of ten cases they returned to the activity on their own.

*Learning numbers*

For remembering numbers, option 1 is a simple method of visually presenting numbers and expecting memory recall: "Bill, tell me the numbers that we studied yesterday." Option 2 is presenting numbers paired with a tactile cue, such as tapping out a count: "Bill, tap out the numbers we studied yesterday." Option 3 is technology-assisted recall: "Bill, type out the numbers that we studied yesterday." It is important to offer mathematics lessons that are specific.

*Providing answers in writing*

I say to the child, "Bill, I need the answers on paper." Option 1 is any standard handwriting method: "Bill, please write what is on the board." Option 2 is typing: "Bill, if writing upsets you today, type on a typewriter." This option worked well in my classroom. Option 3 depends on the technology available at the school. In a school with computers, all technology should be put to use. If there are no computers, option 3 ought to be a paper written with another student or a report the child dictates with a tape recorder.

## Finding What Works for Each Child

Structuring the classroom and giving three options helps to reduce behavioral problem but does not guarantee that the children with FAS/FAE will learn. A teacher needs to find the right strategies—sometimes a family member or specialist can help.

One boy, for example, hated to do his math. When I assigned thirty math problems for homework, the boy immediately became exasperated and began to cry over the assignment. His brother understood why he was crying. The brother's solution was to rewrite the problems onto several sheets, separating the addition and subtraction problems. The boy was able to finish the assignment in ten minutes with no trouble. Conclusion: The page was too busy for him and the combination of addition and subtraction problems too trying.

Another student could never wait his turn and randomly blurted out answers before it was time to do so. We developed a system.

When there were three students to go before his turn, I would touch him lightly on the shoulder and whisper, "There are three people to go before your turn," and I would point to his paragraph. We never had any problems with out-of-turn behavior after that.

### Draw It, Sing It, Anything That Works . . .

Stan was a four-year-old preschooler who rocked, grabbed, and rubbed his face until it was raw. By the end of the year, Stan was a new child. Two forms of communication reached him and other kids with FAS/FAE better than the spoken word: drawing and singing.

During one memory recall session, Stan asked me to "draw my evening." I divided my paper into sections and depicted one evening's activity in each section. My drawings were simple—they resembled stick figure cartoons. At the end of the day we reviewed the events since morning. Surprisingly, Stan remembered little of his own day but recalled all the details of my evening. I spent the rest of the year drawing the world for Stan. He remembered the things I drew, and he began to concentrate on details. Every morning after we ran, I drew each student's activities from the night before.

Stan asked me questions like, "Who was there?" "What was on the table?" If I asked him the same questions as we drew his day, he not only remembered the answers, but he began to understand the concept of a sequence of events. I would check his details with his family or group home parent, and his accuracy amazed me at times.

We expanded this teaching method to illustrate his schedule, the alphabet, numbers, food groups, and other things. I tried using pictures from magazines, but I did not achieve the same result. This teaching method was only successful if I drew the pictures.

Singing also proved to be a powerful tool in helping the children remember lessons and schedules. I sang about lunch, about the desert, about the moon, about cars. Stan, like most kids with FAS/FAE, would frequently stray from his task. Singing was the most effective way to regain his attention. At certain stretches of the day, when it looked like Stan was not going to accomplish a thing, he would ask me to sing to him. I was amazed to find that this hyperactive child would sit still up to twenty-five minutes. If I prompted him with a verse in a song, he could recall details of a lesson or task and was genuinely pleased with himself for being able to remember.

Singing helped Stan remember the time sequences he often forgot. But singing was most effective if I sang to the tune of a favorite song. For example, Stan's favorite tune was "Meet me in Montana." I sang something like, "Meet me in the kitchen; I want you to clean the table now," and he would do it.

### Shut Up and Talk to Me

The staff assistants in my classroom and I noticed Matt stuck his fingers in his ears before an "out-of-seat" behavior occurred. During structured activities, even when no one was speaking, he pleaded, "Be quiet!" He talked to himself all the time. Finally, during one math lesson, he demanded: "Shut up and talk to me." At first, I considered this an inappropriate remark, but then I realized his remark was a cue to something more important.

He was trying to communicate that he could not hear me through all my words. Sounds were swarming him. I thought about his reactions to music. He professed to love rock-and-roll, yet when he heard the music he lost control and often had to be removed from social situations that included music. His reaction to country western music was different, however; he was able to maintain his composure.

That day, I understood how easy it is to misinterpret the behavior of alcohol-affected children. I learned to listen closely to the children's needs. I was fortunate to have a small classroom and had the flexibility to tailor my lessons according to the children's individuals needs.

### Teaching real skills in real life

For children with FAS/FAE, school should focus on life skills—handling money, telling time, how to behave in social settings. To teach the child how to handle money, take a field trip to a store or to a bank. Give the students opportunities to talk with people in the community. Role playing is an especially effective way to practice life skills, for example, playing store, conducting a mock interview for a job. Role-playing is also valuable in showing the teacher just how a child perceives things and what you need to do to help him see things more appropriately.

Of all the difficulties of alcohol-related birth defects, the behavioral problems cause people the most trouble throughout life. We would assume, for example, that every child ought to know the multiplication tables and using a calculator is cheating. But for children with FAS/FAE, memorizing the multiplication tables is a monumental task, and they are not likely to remember them for long anyway. Learning to use a calculator or learning exactly how to ask for help are more productive uses of school time, as well as being easier on everyone.

### Conclusion—Finding the Hippity Hop

Children with FAS/FAE need teaching approaches based on understanding the nature of their problems. They chat frequently without much substance to their rambling. They ask the same questions every day. They forget lessons from one day to the next. They are hyperactive and everything distracts them. They are constantly touching others and are overly trusting and gullible. We have come to recognize that much of their behavior stems from organic brain damage and is largely beyond their control.

My advice to parents and administrators is to search out creative teachers who delight in inventions. The occupational therapist at my former school, for example, thought up an ingenious idea for a child who could not stay still. She constructed a chair that bounced in place. The therapist used for seating a large rubber ball with a handle (a "Hippity Hop"), secured it to the floor with Velcro, and surrounded the ball with a tire. This bouncing but unmovable chair allowed the child to meet his need for stimulation and me to meet my need to conduct an art lesson.

I offer here my own discoveries—my options, ideas, and solutions. Every day I hear new ideas from new people, ideas that are creative and fun and that I want to try. That is the way we grow, we teachers as well as our students.

# Snagging the Kite String
## The Elementary Years
PATRICIA TANNER-HALVERSON

*Patricia Tanner-Halverson, Ph.D., a practicing psychologist for nineteen years, is currently in her fifth year as a district psychologist for the Indian Oasis School District, on the Tohono O'Odham Indian Reservation. She is the primary author and project director of a grant funded by the state of Arizona for a pilot project to educate children with FAS/FAE. A nationally recognized speaker on practical methods of working effectively, both in the community and at school, with these children, she has also been an invited speaker in many Native American communities throughout the United States and Canada.*

EIGHTEEN YEARS AGO I LAUNCHED MY CAREER as a school psychologist in Anchorage, Alaska, where Alaska Native students were brought from their homes in the bush to attend high school. Back then, I worked on a shaky wooden trestle of knowledge, hastily constructed, giving achievement and IQ tests and doing my best to develop an appropriate education plan for each student. Like a bespectacled general on a two-day fact-finding tour, I waded and bumbled through each evaluation.

Today, I venture forth five days a week, through a Sonoran Desert humming with flowers, to the Tohono O'Odham Nation about sixty miles southwest of Tucson, Arizona. From my four years here, I have learned a great deal about what works with alcohol-affected children. During my first weeks at the schools, I frequently walked the halls, visited classrooms, talked with teachers and students, and spent time in the cafeteria. Compared to my previous

201

experiences in non-Native schools, the activity level of these children appeared higher. It was not unusual to find several children roaming around a classroom for no apparent reason or purpose. Often, they were bothering other students who were working, despite the teacher's continual attempts to get and keep the wanderers on task or at their desk.

Like George . . .

George propels himself down the hall, like a Ferrari-red race car jetting down the track. His hand has to be captured and imprisoned by a teacher or an aide, or he is literally climbing the light fixture in the classroom, on top of the cabinets, out an open window. Like the shifting, drifting sand of the Sahara, one day he is this way, the next day another, never remembering what he was the day before, what he learned, or where he is going. George does not understand he can travel by jet or by stagecoach through life, and there are advantages to both methods of travel. The only way for George is jet, leaving all the small details behind.

Although there were other similar children in the classrooms, George stood out as the most unmanageable. Children like George, whom I later found had FAS, did not seem to respond like other children I was used to working with. When I entered a classroom to fetch a child for testing, for example, I was often mobbed by children, grasping my arms and body, crying "Oh, take me, take me!" Prior experience had taught me that children might look up at me hopefully, but they would not plead with me, in chorus, to choose them.

Well, I thought, perhaps this was a reflection of cultural values or child-rearing practices. Perhaps parents encouraged their children to learn by experiencing logical consequences, instead of strict adherence to rules. Following this hypothesis, I designed some behavioral programs to increase the attention and compliance of selected children. Stars went on charts and stickers went on shirts, for small gains. But there was no generalization of behavior or long-term changes.

Behavior modification was unusually ineffective and so was pointing out logical consequences. Thinking to win them over with my charm, I tried to reason with previously retained third graders, who were ten years old, had five years in the school system, and by now knew what was expected of them by their teachers. Pointing out logical consequences and causes and effects, I talked with them in a small group. (If you do thus and so, what could happen? What else could happen? What might be a better way to handle this situation?) Still no generalizations occurred to the classroom.

Some of the parents worked with their children at home to gain compliance. We sent a report home each day for selected children, which needed to be signed by the parents. As all teachers find, some parents followed through with their children, some did not. Still nothing much happened in the school environment, whether or not parents followed through.

Increased behavioral problems and very slow academic progress, sometimes even for children placed in special education, has been noted in many school districts in recent years. At the same time, FAS/FAE has been on the increase. According to some authorities, children identified with FAS/FAE and/or drug effects from substance-abusing mothers have increased tenfold in the past two years. Children may have difficulty in school because of other factors, such as coming from bilingual, bicultural, or rural backgrounds, low socioeconomic conditions, lack of educational materials in the home, and so on. These factors were a common thread in the background of the children who were having academic difficulty in our district, but so was maternal alcoholism.

Like concentric circles formed when a pebble is tossed into a quiet pond, my awareness of the characteristics of fetal alcohol syndrome spread out, eventually overlapping with the characteristics of those children who were having academic and social difficulties, even in special education programs. The obstacles had to do with much more than just poor attention, generalization of behaviors, or compliance. As Michael Dorris, who raised a son with FAS, puts it, "An intoxicated pregnant woman may be sick all the next day. For the unborn fetus, the hangover lasts a lifetime."

We had the "hangover" to deal with on a daily basis. This situation was our carnival, like it or not, and no one but our staff was going to train the lions or tame the tigers. It was time to abandon traditional methods of treatment for remediation of problem behaviors and slow academic progress. Envisioning a unique classroom where we could start from scratch to discover what works, I wrote a grant for the Arizona State Department of Education to fund a special education class for children with FAS/FAE. The purpose is to find methods and strategies that work to increase academic success and improve social skills and behavior for these special needs children. The project has two major components: (1) cultural awareness and (2) attention deficits.

Six students, one teacher, and one aide inhabit this "Cross/ Categorical Special Education" classroom. The children are between six and nine years old. Most of the children have such problems as:

1. Poor judgment in social situations and difficulty in learning from their past mistakes.
2. Impulsivity and difficulty in staying on task as well as serious problems with memory.
3. Skills and knowledge that do not generalize and impaired rates of learning.
4. Lack of problem-solving strategies as well as an inability to understand the consequences of their behavior.
5. Need for continual monitoring and motivation.

For children to learn, a teacher must gain and hold their attention. The first and major focus of our project is the difficulty children with FAS/FAE have maintaining attention and the other behaviors closely associated with attention deficits, such as hyperactivity, distractibility, and impulsivity. Many of the characteristics and specific behaviors of alcohol-affected children are symptoms of an underlying attention disorder, and it is the attention deficiency that initially needs to be treated.

The second major focus of our project is to empower students and communities by expanding the student's sense of identity through the continual inclusion of cultural components in the educational program. The project encourages active parental participation. We also weave culture into the classroom. We have an O'Odham teacher aide in the classroom. Within the classroom

---

CULTURAL AWARENESS IN O'ODHAM CLASSROOMS FOR ALCOHOL-AFFECTED
CHILDREN

The Tohono O'Odham (pronounced ah'thum) Indian Reservation in
Southern Arizona is almost the size of the state of Connecticut. Approximately 1,800 families live on the reservation with about 4,800
children under sixteen years of age.

Cultural awareness is a major emphasis in the special classroom
developed for alcohol-affected children. Parents and teachers want
children to know their O'Odham history, culture, and traditions. Using
the student's culture, the program hopes to develop students' self-
esteem and self-identity as well as increase their attention and interest
in academic subjects through culturally relevant educational
activities.

The special classroom integrates the O'Odham language as much
as possible into the curriculum. Both the teacher and the aide in the
classroom are O'Odham speakers who are familiar with the history
and traditions of the Tohono O'Odham Nation.

Culturally relevant materials are especially valuable to students with
FAS/FAE. Here is an example of a legend the teacher told: "A witch,
who disguises herself as a kind old woman, kidnaps little boys. When
the children come up to her, the witch puts them in a big bag that she
carries on her back and does away with them."

The students paid attention and were active listeners, behaviors
not often seen in their regular education classes. This story also has
a moral pertinent to alcohol-affected children, who are sometimes
overly friendly to strangers. The teacher used the lesson to discuss
not only culture but also behavior—learning caution when approaching strangers.

—Rick Lucero

*Rick Lucero was director of special education at the Indian Oasis-
Baboquivari Unified School District in Sells, Arizona, during the first
year of the grant.*

---

are signs labeling objects with O'Odham words as well as English
labels. In this paper, however, I describe not these cultural elements
but the way we identified the behaviors and characteristics of our
specific FAS/FAE children, so that behavioral and academic

prescriptions could be formulated. The child with FAS/FAE often has a myriad of stumbling blocks to overcome. Let me share with you some of the students I have come to know. Then I will describe the strategies that were developed to compensate for some of their difficulties.

## Portraits of Children with FAS/FAE

### Sammy

Sammy beams at me as I slip into his classroom. He is an energetic, dark-haired, ten-year-old boy, small for his age, with magical chocolate-brown eyes. Hand in mine, his eyes crinkled against the noonday sun, he assails me with a rapid-fire barrage of questions as we walk to my office. Am I married? Do I have kids? How old are they? Where do I live?

He presented himself this way from the start. Like many FAS children, he is indiscriminately friendly, initially charming, but then overly inquisitive, and will go with almost anyone, anywhere. The majority of O'Odham reservation children will fall back, five to twenty steps behind me, on the walk from their classroom to my office. Not the child with FAS. Most of them want physical contact, and give me the feeling of being mobbed by a crowd of one when I enter their classroom.

Sammy presents a picture of disorganization in all facets of his behavior. His third-grade teacher complains: "Sammy just can't seem to get it together. It's like he runs out the door, jumps on a horse, and then rides wildly off in all directions." His teacher also reports,

> He is careless and messy in his work. He cannot tell or write a story with a beginning, middle, or end. He has trouble with abstract concepts, so I use manipulatives when teaching math or he is lost. He does not remember math facts from one day to the next, and I worry he will never know his multiplication tables automatically.
>
> He looks puzzled or confused when I use metaphors or expressions like "take the fork in the road" or "don't burn your bridges." Sammy does not trust his own judgment, making it difficult for him to make a decision or choice. Even when he is right, he will say "This is right, I think, isn't it? No . . . "

It is difficult to keep Sammy's attention, especially if there is more than one thing going on in the room at the same time, or something happening outside the room he can see or hear. He seldom finishes his work and learns new material very slowly.

Sammy complains when there is any extraneous noise, "I can't concentrate when other people are talking." But he continually distracts other students. Lately, it seems he is always in trouble. In fact, Sammy is often scapegoated by the class because he is noisy and noticeable, even though he complains that others are noisy when he is trying to concentrate. As a result, he has a low self concept.

How can I help Sammy?

## Marilyn

One of our regular second-grade teachers has requested a comprehensive evaluation for one of her students who is having difficulty learning in all academic areas. She has this to say about the child:

Marilyn is very inconsistent in her classroom performance. She reminds me of a piece of Swiss cheese. The information slides down one hole in her brain, only to slip out of another hole. She often does the work we have gone over that morning, but in the afternoon, or the next day, she remembers very little. Then two days later, she can do the work again, with no new instruction. She repeats this cycle over and over. If we can fashion a piece of cellophane to stretch over the holes so the learning will stay in, the memory problems will stop.

Brain cellophane being unavailable, I worked with Marilyn, looking for alternative, practical suggestions for her classroom teacher. Perhaps the information was there; it was a retrieval problem. However, once I begin to work with this child, I found that Marilyn also had serious problems with sequencing and understanding time concepts. She did not understand a progression of ideas and was not able to plan. For instance, she could not grasp that there was an order to things, so first you do this, followed by that, and so on. She did not know where to start, even though we went over the sequence many times.

Marilyn also had trouble organizing her thoughts—a story came out in a jumble. Her stories went like this: "First the boy is walking the dog, then he gets his coat, then he meets the mailman, then the mailman gets mad, then the dog jumps on him." The proper sequence, which the pictures illustrate, is:

1. get coat,
2. walk dog,
3. meet mailman,
4. dog jumps on mailman, and
5. mailman gets mad.

The proper sequence would be demonstrated, and then she would start again, now in another mixed-up order.

Her teacher reported other frustrations, "Marilyn is really a sweet child, but she typically acts without thinking. I often find myself saying to her, 'You just don't think, Marilyn.' She is always losing things. It is difficult for her to take turns because she has trouble waiting. To her ten minutes may as well be an hour."

### Joshua

Joshua, a short-fused, seven-year-old fellow with a quick and easy smile, was easily frustrated and overstimulated, at times resulting in temper tantrums. He became distressed if the teacher departed from familiar routines, and he had difficulty shifting from one activity to another, especially from recess to reading or from physical education to math. He tended to avoid new challenges. He would flit from one place or activity to another. (Noted expert on FAS/FAE, Dr. Ann Streissguth of the University of Washington, describes children like Joshua as "butterflies.")

Joshua loitered over every conversation blade of grass. His mother complained that he talked too much and often had trouble falling asleep at night. She confided that when she was a child, she also had trouble paying attention. Joshua was always tapping a pencil, jiggling, swinging his leg or arm, or moving his head. Adults grew tired just watching him.

Joshua's teacher reported:

> He is always punching, hitting, or touching another child. But if another child accidentally bumps him, Joshua immediately responds with aggressive behavior. Joshua has a low aggravation and stimulation tolerance. His nerve endings appear to be three times

as sensitive, or closer to the surface, than other children. He just can't tolerate much tactile stimulation and translates what to other children would be a little bump as a HUGE transgression into his space.

Where Joshua resides, chaos reigns. Being with Joshua feels like Pledge Week at a sorority house—noisy, emotional, and lots of rushing from one event to the next. Joshua has trouble predicting consequences and has limited ability to reason. He cannot delay his responses sufficiently to allow problem solving to occur. He has serious social problems, in part because he misses minimal social cues. He blurts out his thoughts, often saying things that he should not. Unlike his peers, Joshua does not seem to recognize those things we may think but do not say. He continually interrupts or intrudes on others. He does not see clear boundaries between himself and others. He is always in someone else's space or complaining they are in his. His behavior is sporadic and unpredictable. We never know what Joshua is going to do next.

### Rose

Twelve-year-old Rose was like Joshua and Sammy in many ways, except her behaviors were more feminine. She twirled her shining black hair with her finger or a pencil and fussed with her clothes, rather than tapping a pencil and swinging her legs. An active child, she romped around the room in a gay swirl of movement. She was inconsistent in motor coordination and organization. She could do some things but not others requiring the same muscle groups. She had trouble with tasks that required precision or speed, for example writing, knitting, typing, and working mazes. It took her a long time to complete tasks, even those that were not motor related. When moving from one place in the room to another, she bumped into desks, chairs, or other students. During exams she demonstrated cognitive fatigue by putting her head on the desk while she worked.

Her parents thought she was "addicted" to adrenaline rushes, as Rose was constantly seeking thrills. She sought out activities that were emotionally intense, such as watching scary films, riding her bike at breakneck speed, or otherwise placing herself in danger.

She was unresponsive to verbal cautions of danger. One time, when the family was visiting a relative in Tucson, she ran across the tracks when a train was coming to "see if I could beat it." No doubt she got quite a "rush" from this behavior. Having little sense of fear, she did not understand why her family was so upset. Rose was bored when her life was not a Barnum and Bailey circus show.

Rose also showed an impaired ability to elaborate on or generalize learning. Just because it was dangerous to run in front of a train did not mean she understood it was dangerous to run in front of any rapidly moving vehicle such as a car on the highway. For Rose to go unaccompanied to her friend's house across the highway, which crossed the reservation, was dangerous.

Rose had a language delay of approximately three years. She did not have the verbal tools needed to put her life experiences into pigeon holes—concepts and abstractions were beyond her. Inability to structure and categorize made it especially difficult for her to learn from previous events.

### Strategies for Educating Children with FAS/FAE

The behavior and characteristics of these children may be familiar to many of you who are well acquainted with the frustrations of trying to teach and live with the FAS/FAE child. We now turn to the question of what to do about it. In considering these strategies, keep in mind that some children with FAS/FAE are mildly to severely retarded. But the children I described here are all of relatively normal intelligence, with IQs between eighty and one hundred and ten.

Over the last year and a half, many old and some new methods of working effectively with children with FAS/FAE have been field tested in our program. We found the keys to working successfully with children with FAS/FAE are structure, consistency, brevity, variety, and persistence.

### Organizing the Classroom Environment

It is important to give careful consideration to the physical environment of the classroom in order to minimize sensory overload and provide multisensory reminders of classroom routines. In our classroom we use well-defined areas that are labeled in several ways. For example, the teacher might use a green triangle, label it "reading" and paste it on the table that contains reading materials. A stamp and a stamp pad with a green triangle is used to mark reading papers. A red square is used for math materials. This approach increases the children's memory. Avoid open classrooms, as these children need structure, routine, and predictability.

To minimize the amount of material children must deal with at one time, remove any materials not needed for a specific lesson. In a classroom with many mobiles hanging from the ceiling, the effect is bright, lively, and colorful. But imagine the difficulty a distractible child has looking through a sea of paper to focus on the teacher or chalkboard. Use visual displays, but then remove them. We keep work areas cleared off except for the materials we are using. For example, worksheets and other materials children are working with should be uncluttered, with lots of white space on the page; instead of twenty-five pictures on a page, use only five.

Use special seating to help the child pay attention. We all know that having a child sit up front, next to teacher, helps the child maintain attention. Consider as well where to place the child with FAS/FAE when in small groups. At the reading table for instance, have the child sit directly across from the teacher's seat, looking directly at the teacher. If the child is seated right next to the teacher, eye contact cannot be maintained as easily. Children with FAS or FAE should be put at the beginning or end of the line or seated at the edge of a group of children on the floor, to minimize accidental bumping or touching and to give consideration to their need for an expanded "personal space zone."

We use the same staff consistently, avoiding the use of different support staff. Limiting visitors and reducing classroom interruptions is also helpful. Although we have not turned off the loudspeaker in the FAS/FAE classroom, it would lessen distractions to do so. Some teachers have found soft background music on the radio calms alcohol-affected children. Administrators should hire educators with great attendance records to teach these children. Alcohol-affected children do not do well with substitutes.

Put up pictorial cues as reminders of the class routine, such as stick figures that illustrate the routine of going to the bathroom. Pictures can also be used to identify work areas, such as a picture of a child reading to identify the reading area. Focusing attention with pictures, objects, or facial expressions is especially helpful because visual and kinesthetic cues work better with most alcohol-affected children.

### Handling Transitional Periods: Change and Time

Children with FAS/FAE have trouble with activity changes and with marking the beginning, middle, and end of activities. They have difficulty understanding time. We use several strategies to help us lessen the disruption that follows when change overwhelms children.

An egg timer can be used to define clearly the ending of activities. Set the clock for the desired time and the ring of the bell signals the end of the period. Older children can time themselves with a digital watch. Puppets can be used as a visual cue that the activity is about to change. The teacher puts a clown puppet on her hand when it is time to get ready for recess and holds her hand up in the air. The children see the puppet and know it is time for recess, without any auditory cue.

Using transparent plastic cups also helps children keep track of time relationships. The teacher puts three identical items in the cup and removes one when the beginning is over, two when the middle is over, and so on. Paper chains are useful to mark time. Cut or tear one link off as each task or period ends.

Most important, we explain new situations thoroughly, several times, before they occur. We alert the children in advance of activity change. "We have ten more minutes to finish up. We have five more minutes! . . ." If it looks as if the child's negative behavior is escalating or as if the child will have trouble making the shift, have a respite plan in place for when the child becomes overwhelmed. In our program, the teacher aide will leave the classroom with the child and walk down the hall or go out onto the playground or sit on the steps, talking quietly until the youngster is ready to return to the class.

Alcohol-affected children become easily overwhelmed, resulting in misbehavior such as temper tantrums or a complete shutdown. Limit the type and number of new situations encountered at one time. Explain changes in advance. We break anything new into very small pieces and do not assume the children have prerequisite information. In advance, we cover as many contingency cases as we can, talking about the "What ifs."

## Managing Impulsivity

Many noncompliant behaviors are actually only symptoms of learning problems. Suppose children cannot wait for their turn. We must perform a task analysis and determine what a specific child must learn. We cannot just teach a rule, "Wait your turn." We must also teach:

- Another word for WAIT (patience)
- To delay gratification
- Time concepts
- Impulse control
- Habit

Children affected with FAS/FAE are often seriously affected by problems with impulsivity, due in part to their difficulty grasping the concept of time or temporal relationships. To help them understand the concept of taking turns, a routine can be quite helpful. For example, we use the Queen of Hearts from a deck of cards as part of our turn-taking routine. Given to the child who starts, the Queen of Hearts is passed to the next child when the first child has finished his or her turn. The rule is simple: When the card is in your hand, it's your turn. If the card is not in your hand, it is not your turn. When a child responds out of turn, instead of a lecture, we politely ask, "Is the card in your hand?"

Impulsive behavior is also improved by modeling and rehearsing social skills. Teach children directly what to do in a restaurant or in the movies, how to ride a bus, how to greet someone, and how to thank someone.

A tendency to respond impulsively has resulted in people claiming that these children steal. Stealing requires the intent to take something with the knowledge that it belongs to someone else and that it is wrong to take and keep something that belongs to someone else. Children with FAS/FAE engage in behaviors often labeled as stealing because of poorly developed impulse control. In their minds, the scenario runs "I see, I want, I reach out and take." That is not stealing. There is no critical thinking about the behavior and no recognition of wrongdoing.

### Teaching Generalization

Alcohol-affected children may fail to see the silver thread that binds experiences together to form a complex tapestry of life. As parents, caretakers, and teachers, we need to help these children build the configuration of ideas that fashion people into French, American, Navajo, Chippewa, or whatever. These kinds of activities, I find, build scaffolding so children develop better skills at generalization:

1. Give the child a pair of objects and ask his or her to name all the ways that they are alike and then all the ways that they are different. Repeat, repeat, repeat. Start with simple, observable things, and move to complex, abstract similarities.

2. Brainstorm with the child. Start like this: Tell me everything you can about a tree, a mountain, a house, a dog, and so on. Place the ideas into different categories with a diagram showing the connections.

3. Play twenty (or thirty) questions as children get older and more knowledgeable about their world. What are you thinking about? Is it animal, vegetable, mineral? Give the child twenty tries to figure it out.

4. When children learn to count by five or ten, have them practice by using dimes or nickels. This way the knowledge is tied to daily living skills.

5. Play a "What if . . ." game with the child. What if there were no rules or laws? . . . there were no cars or streets? . . . there were no houses? . . .

6. Compare what to do in various situations. You are supposed to come right home after school. How about when you go to Tony's house? How about when you go to the trading post? How about

when you go to church? How about the Pow Wow? When would be a time when you would not have to come right home? How should you find out? (Ask.)

## Teaching Organizational and Analysis Skills

In our classroom, the teacher assigns short tasks with clearly defined objectives. It is best to avoid open-ended assignments and activities. A schedule for the day's activities is posted in the room. For older children, teachers can use calendars and assignment books to help students get organized. Teach students how to use these organizational aids, review the use of them every day for the first two weeks, and then review once a week.

Putting important papers in a giant paper clip also helps children with organization. "This is where the papers go." Then they can not only be found but they will not be crumpled up. Provide lists of homework, readings, and rules for older children. Using note cards to write facts on also helps organize older children. Matching and sorting teach organizational skills, as well as other psychological processes needed to learn academic material, such as visual discrimination and concept formation. A teacher can also use a running dialogue about the environment to increase the child's conceptual knowledge and language skills. For example, fully describe a picture of a dog with as many descriptive words as you can: "This dog is big, black, has short curly hair, one brown eye and one blue, a bushy tail, drools, and has ears that flop down on the sides like a bunny."

Keep in mind that children with FAS/FAE may have figure/ground or foreground/background confusion. Use a blackboard if one is available, as black gives better background contrast than a green board with yellow chalk. Using tapes and listening centers helps children with auditory figure/ground problems. Another technique is to read a passage with the same word repeated. Have the children hold up their hands every time they hear the word. To teach visual figure/ground distinctions, draw outlines of figures that overlap. Have the child trace the outlines with a finger. Start with two simple figures overlapping slightly and proceed in gradual steps to several figures overlapping. Use "hidden pictures" puzzles and color-by-number pictures.

The teacher should specifically teach analyzing and synthesizing skills. Have specific lessons on whole-to-part relationships, and when that is mastered try part to whole. "Look at the whole picture." Then ask about the details in a picture before a story is read: "Where is the little girl in the picture? What is she doing? What else in the picture gives you clues?"

We avoid phonics to teach reading, unless we know auditory processing skills are adequate, which they usually are not for the child with FAS/FAE. Phonics requires analyses and synthesis, something children with FAS/FAE are not good at. Instead, we have found a whole language approach works best.

### Getting and Maintaining Attention

Difficulty paying attention, poor concentration, and a tendency to be easily distracted are some of the most serious and consistent behaviors of children with FAS/FAE. All of the children in our project have difficulty in this area. When an exam or test of any sort is given (including intelligence tests), it is important to make sure we are testing knowledge, not attention span. Avoid timed tests, if possible, make tests short and, in some cases, give the test one-on-one. We watch carefully to make sure students are working and not staring out the window.

Using a tape recorder increases the child's attention, both when they are recording and when they are playing back material. They can listen over and over again to the same material to reinforce important information. Using ear phones is also helpful as it screens out extraneous noise and increases attention on the target auditory stimuli. If necessary, teach children to close their eyes when surrounding visual stimuli is distracting. We have a study carrel in the room that is used to help a child keep focused on schoolwork when other methods fail. The study carrel is never used as punishment, but instead the carrel is presented as a special place that will help the students get their work done sooner.

Songs or music and rhythm cues also help children focus their attention. If the teacher sings, "DA, DA, DA, DUM," this is an instant attention grabber. Unusual environmental sounds, such as horse clopping, whinnying, and popping sounds also keep the children on task.

We are careful to use eye contact, touch, or the child's name before giving directions, to make sure that the child is listening. Using focus words and phrases, such as "Do it NOW," and "One, two, three, look at me!" gets their attention. Avoid group directions and give directions individually when the children are in a large group. Novelty is also an excellent attention getter. Reduce the tempo of speech, then speed it up. Varying loudness, inflection, and quality of the voice is another attention-getting method.

Since alcohol-affected children have an even higher natural level of curiosity than other children, present material beginning with a riddle, or put something in a box and let them guess what it is. Bring unusual things or gadgets into the classroom and talk about them.

Using incomplete sentences, with key words omitted, forces students to pay attention if they are to participate. For example, "Listen carefully and fill in the blank with the right word: Simple Simon ——— a pie man, going to the ———."

Our children often find it more difficult to maintain attention when only the auditory channel is used. Teachers and caretakers need to keep in mind that information needs to be presented visually and kinesthetically to supplement the auditory channel whenever possible. Using music and rhymes for a rhythm stimulus adds a haptic or kinesthetic method of learning. Use sensory stimulation whenever possible in teaching: for example, "Feel the difference between hot and cold." Begin with concrete vocabulary that can be demonstrated with tactile or kinesthetic means, such as big-little, loud-soft, high-low.

Teachers should consider length of attention a developmental skill. Gradually increase the period of time for sustained attention. Having the children mark their own chart to graph their progress gets them actively involved in the process. We avoid long periods of desk work and balance structured and free time.

### Rewards and Discipline

Redirecting behavior reduces the amount of negative attention many children with FAS/FAE receive. When they tattle, redirect their behavior by turning the focus of attention back on them. Ask, "What were you doing when this happened? Good—you knew what to do, didn't you?" This technique gives positive feedback about doing the right thing, while at the same time redirecting behavior. We want to minimize attention to problems and instead focus on solutions.

It helps children with FAS/FAE to separate themselves from others by stressing what is theirs. "This is your desk, chair, or pencil." Avoiding sarcasm or nagging helps us to keep a positive approach.

Make lists of things the child needs to do, with visual cues. Use markers to cross items off the list when done. Crossing off items from the list is, in and of itself, a reinforcement. Making "my choice" cards also rewards children. Complete a reinforcer survey to determine a child's interests and favorite activities. Write activities on thick pieces of cardboard and punch a hole in each card. Put them on a ring, so they stay together while students choose an activity as a reward. Providing positive incentives for finishing, instead of focusing on those who do not finish, increases their interest in getting their work done. For the child who just cannot seem to get any answers right in a particular area, we can recognize the child for partially correct responses, thereby increasing self-esteem and confidence.

We focus on helping our children see the value of failure. Mistakes are an opportunity to learn and grow. If children become discouraged because they did not learn from past mistakes, stress what they are getting now is another chance to learn. We maintain a philosophy of guiding children towards solutions and thus minimizing time spent on the problem. It is important to listen to children when they need to talk about what has happened. However, once they begin to repeat the story, simply remind them, broken-record style, "Well, that's in the past now, that's over. What can you do now?" When looking for a solution, we ask, "What could you have done differently? How else could you have handled the situation? What will you do the next time?"

When something goes wrong and the teacher is trying to figure out exactly what happened, avoid asking "Why . . ." questions. Often children with FAS/FAE will either shut down or keep repeating "I don't know" to a question that starts with "Why?"

Be firm, but supportive. While we ignore negative behavior when we can, sometimes punishment cannot be avoided. Firm rules, consistently adhered to and with clearly understood consequences, reduce confusion about discipline and rules. We use pre-established consequences for misbehavior. The rules are set at the beginning of the year and gone over periodically (every day at the beginning of the year). We have children tell us, in their own words, their understanding of what will happen when they engage in various behaviors. We stress that they chose their own consequence, and we are not punishing them. They are responsible. And then we repeat, repeat, repeat.

We make great efforts not to debate or argue over rules or infractions. It is best to avoid generalizing. We specifically identify behavior, for example, "When you scream at me like you are doing right now, that is really obnoxious. It hurts my ears, it bothers other students, and it is rude behavior."

Negative behavior can be a symptom of unmet needs. Ask the child, when they exhibit the same behavior over and over again, "What do you need right now?" Talk with the child about "Have you felt the same way you are feeling right now before? What would have made you feel better?" Talk with parents and others who know other situations the child is involved in to try to discover what the unmet need might be.

When the child feels angry, acknowledge it and then go on. Sometimes you may need to help children under seven years of age to get back under control. Wrap them in a blanket and hold them, or put them in a quiet room where they can "detox" emotionally.

If children become frustrated and give up, we have not only lost the opportunity to teach, but also increase the likelihood of negative behaviors, such as tantrums, hitting, grabbing, shoving, or pulling hair. We routinely adapt tasks and materials to each child's frustration tolerance. The amount of required work time may be shortened and the number of problems may be reduced. Material may need to be less complicated or presented in stages.

Encourage the child to develop a success orientation through positive self-talk. When you hear a child say, "Oh no, I'll never learn this, I'm so dumb," say quietly in his ear, "Don't even think that. Say to yourself quietly, 'I can do this. I'll give it another try.'" Make it a practice to point out and notice what children do well. Teach children to monitor and reward themselves. ("Let's see, how am I doing right now? Well, I need to quiet down a little bit, but otherwise I have had a good day . . . I got along with everybody today. Good for me.")

Try to anticipate negative behavior. After the first few weeks of school, we know most of the danger signs and situations which will set off each child. When Mary starts tapping her feet and drumming her fingers, she needs to discharge that energy or she can erupt into aggressive behavior. We send her with a note to deliver to the office, or tell her to "take a little break now" and speed walk around the playground until she feels calmed down.

### Getting Hyperactivity under Control

Providing lessons that emphasize manual or physical expression helps diffuse excess energy in a positive way. When the children draw the activity or lesson while the teacher talks about it, attention increases. Regularly schedule walks and other physical activities and build relaxation time into the program.

Finally, only when all else has failed, you may want to consider medication. Several of our children have been medicated for hyperactivity and have shown dramatic improvement. These children are carefully monitored, on a twice-daily basis at first, and then weekly. One especially hyperactive child ran out of his medication or forgot it from time to time. During these times he found it hard to pay attention, and his social problems dramatically increased. Please do not consider this a blanket recommendation for medication for all children with FAS/FAE. For some children, it produces a marked improvement. For others it has no effect or a bad effect. Each case must be evaluated individually. But when medication works, the results can be phenomenal.

## CONCLUSION

Our program for children with FAS/FAE has just completed its second year. We cannot determine the long-term effects yet but feel encouraged when regular teachers comment that now, when the special education students with FAS/FAE come to their classroom for mainstreaming activities, these children blend in with the other students.

Although the children still have some social problems in the cafeteria or on the playground from time to time, these problems do not occur nearly as often, nor are the problems as serious. When I walk by or go into the special classroom, I generally find the children quietly working or actively listening to their teacher.

Many people believe that the effects of fetal alcohol syndrome cannot be ameliorated. I do not believe it. That was also thought about severely retarded people thirty years ago. When these people were treated as if there was no hope, there was no hope. The truth is, we just did not know how to educate these people. I believe the same can be said for alcohol-affected children.

## EPILOGUE: A LOOK AT OUR CHILDREN TWO YEARS LATER

George, our Ferrari race car, has experienced remarkable progress. When he began a trial on Ritalan, the difference was unbelievable. He learned. He could now sit and listen. Unfortunately, his family did not feel comfortable with the idea of medication, so he only made one month's gain over one year in reading and math, mainly because he just could not pay attention. His behavior did improve and became much more controlled. George would start to do something wrong, stop, and tell himself "No!"

Sammy, our scattered, disorganized student, attends middle school now. He made four months' progress in math and reading over the year. Problems surface when he is not closely supervised.

He showed the best behavior in the class by the end of the year, even though he started the year crawling under tables, hiding, and pretending to be a dog.

Marilyn, with major impulsivity problems, is having serious difficulties at this time. Her mother is still a practicing alcoholic and the home environment is in a turmoil. While Marilyn made behavior progress over the year, her academic progress was slow. Two weeks before the first year of the program ended, her mother was arrested and spent time in jail. Marilyn began acting out again and has been very difficult to control, even in the special education classroom. Some days she is unable to accomplish any work at all.

Joshua, one of the most serious problems when he entered the program due to inappropriate touching, has become a wonderful success story. When he entered the program, many parents of children in his former class were in an uproar over his sexual touching of their sons and daughters in the classroom. This behavior totally stopped within two months, probably because of the structure, individual attention, and close supervision in the program. Not one new complaint has been made. He had previously been arrested several times (at six and seven years of age) for this behavior. He made an excellent six months of progress in one year in reading and math. His behavior has improved so dramatically that he will be in a resource room program next year.

Rose, our more-bounce-to-the-ounce child, who loved the excitement of beating a speeding train, has not been placed in the program because it is at maximum enrollment now. Learning comes very slowly for her, even though she is in special education. Perhaps next year . . .

# Mainstreaming Children with FAS in a Small Rural School

PATRICE WINICK

*Patrice Winick has taught for several years in northern rural communities. She has been a consultant on fetal alcohol syndrome and specializes in mainstreaming students with FAS through a community-based, multicultural curriculum.*

MANY SPECIAL EDUCATION PROGRAMS PULL STUDENTS out of the regular classroom into a resource room where they do drills on their weaker skills. This model carries serious flaws for alcohol-affected children. Children struggle to stay on task with seemingly endless drills that lack concreteness or connections to real life dilemmas. The resource room approach also concentrates attention on children's shortcomings, not their strengths. In some small schools in rural communities, moreover, a resource room is a luxury that these schools cannot afford.

In our K–12 school, we mainstream the alcohol-affected children—numbering five out of a student body of approximately 120—with success. Danielle, a student in her teens, for example, manages to overcome her FAS-related difficulties so well that some of her classmates appear unaware of her condition. One of her classmates asked another why Danielle spends time every day as a preschool aide in the elementary classroom. "I think she's in some gifted program," the other student replied.

223

Danielle is well adjusted largely because of the efforts of her adoptive parents, who are from the same region and Native group as Danielle. They are poignantly aware of the challenges that have faced Danielle since she was born prematurely. They recently explained this history to her so she would understand her difficulty with otherwise simple tasks and routines. Her mother, an observant woman, helped me tailor the classroom for her daughter based on her years of work as a special education aide at the school.

Our village still relies heavily on a subsistence style of living, which offers innumerable opportunities to teach with hands-on projects. A math lesson for the older kids might be calculating the current in the nearby river so that fishing may be done more effectively. Danielle needs this kind of concrete instruction to learn, but the rest of the children also gain from learning practical, fun things.

Employment in the nearby city or hunting trips take whole families away from the village for weeks or months. To accommodate the needs of such a mobile student body, we use multilevel materials, which sequence what the children are to learn. Those children who travel with their families are welcomed back to the classroom at the level they left off. Having students work at varying levels comforts Danielle, who might otherwise appear to fall behind her classmates.

Danielle's day is very similar to that of her classmates, with the exception of spending time as an aide in the elementary classroom. Her classmates consider her lucky, and the elementary kids look up to her. She works with a ten-year-old who also has FAS, in an arrangement that bolsters both of their lives. Danielle recognizes the needs that motivate the younger child's behavior; at times Danielle will let the child bounce or jump for a half a minute and then they are both back on task. The responsibility she demonstrates with this position is admirable; she has learned to present herself well in front of others and keep their attention.

Danielle is doing well, but every once in a while I see a glimpse of how fragile her control actually is. This spring, the Iowa Test of Basic Skills caused her great concern because she thought that her classmates would discover she was behind them in ability. She considered not taking the test, since those in special education are not obligated to. Danielle debated until she finally decided to take it, and then stayed stressed the entire week of testing. The whole episode verified my suspicions about what the wrong classroom setting can cause for children with alcohol-related birth defects: stress, insecurity, excitability, and a complete inability to learn.

## HOW A SMALL CLASSROOM CAN MEET THE NEEDS OF STUDENTS WITH FAS

Danielle, of all the students in the upper grades (with seven teachers for K–12 in our small rural school, we must group several grades together for each teacher), has the most specific and demanding needs because of her FAS. Pinpointing her needs was one of the first things I did.

In such a small village, getting to know the family outside of the school setting happened quite naturally. In fact, Danielle was one of the first people to greet my family when we moved here. When we went for walks, she often came with us and answered our questions about the village and the region along the way.

Now an adolescent of fifteen, Danielle is outgrowing some of the physical features characteristic of children with FAS. She is thin, but getting taller. Although her eyes are set rather far apart, she is attractive, and her face is filling out. Like many teenagers, she is concerned about her looks and tries hard to dress and act like her peers. Because of her outgoing personality and pleasant nature, she is popular and well liked by young people her age.

Her love of sports highlights how unaware she is of her limits. She channels a tremendous amount of energy into cross-country skiing, for example, not only to do her best but to compete with students her age. At times she has to be reminded when to stop; after finishing a ten-kilometer ski run she wants to do another. When the routines change, she can get overly excited and impatient.

Several in-service training sessions armed me with the general ideas for teaching children with FAS. But the specifics of teaching Danielle came from both her mother and the special education staff who have worked with her since she began school.

In previous years, Danielle studied in a more conventional learning environment. The classrooms were often teacher-centered. She was expected to memorize names and dates, do worksheets, remember details from teacher-centered lectures, and then take tests that measured the ability of rote memorization. Students worked competitively as individuals in a large group; small group activities did not include learning cooperative skills first. Learning usually took place through listening and watching (with little or no kinesthetic learning experiences). Appropriate behavior in school was implied or explained verbally, with the rules posted on the wall.

With helpful suggestions from the people who had watched Danielle through her educational career, I set up a classroom that is structured to be clearly defined and predictable. Techniques include: role playing, peer tutoring, cooperative grouping, a curriculum that integrates different subjects, project-centered activities that relate to real-life experiences, environmental projects (sometimes run by elders and other skilled community members), kinesthetic learning, and tactile stimulation. I use role playing to communicate exactly what I expect from the students, rather than giving abstract directions and assuming they will figure it out. Instead of addressing the needs of one child, all of the students gain from the clarity of the directions, consistency of the schedule, and the usefulness of real-life related lessons.

## ROLE PLAYING

Many of the teenagers in our community tease each other with put-downs. Statements like "you're such a nerd" are commonplace in the hallways and sometimes in the classroom. Often the students do not realize that teasing, pushing, and shoving make others (especially younger students) feel uncomfortable. Nor do they recognize how disruptive such behaviors can be in the classroom—or in any other group of people.

For Danielle especially, role plays of classroom problems drive home the rules that she might not otherwise understand. In the first two weeks of the school year, time is devoted to acting out typical scenarios. I select students from the class and we enact a situation of teasing, as well as the other behaviors listed in the rules. Consequences are written into the role plays. The discussion afterwards focuses on what will happen in real life, like the different ways we do things at home and at school. In a family situation, informal teasing is often harmless and fun. At school, on the other hand, teasing can be disruptive and hurtful.

I point out to students that they will need to follow similar rules of behavior when they attend gatherings such as a village council meeting. The rules become more important than just words posted on the wall. The children accept the rules as a familiar way to act and be acted upon.

If a breach of the rules does occur, the student is first given a verbal warning. This one reminder is given without consequences. After the first reminder, the student sits at the desk in the hall to write an answer to "A better choice in a group situation would have been . . . ." After two warnings, the student visits the principal, who is more concerned with problem solving rather than with punishment.

For the rules of responsibility, I explain that since students are responsible enough to come to school with clothes on, they should also be responsible enough to come to school with a pencil and the necessary equipment they will need to do their jobs. We compare this to taking the correct materials to go trapping, bake bread, work in the wood yard, or fix a snowmachine.

I also give the students the opportunity to create rules for me (see below). We call this "structured freedom," because it allows movement around the room, opportunity to use the restrooms, and drink water when necessary, and yet gives everyone the right to learn, feel safe, comfortable, and to be treated with dignity.

## Teachers' Rules
- Teachers will give reasonable amounts of work to students.
- Teachers will let students go hunting with their families if the school is notified and if they make up the school work they miss.
- Teachers will let students eat snacks at a specific snack time.

- After school, teachers will let students give their reasons for deciding to break a rule.

For Danielle, the role-plays help her really understand what is acceptable and what is not. Few teachers had explained these to her, and she had never picked up the cues from her peers. At the beginning of the year, Danielle was sent out to the hall frequently, where she wrote impressive answers to the "better choice" question. After one month, she began to grasp what she was doing wrong and learned to stop and think about it before repeating the same behaviors. For the remainder of the year she was sent out only on rare occasions, usually because a schedule change upset her.

## TEACHING COOPERATION IN THE GROUP

Over the years, I have shifted my teaching style to concentrate more on project-centered activities than on lectures. Many of the activities in a subsistence lifestyle require cooperation to succeed. Cooperation, however, is not an innate skill.

All students, especially ones with FAS, need to have the process of "cooperative learning" explained and modeled. A teacher cannot assume students know how to cooperate just because they have been told to do so. I built this teaching into the curriculum by breaking up the students into pairs at the beginning of the year. One person may be assigned to the role of "researcher," responsible for looking up materials in a given resource. The other person would be the "recorder," responsible for writing down all the important information found. Together they make the finished product. Roles are varied with each project so that students get practice doing more than one of the skills or activities.

Role plays of working-together skills lay out the expectations of what the roles are, how students in the group will be assessed, and what the finished product should be. Gradually, the group size can be expanded once the tasks are learned successfully in smaller groups.

In small, cooperative group learning, students come to understand the importance of individual accountability, as no one is allowed to do the work for them. I emphasize that they will need to know how to work in groups to serve on committees in our community, work with other staff members in real-life jobs, and get along with family members.

Even better than telling the students that they will need cooperation skills in real life, we do community activities requiring cooperation: making fish traps, story telling, traditional singing and dancing, and camping out at traditional camp sites. Elders in the community orchestrate some of the affairs, but the concept of structured freedom is maintained. The focus on traditional technologies and the hands-on experience helps students like Danielle who enjoy familiar interaction, learn kinesthetically, and require tactile stimulation. Danielle tends to remember what she learns when she can participate in real-life experiences.

One particularly memorable community project was building a fish trap. Traditionally, underwater fences were used to corral fish into one spot in the river where a basket-like trap kept them from escaping through the cold winter water. The students helped cut holes in the ice for submerging the fence poles. Each person had to hold a pole as this fence went down at the same time. After submerging the trap, the kids helped fling the fish onto the ice with spear-like poles that hook the fish in the gills. It is just one example of how the region around us provides a fantastic classroom.

## DEVELOPING RESPONSIBILITY AND WORK EXPERIENCE IN THE PRESCHOOL

Since Danielle enjoys working with younger children, and because of her need to develop skills of responsibility, we decided to take her out of the language arts classroom for thirty minutes daily so she could be a peer tutor to the preschool teacher. She assists with group time, P.E. activities, art projects, and helping the students brush their teeth and wash up. Detailed objectives, in the form of a checklist of items, helped Danielle remember her responsibilities.

At the beginning, the preschool teacher assisted Danielle, but gradually Danielle became so well versed in the routine of carrying out the activities that the teacher spent very little time assisting her. It is heartwarming to see someone who struggles with simple tasks such as finding a letter in the alphabet stand up in front of younger children and teach these same tasks, while reinforcing the skills of the person instructing. In February, Danielle told the students that Valentine's Day was coming by marking it on their calendar. After completing a class recital of the alphabet, she wanted to point out the letter V for Valentine on the cardboard alphabet. But she could not locate it instantly. So she picked a point along the alphabet—the letter S—and, while moving her finger along the alphabet on the cardboard, she recited each letter until reaching V.

The commitment and responsibility of this job are important to Danielle, and she enjoys the job immensely. Before Christmas time, the preschool teacher needed extra help with her students. Danielle decided on her own that she would work in the preschool rather than go to her own P.E. class, which she treasures dearly.

This semester she has decided to work twenty minutes longer with the preschool students and not go to the gym. During this time, she tutors individual students in math readiness activities, and reads to the group as a whole. For the last three years, she has read to the preschoolers on a casual basis. This adult role gave her a real reason to practice reading, as well as learning how to keep the young children's attention during story time.

The experience has done wonders to improve the way Danielle presents herself. She has learned to hold herself up when standing in front of the class and refrain from distracting behaviors. It has helped her in many areas of difficulty, such as short attention span, hyperactivity, fidgeting with nearby objects, and poor body language (continuously keeping her head down in her jacket or sweatshirt and slouching). Her mother noticed the change in her attitude toward school and willingness to apply herself as the year progressed.

## CLOSING WORDS

Her mother, and now Danielle, are painfully aware that students who have special needs are often labeled in schools. Even though labels can be useful in problem solving, they can also be disabling for the children. This is not the children's disability, but ours. For this reason, the school staff are the only members of the community who have been told that Danielle's diagnosis is FAS.

I feel Danielle has taught me a lot about how to teach—all children benefit from the kind of curriculum that is demanded for Danielle to learn. Rules in the form of structured freedom give students responsibility for themselves and their behavior, and keep me from becoming simply a law enforcement officer in the classroom. Danielle gives me reason to grow as a teacher. I think about the caregiver that Michael Dorris writes about in *The Broken Cord*—the one who celebrates every success, dismisses every failure, and strives to become eternally patient.

# A One-Room Schoolhouse for Children with FAS/FAE

BEULAH PHILLPOT AND NANCY HARRISON

## Setting up the Learning Centre

BEULAH PHILLPOT

*Beulah Phillpot is a teacher and long-term member of The Learning Disabilities Association of the Northwest Territories and the founding teacher of the Learning Centre which provides regular day programs for FAS/FAE children and others. In addition to nine years' classroom work with these children, she is active in promoting awareness of learning difficulties, including support and counseling for parents and students. She shares in facilitating weekly social development groups for young teens and writes columns on the subject of learning disabilities for a local newspaper.*

FOR CHILDREN WITH FAS/FAE, we cannot leave learning to chance encounters in a school setting filled with rich but vague educational possibilities. What most students take for granted—the ability to learn spontaneously from their experience—must be painstakingly taught to alcohol-affected children. Public schools can fail to provide the right education. Overworked teachers often do not have the time nor the energy to ensure that a child with FAS/FAE gains rudimentary skills.

233

Another serious problem is the way teachers sometimes react to small, cute, sociable children with FAS/FAE: they reduce expectations and make academic tasks too easy and undemanding. The teachers may make excuses for the children, for whom they have genuine feeling. The children are then free to develop an avoidance style, such as settling into helpless postures or refusing to put anything down on paper.

In these school situations the alcohol-affected child is not learning. The teachers often send the schoolwork home, with no concept of the monumental workload they are foisting on parents—even if it is only a few worksheets every day. Parents become the work enforcers, causing innumerable strains on family life.

Ten years ago, a few parents in Northwest Territories decided that they needed a school where their learning-disabled children, especially those with FAS/FAE, could gain fundamental academic and social skills. Knowing that I had experience, these parents convinced me to devote a corner of my living room to educating their children. Five years ago, a report from the Learning Disabilities Association of Northwest Territories gave justification for the establishment of such a specialized school, called the Learning Centre.

Our school is not all sweetness and light, but it is a consistently safe, orderly, encouraging space. While I know without a doubt that some of the Learning Centre students have FAS/FAE, I am equally certain that some do not. Yet, all the children work and play comfortably and profitably together. The methods and techniques I use are valuable for all students and invaluable for our students with FAS/FAE. Several visitors noted that I use old-fashioned methods that provide structure, emphasizing mastery of basic skills. This makes me smile since many of the ideas I have honed and incorporated into the program are, to say the least, new age.

Parents are the first and only on-going teachers of their child. They are the only people who can coordinate and monitor all the many services the special child needs and receives. I do more than just accept their advice, I respect their goals for their children and attempt to work them into the program, including the moral values they wish to instill. Parents often drop in to spend an hour or a morning, especially with new and young students.

The need for our school has grown over the years, and today we have two teachers and nine half-day students (ages six to sixteen). Twelve other students come for tutoring after school or on Saturdays. There are never more than five students, and often only three or four, in any learning group at any one time. Also, each learner must help another at least part of each day: listen to their partner read, edit their news, hold their flashcards. All classes are ungraded, with skill checklists used to record progress.

In this way, our one-room school, with its small, multiage classes, is ideal for children with FAS/FAE. The only divisions are "big kids" and "little kids." Big kids watch out for the little kids and little kids look up to big kids.

Our type of teaching need not take place in a special school like the Learning Centre, as small schools in reservations or villages may be able to adopt a similar curriculum. I will first discuss our basic principles and then show you some of our daily routines and setup.

## FUNDAMENTAL EDUCATIONAL PRINCIPLES FOR TEACHING CHILDREN WITH FAS/FAE

Children with FAS/FAE learn well in small, personalized classrooms where they can receive careful attention. We cannot rely on the busy public school where these students are tested but not explicitly taught how to learn. The students need very careful, precise teaching and monitoring.

What is critical is to teach children with FAS/FAE how to go about learning. The adult needs to *mediate* the learning experience to show children (1) how to keep themselves on a task, (2) how to remember, and (3) how to look like effective learners. We cannot rely on the children learning these skills spontaneously. The children must be taught these skills directly, and we do so at the Learning Centre.

## The Scene of the Modern One-Room School

The Learning Centre is now nestled in a modern apartment building near a large elementary school. The southeast location gives bright natural light most of the year, with such spectacular sunrises and sunsets during the short days of December and January that we feel compelled to paint them almost daily. Mature trees reach to the balcony, bringing the splendor of our hardy flora and fauna into our room. The balcony is also the perfect spot for keeping an eye on our neighborhood, including migrating birds, visiting hot air balloons, or F-18 fighter jets. It is a place to eat lunch or catch the first snowflake.

I can no longer imagine having to cope with teaching in one of the windowless spaces many classrooms have become in our pursuit of energy efficiencies.

Apart from a few art prints, the room is filled entirely with the work of the students. The children do everything necessary to mount displays: plan, prepare, and execute. They decide if they will work alone or with others. I am always available to assist, especially for those children who can plan beyond their ability to execute. All walls and pin boards are white, but the person using a particular space can choose the background color from many shades of crepe paper. Always available are large rolls of paper, many shades of marker and, most fun of all, real paints that can be mixed to any hue.

I like to have a monthly theme that has enough depth to include all the children. Right now we are doing family trees, which is a topic simple enough for the six-year-old yet challenging enough for the sixteen-year-old. We will extend our work to include the study of migration patterns into and out of our territory, reaching back through time to the arrival of the indigenous people and forward to the debate now raging about sovereignty of Native people.

The children's desks are their castles. The skills being learned are taped to the top, the student's books are kept in the shelf space, and its physical location is usually chosen by the child. Some children build elaborate screens around their work space or place their desk in a corner or even in another room. The children's desks can be moved very quickly from one place to another to allow groupings or regroupings throughout the day.

When children are having a particularly difficult time settling down, I will move the desk to another room and the children will move them back as soon as they feel they can manage in the group. Occasionally a child is placed entirely out of the group, without work, to return when ready to participate appropriately or at least refrain from disrupting.

Color influences our feelings and our thoughts and organizes the world in an easily recognizable way for children with FAS/FAE. With this in mind, we allow the students to choose the colors of their space, the colors of their workbooks, their word cards, their highlighters, etc. Each child is offered colored plastic sheets (available as report covers in any stationary store) that can be placed over a page of any text to change its color and contrast. Some children use these overlays extensively, others only until the novelty wears off. Some children cannot work with pencils so they use pens or colored pencils. All beginning vocabulary is written with thick red marker on pure white cardboard that is filed in a shoe box file. Older children use colored index cards that are filed in recipe boxes.

Baroque music is often playing quietly; we encourage the children to bring their classical favorites to share. Almost the only time we refrain from music entirely is during math lessons, which usually become lively, noisy affairs with people shouting out answers or counting aloud as they leap up and down on the rebounder, a small trampoline.

## A DAY AT THE LEARNING CENTRE

8:30 A.M.: *Arrival and Organization.* Children arrive and produce their homework. We ask about any triumphs or problems while they have been doing homework "on their own." The students gather together at their desks, placed in the center of the room, and chat. If children have brought items from home, the items are discussed and then these distractions are put away (in their backpacks, on the shelf, or on the bulletin board). After about fifteen minutes, the teacher reminds everyone what will be done that day. For example, we have food every Friday, and the students take turns planning, preparing, and serving it.

*About 9:00 to 10:30: Language Arts Block.* We begin with a group session on important ideas about reading, why we read, how we read, and so forth. Then there is a quick drill or the introduction of a new book or magazine.

All students must do at least four kinds of language arts each day: reading, writing, listening, and speaking. The core activities, reading, speech training, printing, and hand-writing, are taught in very structured ways. We use readers, workbooks and phonics books as well as Barnell Loft Specific Skill and Multiple Skill books.

Since many of our children have auditory difficulties, everyone works out loud, as softly as possible. Working out loud, as I explain later, helps students with FAS or FAE keep their attention on task. When their skill level matches their age, they are asked to find strategies to begin learning "the way they have to do it in the big school."

Everyone keeps a journal and enters personal news three or four times a week. Older students read a daily newspaper, and younger students read the local weekly paper.

*Break: Outside for at least fifteen minutes.*

*About 10:45 to 11:45: Mathematics.* Again, students learn through much talking out loud. Each period begins with the teacher talking about some principles of mathematics: What is our number system? What are fractions? How do we solve problems? We then count vigorously in chorus and then alone. Afterwards, the children do exercises from their textbooks.

The older students help the younger ones memorize their times tables, use a calculator, and so forth. I try to check everything immediately so all corrections are done before the period is over.

*About 11:45 to Noon.* At the end of the morning, everyone puts their homework in the backpack and tells me one thing they remember learning that day. I tell them if I have something I want them to focus on. I check to be sure that children are making the transition to the next activity and that they are confident that they can cope with what it will bring.

If the day has been difficult for the child, as it sometimes is, we reaffirm that difficulties are part of the human condition, that we did overcome the problem, and that usually there are ways to avoid the same problem again. I will often hear, as they prepare to leave, children telling each other how "that" happened to them one time, too.

**Afternoons**

When full-day programs are offered, afternoons are similar to mornings. I have found excellent social studies and science/health books full of exciting projects and experiments at different levels of the same concept. *Science* (Modern Curriculum Press) is excellent for grades K–7.

Every day is a completed day. Children do not go home or to their next activity without finishing their duties. On one occasion, a child did not finish his work before his bedtime, so he slept over. (This, incidentally, proved to be an inappropriate consequence since he liked it.) In this way, the responsibility of working on school chores is removed from the parents, a burden that often consumes households. Homework is assigned, but the child is completely responsible for doing the work. If a student cannot remember what to do or how to do it, he or she must phone the teacher for help or wait to do it first thing in the morning when everyone else is enjoying "gossip time," one of the best parts of the day.

### WHAT UNDERLIES THE LEARNING CENTRE'S CONVENTIONAL APPEARANCE

A superficial look at the Learning Centre leads many teachers and other professionals to observe that "You don't do anything too differently here."

The similarity to regular classrooms and teaching methods is quite deliberate. The capability to participate in the ordinary school settings and life situations is fostered in all our students by teaching basic cognitive strategies that students can use to guide and monitor themselves outside the Learning Centre.

On a more fundamental level, the Learning Centre goes way beyond the traditional classroom because every aspect of the child's day at the Learning Centre is thought about and planned. While on the surface the work looks like the same old drills that we and our parents were presented, the objectives are very different.

Our program is based on Reuven Feuerstein's Instrumental Enrichments, which offers an information-processing framework for testing and teaching children. Instead of measuring past learning and inferring ability, Feuerstein thought that one ought to measure learning ability directly through a Learning Potential Assessment Device (LPAD). He found that adolescents ignorant of basic facts in the test could learn them. Those who were unable to reason abstractly could do so. The LPAD test results revealed serious flaws in basic thinking skills among slow-learning students, with the most common being impulsiveness, failure to recognize problems, episodic grasp of reality (aware only of the here and now), failure to make comparisons, and inadequate spatial orientation. Feuerstein was able to detect one constant attitude underlying these flaws: *a passive approach to the environment.* Many slow learners seem unable to realize that their own intellectual effort could indeed solve a problem. The student who replies "I don't know" when asked to recall a fact is unable to realize that by working or thinking a little, the answer would come to mind.[1]

Feuerstein's concept of mediated learning experience (MLE) helps me teach children with FAS/FAE to learn. Feuerstein distinguishes two types of learning: *experiential learning*, the familiar, natural learning that occurs as people engage with their environment; and *mediated learning*, where adults deliberately place themselves between the child and the environment to produce a specific learning experience.

Mediation includes focusing the child's attention, using sequential patterns and routines, repetition, and demonstrations.

---

1. Feuerstein's teaching materials are only available through attending his workshops, and for those who have the opportunity, I highly recommend it.

Alcohol-affected children need considerably more mediation than other students do, as they are far less likely to accomplish experiential learning. The skill of staying on task is one that can apply to all situations outside the Learning Centre.

With the knowledge that inefficient learners have a passive approach to the environment, we searched out already existing teaching methods that actively engage the learner. We stay away from gimmicks or special techniques that can become another handicap in favor of cognitive strategies that become a way of life for the learner. Teaching techniques such as relaxation exercises, rhythmic breathing, and multisensory strategies designed to engage the whole brain are woven through the carefully paced activities.

Teaching at the Learning Centre is not lectures droned into the children; apart from group lessons, I try to listen and question

---

A LEARNING CENTRE ROUTINE IN MATH WHERE STUDENTS TALK ALOUD

Focus and get ready: Relax, breathe gently but deeply once or twice. Think—talk it to yourself.
1. This is math—numbers. We learn this because . . .
2. Now what did the teacher say?
   Oh, yes. Do page 63.
   Oh, no. So think again or ask teacher.
3. Read instructions. What do I do? Tell myself.
4. Do first example.
   Oh, yes.
   Oh, no. Think again or ask teacher.
5. OK. I know how to do it.
6. Spurt to end. (Sometimes we time. Sometimes we invent other techniques.)
7. RELAX (3 or 4 seconds).
8. Check. Did I do everything? Do I need help?
   Yes, I need help. What did the teacher say? Should I ask a partner?
   No, I don't need help. I'm done. I'm proud of myself. I did a good job. Pat myself on the back.
9. Now what am I supposed to do next?
And so on, back to the beginning.

rather than tell. My lessons and contributions are always as short as possible and point out the ways in which the new information relates to that already known. Children are taught systems to use when seeking information: "What do I know?" "What do I not know?" "How can I help myself?"

## Teaching Students How to Keep Themselves on Task

An example of how we encourage the students to help themselves is the math lesson dialogue, in which students talk through the lesson. The self-directed conversation keeps them on task. The math lesson (in the box) gives one example of the self-directed dialogue we teach.

To take another example, of mediation, a child may say, "I don't know that word." A beginning reader would be told immediately what the word is. Someone who has been reading for a year, on the other hand, would be encouraged to be specific and say, "I don't know what the vowel in that word says." Often all that need be done by the teacher is to point to the information on the desk or at the front of the book or on the lesson sheet. If the question required new information, I tell the student to make a quick note so we will not forget to learn and practice it.

## How We Get Children to Surprise Themselves with Their Ability to Remember

Every lesson ends with a review of the skills being learned, the strategies that might be used to remember them, and a little bit of key information to remember for the next day. This bit is often put on a little card and left where it can be looked at many times during the day. Sometimes the child decides what to choose to remember, sometimes I do. Regardless, the beginning of the lesson the next day will be recall of the bit remembered. If it is not learned, it will be practiced many times during the day: before leaving for break, when putting books away or taking them out, before eating lunch, or leaving for home. Using these repetitions becomes habit within six weeks and the children are so pleased to discover they can remember, that they often devise their own strategies for practice.

## TEACHING STUDENTS HOW TO
## LOOK LIKE EFFECTIVE LEARNERS

Effective learners focus their complete attention on the task, follow suggestions and instructions, give appropriate eye contact, smile, work quickly and neatly, set goals for themselves, say work is easy or manageable, accept correction, display insight, and practice.

Ineffective learners wiggle, fidget, twitch, look out the window, resist suggestion ("but," "except," "you said"), look disorganized (no pencils, lost books), resist practice (we did it before, last week, when I was five), give excuses (too hard, too easy, too long, too much . . . ), cannot remember, do not care, etc. School is not something they pursue but something imposed by others that they must endure.

While we carefully monitor everything the children do, we do not want to make them overly dependent on one-to-one tutoring by an ever-present adult, fostering learned helplessness. We believe that the child's success depends upon how creative and tenacious we mediators are in preparing them for other environments.

The most important skills we teach children with FAS/FAE are social skills. These include making eye contact, using appropriate nonverbal language, understanding personal space, expressing feelings, learning how to open conversations, doing your part in keeping a conversation going, knowing how to change the subject, and knowing how to close a conversation. We teach old-fashioned manners but try to be up-to-date, especially with the "big kids."

Infringements on the rights of others are dealt with immediately. The key phrase in this program is, "start with I." Starting with I eliminates most of the negative blaming and self-pity that interferes with problem solving. My job is to help the children learn their roles by providing vocabulary, illustrating, or reenacting: staging the scene to ensure that resolution is achieved. Sometimes in the early days with a particularly bullying or insecure child, we spend

---

### A WORD ABOUT THE LOGISTICS OF THE LEARNING CENTRE

In the Northwest Territories, parents apply to the local superintendent of education for permission to enroll their children in this special school. To cover the expenses of operating the program, parents pay a fee: in 1990–1991, the program cost $8,000 for a full day and $4,000 for a part day. Social Services and other agencies provide half this fee, and the Learning Centre Society raises other funds to make ends meet.

As more children joined our school, parents and other concerned citizens realized the need for a nonprofit organization—the Learning Centre Society—to guide and manage the various programs we offer. The Learning Disabilities Association of Northwest Territories also runs Project Change Training Centre, providing academic upgrading, life skills, job search and work experience for youth sixteen and older. The Learning Centre and Training Centre are meant to try to reach those children and young adults who might otherwise never find the right setting to learn or grow.

Either or both type of programs would be easy enough to duplicate in either a rural or urban setting. The impetus for such change generally comes from parents, who know their children the best.

---

most of the day "starting with I." The time is well spent, however, since we establish the ground rules for the newcomer and confirm for all of us that people can act cooperatively, even if some have never done so before.

The principles of the Learning Centre can be used by teachers in public schools. This way of learning is especially well suited to small rural schools. But if such a school is not available, you can start your own. We did.

# Successes in the Learning Centre
NANCY HARRISON

*Nancy Harrison has adopted three children with FAS/FAE and has been foster parent to thirteen other alcohol-affected children. When the public schools ignored her daughter, who was not causing the school any problems, Harrison took action. She asked her friend Beulah Phillpot, a retired teacher, to start a school that would focus on the needs of children like hers. Harrison and other parents funded the school through a combination of donations, tuition, and government funds.*

IN 1977 OUR SECOND ADOPTION WENT THROUGH, and Social Services called me to say that they had a beautiful little girl in perfect health for us. We imagined the wonderful experience of picking up our daughter at the airport, only to find our hopes dashed, as she obviously suffered from FAS. We could tell by this time because FAS was better known and all reports indicated the children were retarded. As we had little interest in adopting a mentally handicapped child, we went straight to our pediatrician to have a proper assessment done. This diagnosis would become part of her record, thus preventing another family from sharing our disappointment. Three pediatricians saw her as well as a child psychologist—all with the definite diagnosis of FAS.

Our conviction to return her was not iron clad, and the last visit with the psychologist became a turning point. We concluded that our willingness to adopt was really based on the child's ability to live independently upon reaching adulthood. Was she capable of living on her own happily, in a reasonable amount of time? After much IQ testing and psychological evaluation the psychologist felt this little girl would be capable of living independently. Her IQ was eighty and she appeared to have a good attention span for things she was interested in. On this basis, I called my husband to say we were keeping her. We named her Julie.

Julie is now one of our ten children: two I had on my own, four are adopted and four are foster children. Their ages range from one to sixteen years, and all but the youngest are with us permanently. Three of these children have FAS. I believe they are second-generation FAS, that is, their mothers suffered the same plight. Over the years, our family has hosted twenty-four foster children, thirteen of whom had FAS or FAE. In this chapter, I will share our experiences in raising alcohol-affected children, highlighting the vast personality differences I have seen between boys and girls with FAS.

Poor coordination plagued Julie and became one of our first areas of concern. We put her in swimming classes, encouraged her to do a lot of walking and, in her early years, emphasized dance classes, gymnastics, and skating (any sport or activity that was not team oriented). Her coordination improved vastly with glasses and corrective eye surgery.

We also learned that we had to feed her frequently, because a low blood sugar level resulted in her dissolving into a whimpering blob. At first, I considered these outbursts as temper tantrums, and put her to bed or out of the room. But it did not take long to notice the tantrums occurred just prior to meals. I had to give her a snack to hold her over until mealtime. I also learned that if I wanted optimum performance I had to feed her first, regardless of the time—a quick peanut butter sandwich before swimming tests or cheese and crackers before music. As Julie surmised, snacking made her smarter.

We noticed other behaviors which set her apart from our other children: (1) extremely possessive behavior—if she touched a toy she regarded it as hers; (2) inflexible and rigid—she could not adapt to changes in situations; (3) impulsive and explosive—a tantrum could occur at any time; (4) indiscriminately friendly—she would drape herself on anyone who would let her; (5) unaware of social cues—subtle signs in expression passed by her, so everything had to be clearly pointed out; and (6) her laugh and cry sounded the same.

The preschool years put us through the wringer. We recognized early on that structure and repetition were the most successful teaching tools and tried as much as possible to choose these routes for Julie (i.e., Montessori over play school). We had to change our parenting style radically for her. For our other children, tantrums could be quelled with a simple "stop that," or "you'll go to bed. . . ." Julie did not respond to anything but the tightest discipline—we had to remove her and wait until she quit, no matter where we were or what was going on. Otherwise, she inevitably held her breath until she passed out (sometimes wetting herself). Once at the beach she was splashed while walking in the water, resulting in a passing-out fit. She fell under the water and would have drowned if we had not seen it happen.

Julie blocked out threats by screaming louder; a disciplinary smack only aggravated a bad situation. What worked best to stop the tantrum was not external punishment but rather teaching her *internal ways* to control her own behavior: "Julie, close your mouth—open your eyes—look at what you're doing."

As it turned out, these years were a piece of cake compared to what was to come. Julie versus the public school system was yet another wonder. By grade one she had attained a reasonable ability to get along with others; she was eager to please and stuck to a task until Hell froze over. If the job was to cut strips of paper, she cut paper and a simple thing like recess would not stop her. Once back in the class she would start again until the teacher told her to move on to the next step.

Her speech was somewhat hard to understand but her perseverance paid off. She would repeat the same unintelligible sounds until someone understood. Julie did attend speech classes twice a week from kindergarten to grade four, but to this day still has trouble with her *R*s and is teased about her speech.

The need for alternative schooling could not have been made more obvious to us than at the open-school Christmas gathering. Julie's class had been videotaped, showing the daily class routine, and the film was displayed on a large screen in the library. As the class gathered early around the teacher's feet to listen to a story, our daughter was facing in the opposite direction and diligently gnawing a piece of tape off the top of the desk closest to her. The video clearly showed her being off task for at least fifteen minutes. In reviewing it, even the teacher was surprised at her inattention, as Julie was not a class disturber and therefore the teacher did not notice when she was off task.

It became clear by the middle of grade two that she was not keeping up. Although the teachers were pleased with her performance, we were not. In this class her average marks were at the sixty percent level, a drop from the seventy-five percent level from the year before. She was not paying attention and required more and more teacher intervention to get her work completed.

Fortunately for all of us we met Beulah Phillpot, who at the time was a housewife with fifteen years' experience teaching disabled children. I found other parents with adopted children failing in the school system, and together we coerced Beulah into starting a school in her home (the Learning Centre).

It was to be the start for Julie of a five-year program from which she would emerge capable of entering a regular grade seven program unassisted.

Beulah let me know what was going on, not out of despair, but as a way of requesting ideas and information so we could work as a team. At the Learning Centre there was only one teacher. Julie is a wonderful manipulator (although an amateur compared to John, one of our other children with FAS), and the more people she can put between her and the source of what she does not want to do, the better. As Beulah and I frequently talked, Julie could not get lost. The control and responsibility for what she did was placed on her, not pawned off on someone else. Here is a typical telephone conversation to give you an idea:

"Hello, Nancy. Julie says her homework isn't finished because you wouldn't let her go to the library and get the proper books."

"That's true, but she didn't decide she needed more books until 8:00 P.M., her bedtime."

"Julie, your mother says you waited until bedtime to ask to go. Why didn't you go earlier?"

Julie shouts, "Because I had to do my supper job."

I interrupt, "Why couldn't you have gone after school?"

"Because I was watching TV and cleaning my room."

"That doesn't answer my question."

Beulah asks, "You mean you chose not to go. Tell me again why your homework is not done."

"Because I chose not to do it," says a tearful Julie.

We had this "tag team" approach to a patterned dialogue two or three times a day. Nothing was too trivial to warrant mentioning. In this way we always knew what the other was doing and did not have to rely on the student to relay a message or explain what was to be done.

I had a difficult time dealing with teachers previously because they did not see the whole picture. They saw Julie as a cute little person who needed to be loved, not pushed. They saw a student not really capable of coping. We as parents were labeled bossy with too high expectations, pushing a child beyond her abilities. There were no repercussions in the regular school system if the child did not do the work. The teacher just sent it home. It became the parent's responsibility to make up for the school's failing to see that the work was completed.

## CONCLUSION

Julie and our thirteen other children with FAS/FAE have taught us some basic strategies for success:

- *Spread responsibility and keep in touch.* The success of the Learning Centre with Julie had a lot to do with how closely her teacher and I worked together. Include as many people as you can in keeping your child on track, explaining to others how they can help. For example, when my son John is doing somersaults down a store aisle, others should let you know about it. Many people think of these messages as telling tales but very little is too trivial to mention, either to the child or his parents. I tell them, "Should you see John doing somersaults down a store aisle, tell him clearly this behavior is inappropriate. Dark looks and head shaking are simply ignored. Be clear and concise about the behavior you expect." The more reinforcement of appropriate behavior in different settings by different people, the better.

- *Ensure success.* Julie has always made great progress when two criteria are met: (1) the activity is something she enjoys, (2) she gets immediate rewards for doing well, even if for nothing more than perseverance. Julie, for example, started early in ballet—attending faithfully for four years. Although she was uncoordinated, she learned. The instructors liked and encouraged her because she paid such close attention.
- *Remember you are the parent and should enjoy your children.* It is easy to assume the organizational role for everything in your child's life. That does not leave you much time to be just the parent, enjoying times with them and the rest of your family. Do not allow teachers to push onto you all the responsibility for schoolwork. Limit the amount of time you expect the children to do schoolwork and make sure you all enjoy some activities together during the week.

Our many successes with children who have FAS or FAE were only achieved when our family and the school had the same goals for the child and where we created together a stable and structured environment where our children can thrive. Writing this chapter reminded me of points I already knew but had forgotten. If I, who live with FAS every day, can forget and lose sight of my goals, it is easy to understand how teachers and others can, too. We need to reset our sights all the time and give each other moral support, in order to ensure the best for our children and for ourselves.

# Part IV

---

# Working with Families of Alcohol-Affected Children

# Stereotypes and Realities
## Positive Outcomes With Intervention
### DIANE B. MALBIN

*Diane B. Malbin, M.S.W., is a cofounder of FAS/Drug Effects Clinical Programs in Portland, Oregon, whose preliminary findings on positive outcomes for people with FAS/FAE and their families have been presented nationally. In addition, she provides professional training for educators, clinicians, and health care providers on alcoholism and fetal alcohol syndrome across the country. She serves as consultant on FAS/FAE for various agencies at the local and national levels. She is the mother of a child with FAE.*

WITHOUT IDENTIFICATION OR DIAGNOSIS, parenting a child with fetal alcohol syndrome (FAS) or fetal alcohol effects (FAE) is like trying to find your way around Denver with a road map of Cincinnati. One family, for example, asked that I stop their adopted eleven-year-old son from destroying his room during time-out periods. This family had been to other therapists, who identified hyperactivity, but none of the strategies seemed to work. He kept repeating the same relatively minor infractions of the family rules, so with every time out they extended the length of time he was required to stay in his room. They thought the extended punishment would bring about the change they sought in his behavior. By the time this son was identified as FAE, he was spending three weeks out of a month in his room and was destroying it. The parents felt terrible. They knew the punishment was extreme, but could think of no alternatives.

When the parents understood their son's inability to deduce, make connections, and transfer learning from one situation to another, they were able to reframe their expectations and plan accordingly. Together they devised a simple structure to help him remember to do his chores and stay on task: he developed a list and checked off each task as it was completed.

Currently most individuals with FAE are not identified as alcohol-affected. They may have been identified as attention deficit disordered, attachment disordered, learning disabled, oppositional, or lazy. Accurate identification is the basis for the development of appropriate parenting and professional strategies. Failure to recognize organic brain damage that is part of FAS/FAE may make the problems worse, adding to everyone's frustration.

Until recently, most research has portrayed children and adults with fetal alcohol syndrome or fetal alcohol effects as having limited potential, falling easily into cycles of failure. Media reports have reinforced this impression. Contrary to this image, a picture of hope and success is emerging. Although individuals with FAS/FAE face significant challenges, they are also capable of living successful, happy lives. Personally and professionally I have seen children with FAS/FAE and their families thrive and flourish. Reports from Canada and the United States suggest that success is possible. Early intervention and appropriate forms of support are important for their success.

As any parent, professional, or individual who has been affected will testify, identification alone is not a panacea. Nor is any discussion about enhanced outcomes intended to trivialize the enormous struggles of families who have not had the benefit of knowledge about FAS/FAE.

Early identification is optimal, as with other conditions. The older the individual at the time of identification, the more deeply entrenched the secondary symptoms of psychopathology which develop over time appear to be. These secondary symptoms include low self-esteem, social isolation, and various defensive behaviors—anger, lying, aggression, destruction, and others.

The enormity of the problem of FAS/FAE is matched only by the high degree of fear about this issue. Such fear, which is in part based on the erroneous picture of hopelessness and failure, is a huge barrier to prevention efforts.

Often the identification of at-risk pregnant women and their FAS/FAE children provides the catalyst for parents and families to enter into recovery. Pregnancy, birth, and parenting all represent windows of opportunity.

This chapter will share a case study of Anna, an alcoholic woman, who is the mother of a child with FAE. It shows how late-stage, chronic alcoholism can be interrupted. This case study offers an opportunity to dispel common myths and misconceptions. It continues with a story of Anna's daughter, born with FAE. This case is not unique. It has happened innumerable times throughout the country. The tragedy is that the successful outcomes are not replicated for all women who are alcoholic and their alcohol-affected children.

## CASE STUDY OF ANNA, MOTHER OF A CHILD WITH FETAL ALCOHOL EFFECTS

The following case study challenges a number of prevailing stereotypes that directly and indirectly affect work in the area of prevention and identification of at-risk women and children.

### Early Years

Anna is a forty-five-year-old remarried parent of two daughters. She is white, middle class, and has earned a graduate degree. She is also a recovering alcoholic, with eleven years' uninterrupted recovery. Her children are twelve and eleven.

She was the second of three children born to professional parents; her father was a physician, her mother a pharmacist and musician. She grew up in an affluent neighborhood. Her parents were Jewish, intellectual, and active socially and politically. There was no apparent alcoholism in the immediate family. Social drinking was the norm among family friends.

### Drinking History

Her first drink was taken during high school. Occasional drinking occurred during college; she drank to intoxication a few times.

She married during her senior year of college and divorced in her mid-twenties.

Following graduation, a pattern of regular drinking, mostly of wine, continued. Her drinking increased during her late twenties, with daily use and symptoms of withdrawal also starting during this time. She told herself she "sought oblivion" through drinking after a series of losses including suicide in the family, divorce, pain, paralysis, and surgeries. She continued to work, although the type of jobs she held changed over time, moving from administrative positions to welding. Gradually her circle of friends and interests also changed. Eventually, she was living on a houseboat in a community whose members drank as much as she. She rarely saw her family, and the obsessive preoccupation with drinking was complete despite her firm, daily decisions to stop drinking.

These repeated attempts to modify and then to stop drinking were unsuccessful. She was confused by her inability to accomplish this seemingly simple task, since in other areas of her life her willpower and determination seemed intact. She believed something was wrong with her. She felt like a failure, feared that she had inherited her mother's mental illness, and sought counseling. Anna was in denial about her drinking and ashamed and terrified to admit the degree to which she felt she was crazy. Through verbal agility and minimizing, she earned a clean bill of health from the counselor, who did not inquire about drinking at all during their few sessions.

A few months later, she began to read about alcoholism and even attended a few Alcoholics Anonymous meetings. She could not relate at all to the idea of a higher power, since her beliefs at that time were that reliance on any form of a deity was a sign of weakness and irresponsibility, of abdication and avoidance. She was also riddled with shame and was unable to relate to others in the meetings. She thought those in the meetings were weak and self-excusing. Soon she lost the ability to understand what she read and stopped reading.

**Pregnancy**

Within a few years after her divorce from her college sweetheart, a new relationship developed which for her held the promise of stability and less drinking. Her partner, however, also drank. A first pregnancy was unplanned but welcomed; it was essentially normal. She did drink during the first and third trimesters, although the amounts were considerably less than at other times in her life. She scheduled and kept all prenatal appointments, routinely took prenatal vitamins, practiced natural childbirth, and delivered an apparently healthy infant. There was no talk about her drinking during pregnancy by family, friends, or professionals.

Within months she had resumed drinking, very quickly returning to her old pattern. By now she was a "maintenance drinker," rarely experiencing intoxication, but drinking constantly to maintain a blood alcohol level adequate to prevent the onset of painful withdrawal symptoms. She soon found herself pregnant, with a six-month-old infant, and out of a relationship.

She again went to all routinely scheduled prenatal appointments. As a now late-stage, chronic alcoholic she was flushed, bloated, fifty pounds overweight, tremulous, fearful, and lacked adequate nutrition. Her kind and gentle obstetrician said to her early in the pregnancy, "You don't drink, do you?" Her response was, "No (thanks for not asking)."

During the course of this pregnancy, two ultrasound exams were performed because of the slow growth of the fetus. When she asked her obstetrician about the need for the tests, he stated, "This one won't win any growth contests."

The birth was two weeks early, with a very short labor. This daughter was low birth weight, had a small head circumference, was tremulous and hypertonic (stiff). No abnormalities were noted on the chart. Aside from some sleep disturbance, early infancy was essentially normal.

The two comments made to her directly about her drinking around this time were angry and blaming. The intent of the speakers was to get her to stop drinking. Their tenor reinforced her beliefs about herself as bad, which she already knew and despaired over ever being able to change, and she further withdrew.

### Recovery

When the younger child was four months old, Anna was on welfare and despondent. When she realized her idle thoughts about suicide were serious and they vaguely included the children, she was stunned. She struggled daily with her addiction, loved and cared for her children, and knew she could not harm them. She sought help. Her motivation was for them since she had long since given up on herself. She called a physician friend who, when she heard the history, kindly and immediately recommended in-patient treatment.

Anna was fortunate that welfare at that time subsidized treatment services. (This is no longer available in her area.) She was doubly fortunate that her brother and sister-in-law were willing and able to care for the two infants. Otherwise, she could not have entered the program. There were no treatment facilities that provided treatment for pregnant women and for children.

A month after completing treatment, she took her children to their pediatrician for a routine exam and booster shots. During this appointment she found the courage to speak candidly with the pediatrician about her alcoholism and asked about whether there could have been an effect on her younger child. He appeared surprised by the question and left the room for a few minutes. When he returned, he was very reassuring, stating that since Anna was now in recovery and the care for the infant was stable and adequate, there really was nothing to worry about. In response to a question about the infant's small size, he responded with, "We'll fatten her up." Other questions and concerns were downplayed and went unanswered, often with the dismissal, "Sounds like parental guilt to me." Over time, as her other questions about growth and development were similarly gently dismissed, she decided she was an overly concerned parent and attempted to ignore her concerns. She wrote in her daughter's baby book, "You are a delight, and you're just fine."

## Identifying FAS/FAE

During the course of the next few years, Anna returned to work and eventually to graduate school, which provided her with a solid professional career.

Anna had lingering concerns about her daughter, who was now six, and at one point during a class on human development heard the term fetal alcohol syndrome mentioned, the first time she had ever heard the simple three-word enormity. She decided to research and write a paper on this syndrome in order either to put her vague fears to rest or to clarify what they were. As she wrote the paper she learned not only about the signs and symptoms of the syndrome, but also about the degree of damage caused by alcohol exposure *in utero*:

> I couldn't breathe as I began reading about FAS. The pain of recognition was unutterable. The nature of the grief that came with the realization of what happened to my daughter when I drank during pregnancy is unparalleled. It is profound, all-encompassing, mind-numbing, excruciating, ongoing, and unlike any other. The process of resolution of this particular kind of grief was prolonged: I looked at my children, checked for signs, denied, acknowledged, avoided, and confronted my perceptions. As I went through the grief process, I replayed, wept, became ill, raged, blamed, and feared. I turned yet again on myself, denigrating my own recovery and raging at a perverse deity. How hideous that I could recover and she would have possibly life-long struggles! Over and over I replayed "I love you, I hurt you, I can't kiss it and make it better. It's not fair for you." I read maybe the first word or sentence in a paragraph describing the effects, until my eyes refused to look after the first recognition of familiarity. I looked at palmar creases, wondered if her palpebral fissures were short, remembered the infant growth charts, and recalled verbatim the newly significant comments of the first grade teacher. The "O my god, Omygods" came cyclically with each new awareness. I avoided reference as I furtively and fearfully worked through the process of discovery. I found there are very few "safe" places to talk. I became depressed and vegetative, cringed or defended around fear of discovery, was riddled with more shame, and agonized over whether, what, and how to tell my children. When I did find the courage to tell our pediatrician about my fears, I was initially pleased to hear the misguided reassurance, "Don't worry about head size—one of my most brilliant

professors in medical school was microcephalic." Lulled by the denial from my physicians, I was grateful to have been "overreactive," only to find later that I wasn't. I can only speculate how earlier identification could have spared my daughter from pain and better supported her.

Over time, after the initial grief, loneliness, and pain of her discovery subsided, and as it dawned on her that there must be many others like her, Anna looked further. She found that thousands of articles had been written about FAS by the time her daughters were born, yet discovered no information about remediation for affected individuals. The research articles she read described outcomes that occur in the absence of intervention.

She also learned that she was not unique, that thousands of children had been identified, but that most women who gave birth to affected children had their children removed from their care and that many women died of their alcoholism by the time their children were adolescents.

## STEREOTYPES

We will continue with this case example after exploring some prevailing myths it challenges:

*Stereotype: The population at risk for giving birth to FAS/FAE children is Native American, Black, poor, uneducated, inner city ghetto dweller.*

Anna is none of the above. Her group of white, middle class, educated women is most underidentified and, according to research, most at-risk.

The stereotype is dangerous. It exists in part to meet the need of the dominant culture—uncomfortable professionals and the general population—to have a focus for the problem, an identifiable group on whom to focus the considerable anger, frustration, and moral indignation generated by this hot topic. At-risk families are rarely seen as professional, white, middle class—our friends, sisters, mothers, or grandmothers.

Without exception, within every group of well-educated, white, middle-class professionals attending training sessions on FAS/FAE, a number identify themselves, their children, their nieces, nephews, or friends' children as possibly alcohol-affected. Alcohol and substances use and abuse is the most underidentified condition in the obstetrician's office.

They are us.

*Stereotype: Alcoholics and substances-addicted women are immoral and selfish. They lack willpower. They do not try to stop using—really try—and they do not care about their children. Since they do not care, their innocent children should be removed from their care.*

This myth reflects the long history and enduring stereotype of alcoholic women. Women alcoholics have historically been seen as worse than male alcoholics. Such women are loose, immoral, sexually indiscriminate, and generally unclean. The worst thing that used to be said about an alcoholic woman was that she was a bad mother. Now, the worst thing that can be said is that she harmed her unborn child. To the observer, women's agony over this tragedy appears self-serving next to the permanence of the damage to the child.

The stigma attached to being an alcoholic woman forms an enormous barrier to identification of at-risk women and their children: family, friends, and professionals are uncomfortable and unwilling to ask or talk with women about their alcohol use because of the implicit accusation.

The emotional climate around identifying a child or a person affected by drinking during pregnancy is very different from that of identifying a child with Down's syndrome. Both are difficult to discuss with parents, but in the case of Down's syndrome parents are not blamed. In the cases where alcohol is concerned, professionals often feel angry at the mother and have an urge to rescue the child and punish the parent(s), especially where professionals have not been successful in treating or facilitating recovery for their patients.

This urge to rescue often results in the child's removal from the care of the natural parents, a reactive and short-sighted approach. Indulging in this emotional response creates a lose-lose-lose dynamic. Children who are removed from parental care statistically fare poorly and remain unidentified as FAS/FAE and at risk; parents are not treated and subsequent, alcohol-affected births are not prevented; and professionals continue to experience intense discomfort around their chronic ineffectuality in addressing alcoholism.

*Stereotype: Using the term "disease" to describe alcoholism is just a cop-out. People use it as an excuse in order to avoid having to take responsibility for their actions.*

Anna was one of the last to believe alcoholism is a disease, as her case notes indicate.

There are two basic schools of thought about the causes of alcoholism. One side sees it as a moral issue, that people who continue to drink are weak or immoral, and could choose to stop if they wanted. The other side sees alcoholism as a disease. Where intervention is concerned, the logical extension of the belief that alcoholism is a moral issue is incarceration or punishment. The belief that alcoholism is a disease suggests medical intervention and treatment.

The American Medical Association identified alcoholism as a disease in 1967. In February 1990, a definition was refined by the Joint Committee to Study the Definition and Criteria for the Diagnosis of Alcoholism of the National Council on Alcoholism and Drug Dependence (NCADD) and the American Society of Addiction Medicine (ASAM):

> Alcoholism is a primary, chronic disease with genetic, psychosocial, and environmental factors influencing its development and manifestations. The disease is often progressive and fatal. It is characterized by continuous or periodic: impaired control over drinking, preoccupation with the drug alcohol, use of alcohol despite adverse consequences, and distortions in thinking, most notably denial.

One of the most confusing aspects of alcoholism is the illusion of choice, which exists both for the alcoholic who is drinking and those around the alcoholic who observe behaviors that appear to be based on choice. A nonalcoholic observing a drinking alcoholic simply projects her own abilities and choices onto the alcoholic. ("I can choose whether or not to drink, so can she.") The alcoholic who lacks information shares those beliefs about herself and others. The denial system provides an illusion of choice because denial processes provide ample reasons, excuses, and rationalizations for otherwise inexplicable behavior (i.e., continuing to drink daily after deciding not to). So both the observer and the alcoholic believe she should choose to stop drinking, and that something is wrong with her if she does not.

Only after intervention and a period of sobriety is the alcoholic able to understand she was responding to a biophysiological imperative that was powerful and primitive, and which bypassed the higher cognitive function of logic. The strongest willpower and greatest determination pale before this compulsion.

Alcoholism, in sum, is a gradually deteriorative process characterized by denial systems and loss of choice. Since it happens over time, and since early alcoholism looks like social drinking, people do not know exactly when it is a problem.

Recovery encompasses far more than stopping drinking. Those in recovery often note that in order to begin the recovery process, "All you have to do is stop drinking and turn your whole life around."

The process of recovering from alcoholism includes acknowledging and making restitution for all behaviors that occurred while the individual was drinking.

For Anna, there was no magic time or moment of readiness for treatment.

Consider all the potential points of identification and intervention demonstrated in this case: prenatal exams by the obstetrician or nurses; any time by family, friends, and co-workers; pediatric exams; routine visits to the family practitioner. We are all in positions to intervene, to be effective, to say something. If we wait for someone else to say something, nothing will be said. Choosing to remain silent may temporarily prevent discomfort for everyone, but this avoidance inevitably exacerbates problems in the long run and directly contributes to FAS/FAE.

*Stereotype: The population at greatest risk for producing children with FAS/FAE are those who do not receive prenatal care.*

*Women who do have prenatal attention also receive adequate information about the effects of substances on their fetuses.*

Anna faithfully went to all prenatal exams.

While prenatal care is linked to improved neonatal outcomes, most women are not routinely provided with adequate information about the effects of substances, including alcohol.

Most at-risk women who see their obstetricians are not identified. If screenings are done, they often happen during the first few appointments, before real trust and rapport are established between patient and practitioner. Because of the shame, stigma, and denial structures of alcoholic women, such rapport is vital for candid communication. Physicians are not necessarily knowledgeable about alcoholism and FAS/FAE and are often not able to discuss these topics with their patients.

*Stereotype: Women who learn about the effect their drinking had on their unborn children cannot handle the grief and relapse.*

Women who are nonjudgmentally and sensitively told about the effects of alcohol on their children often enter into treatment, stay in recovery, become better parents, and become the strongest advocates for their children. Abundant data is available about the improved outcomes for children who are not removed from their homes. Subsequent pregnancies are normal, and the women survive.

There are few safe places for women to deal with the grief related to FAS/FAE. Grief is a process. It is addressable. Women who relapse around this issue have generally not received the support they need. Currently few professionals, support groups, treatment centers, family programs, and aftercare programs specifically address this topic.

This is a grief unlike any other. The energy born of this grief is powerful; it may be rechanneled to positive and constructive areas, redirected actively. This is part of prevention.

## EARLY CHILDHOOD:
## UNIDENTIFIED SYMPTOMS AND EARLY PATTERNS

Aside from her low birth weight, small head circumference, tremulousness (which persisted well into toddlerhood), and slow weight gain, Anna's daughter, Devorah, had been on time developmentally. She was friendly, fearless, funny, and determined. Her speech and language development was slow, characterized by long pauses and "Ahs" and "Ums." She had some trouble shifting from one task to another. She loved animals and playing in the garden, and would work on a task for an unusually long time. Her mother remarked on the length of her attention span after she spent a full fifty minutes diligently sawing an old overgrown zucchini from the garden into little pieces with her little saw. (Much later, Anna recognized perseveration.)

By three, however, she was unable to follow consistently a series of requests such as "put your toy on the shelf, wash your hands, and come to the table." Some days she would and some days she would wander off in the middle of doing the tasks. When Devorah did not follow through, Anna thought Devorah was trying to make her mad and punished her. Devorah started having tantrums, and was sent to her room for time out.

### EARLY SCHOOL: DETERIORATION

When she entered school, her teachers saw Devorah as bright and capable, based on her great sense of humor and strong verbal skills. At first, she appeared to be successful in school. She learned to decode words, but seemed to need to relearn basics. Her teacher reported she was cooperative, although she had trouble going from task to task. At home her behavior started to change. Halfway through the year, she started acting out at home. She became sullen, hostile, and uncooperative, not her usual self. Her rigidity and resistance increased. She either raged or shut down.

Behaviors which were cute when she was younger were now intrusive and inappropriate. Her level of activity, need for physical contact, and off-the-wall comments were irritating. She had few friends. Her choice of games were those of a younger child. Her mother, concerned about her personality change and her struggles in school, asked that Devorah be tested for special services. Testing finally occurred during her second grade year. By this time, Devorah was withdrawn. Her self-esteem eroded. She described herself as feeling "squeezed down" in school. She frequently stated, "I'm dumb." She continued to show less and less care and concern for others—sister, pets, toys—and became more withdrawn and less friendly. Consequences at home had become essentially ineffective.

## IDENTIFICATION

At this point in Devorah's development, her mother discovered, researched, and began to come to grips with FAS/FAE. A specialist in the field of identifying birth defects gave Devorah an evaluation of "possible alcohol-related birth defects" since Devorah failed to meet the diagnostic criteria for full FAS. When Anna found the courage to talk to school personnel about FAS/FAE, she was amazed at their denial. As Anna said:

> It was hard to talk to anybody about this being FAE. I knew stigma and judgment intimately, and I didn't want there to be any spill-over effect on Devorah. I introduced the idea of FAE gradually, testing the waters. What I heard back was amazing! Even with all the information, after I found the courage to talk, the teachers and principal just said, "She's just passive resistive," or, "She's smart and has a great sense of humor. Don't baby her."

Anna advocated for Devorah, insisting that she be tested. The problem was that a child had to test three years behind his or her age level to be considered for special services. To Anna, this criterion meant that her daughter had to experience significant failure before she got any help. Anna pushed for the testing anyway, as she did not want to see her daughter struggle with three years of failure before the school would accommodate her needs. As a result, an Individualized Educational Plan was developed, and Devorah spent a second year in second grade with a supportive teacher. By the end of this year, Devorah was again happy, spontaneous, responsive, caring, and curious. Her mother's goals were clear, simple, and usually flexible: "I wanted Devorah to love herself and love learning."

## TELLING HER DAUGHTER ABOUT FAS/FAE

Around this time Anna began talking with her daughter about the effects of alcohol in simple, visual terms:

I agonized over how to tell her. I still wept at the thought of FAE and I didn't want to scare her. I didn't want her to hate me. When I did talk to her, she saw my sadness, and she heard me. Her very first response was, "GOOD! I thought something was wrong with me!" Later she began to talk about her experience, "It's like there's a wall in my head. I know what's behind it, but I can't get there. I have to figure out how to go around it." Now, we don't talk about FAE that much, only when it comes up. It's there.

## SPECIFIC SUPPORTS AND INTERVENTION

Anna began to recognize the tremendous frustration and exhaustion her daughter was experiencing, and she could see her struggles to remember and follow through.

She developed a structure for Devorah. The structure consisted of clear and simple patterns, predictability, simple directives (using few words, giving one instruction at a time), appropriate levels of support for learning new tasks, modification of timelines for achievements, and gradual environmental changes. "Stuck points" were identified and gradually strategies were developed to help prevent her daughter from butting up against emotional walls. This structure was flexible and was modified over time.

Structure, rather than control, made the difference between peace and war in their home. Anna came to understand the distinction between the two environments: Control was top-down, other-initiated directives. Devorah seemed to function best in a contextual framework and did not always understand directions. Control often led her to resist, to feel more out of control and more inadequate.

Structure invited participation and encompassed Devorah's contextual world since she participated in formatting it. Structure gave Devorah respect and built on what she knew. Where breakdowns occurred they were more easily identified and addressed.

Remembering to do chores, for example, was a problem when she was six. To solve the sequencing problem represented by the chores, her mother asked Devorah to draw three pictures representing her tasks and asked her to choose a good place to post them to cue her to remember. By developing a structure that worked for her, Devorah experienced pride and competence in problem solving. She kept the pictures posted until she no longer needed them.

Devorah learned to take the initiative to solve other problems, for example, her problem telling time. Because numbers and time were abstract, she had difficulty figuring out when to go outside to catch the school bus. This was especially stressful for her on the days her mother needed to leave for work before the bus arrived. Devorah could not calculate the difference between the time displayed on the clock on the microwave and the arrival time of the bus. She would wait outside for a long time, afraid she would miss it. Devorah solved the problem by writing the time the bus came on Post-it paper and placing it adjacent to the numbers on the digital clock. When the numbers matched, she left. Her anxiety was reduced, and her problem-solving skills were enhanced. Eventually, she no longer needed the prompt.

Her mother was constantly amazed by her clear and detailed long-term memory, and her apparently poor short-term memory. Devorah's difficulty with abstraction gradually improved in some areas. But, as a fourth grader, Devorah still randomly applied the functions for addition and subtraction to the symbols "+" and "−."

Anna became adept at reading her daughter's verbal and nonverbal cues for stress and frustration. One primary form of shutdown, occurred where Devorah would simply "go flat." Her face would become inappropriately expressionless, or she would laugh and withdraw emotionally. Her mother discovered the degree to which the internalized rage had accumulated when, after observing a minor incident and after learning the importance of keeping discussions concrete, she asked her daughter what that event made her want to do. Gentle pacifist Devorah said intensely, "I want to kill!"

As Anna put it:

> It's as if she'd accumulated all of these experiences and frustrations and none had a way out. When we began to figure out what was happening and figured out how to talk about her sadness, she cried, and her grief went to her soul. Those who talk

about these kids not having a soul haven't walked there with them. They're layered, hidden, the path broken.

I finally figured out what to do by watching, reading, and seeing what didn't work. I didn't find anything in the literature that was written about what to do. It was all about what FAS/FAE is— what it looks like. The key words for me were "keep it concrete," "keep it simple," and "organic brain effects." The last one was the hardest to remember since she looks good. Devorah hated having to talk about the huge feelings she had at first. She had a hard time finding words for feelings. Her feelings had no way out, since putting labels on feelings is an abstract process.

At eleven, Devorah continues to flourish. She has good friendships. Her most remarkable characteristic is her compassion, her spontaneous displays of consideration and caring.

The school environment continues to be problematic, however. The IEP developed for her next school year cannot be implemented in the new middle school environment, and her parents are exploring compromise arrangements with the school. The basic goals of her education remain unchanged—that she love herself and love learning.

### DISCUSSION: IMPORTANCE OF EARLY IDENTIFICATION

As Devorah's story demonstrates, prior to identification she had started out on a cycle of deterioration. When the problem of FAE was finally identified, both Devorah and her mother could see the problem differently.

Identification is pivotal. It is hard to think of a more radical perceptual shift than the one between "willful misconduct" to "organicity," from "bad child" to "handicapped child with potential."

Alcohol-affected individuals are also able to reframe the way they see themselves. When told about FAS/FAE and how it relates to their chronic struggles, they often weep with relief. Like Devorah, they say, "I thought it was me. I'm not the problem, I have a problem! Now things make sense."

Children who are FAS often look clearly and visibly handicapped. Children who are FAE may look perfectly normal. These

*Devorah, age 11*

children are now believed to be at greater risk for psychosocial failure than those with full FAS.[1] When they are not identified, the only available interpretation for their behavior is that they are choosing to misbehave or not comply. As a result, they are often punished.

Prevention of FAS/FAE starts with reducing our own personal discomfort enough to talk about this issue. The discomfort experienced by individuals who are in positions to intervene is tiny compared to the enormity of the outcomes and potential struggles for families and individuals who, without intervention, will develop FAS/FAE.

We are all responsible for addressing the problem of FAS/FAE.

1. A. P. Streissguth, R. A. LaDue, and S. P. Randels, *A manual on adolescents and adults with fetal alcohol syndrome with special reference to American Indians* (Washington, D.C.: Indian Health Service, 1988).

## CONCLUSION

The case presented in this paper is my own, and "Devorah" is my daughter. Long term recovery and productive lives like ours are common. Our story is not at all unique. Professionals from around the country and Canada report similar success stories. Parents in support groups are experiencing positive, sustained shifts within their families following identification and appropriate information. Adolescents and adults who have FAS/FAE are writing, lecturing, participating in panel discussions, and sharing their experiences, strength, and accomplishments with their communities.

# Helping Families and Their Alcohol-Affected Children

RODGER HORNBY

*Rodger Hornby, M.A., is an instructor at Sinte Gleska University of the Rosebud Sioux Reservation who is experienced in the psychological assessment and treatment of children with FAS/FAE. He has taught for Sinte Gleska the past thirteen years, and he provides psychological services to the Indian Health Service, a local community mental health center, and to the Cheyenne River Sioux Tribe. He has worked with individuals with FAS/FAE from infancy to adulthood and with parents, extended family members, and the various agencies associated with the family, such as schools, social services, and the tribal judicial system. He has been superintendent of a state children's institution for neglected, abused, and predelinquent children and the clinical director of an Indian residential facility for these children.*

THIS PAPER WILL EXPLAIN ONE HELPFUL APPROACH to providing services to families who have a child diagnosed with fetal alcohol syndrome or fetal alcohol effects. The ideas and suggestions are based on my work as a psychologist with primarily Native American as well as some non-Indian parents who have a child with FAS/FAE. This paper is based upon my professional experience over the past twenty-five years, of which approximately twenty have been spent providing services to Native Americans. I have worked with Indian peoples including the Northern Cheyenne, Arapaho, Brule,

273

Hunkpapas, Minneconjou, Oglala, Sans Arcs, Two Kettle Sioux, Blackfeet, and Crow tribes.

## Establishing a Relationship with the Family

In dealing with individuals who have a child with FAS/FAE, it is of tantamount importance to establish a positive, nonjudgmental, and supportive relationship. The relationship needs to be strong enough to deal constructively with the problems. It is vital that honest, factual, and encouraging efforts be directed toward both the parent and child. This sounds easier than it is, as one must deal effectively with two basic dimensions of the problem.

The first dimension centers around the problems and dysfunctions that contributed to having a child with FAS. Generally a variety of dysfunctions of which alcohol abuse is primary must be addressed, including alcohol abuse, relationship of family members, inadequate coping skills, and fragmented development and life experiences. As is often the case with alcohol dysfunctional families, children are seldom adequately cared for by actively drinking parents. Frequently, they must baby-sit younger siblings, cook meals, get themselves and their siblings ready for and to school, drive intoxicated parents around, and care for parents ill from too much drinking. It must be kept in mind that the child is the product of a variety of personal dysfunctions which must be addressed if the child is to be appropriately stimulated and cared for. These dysfunctions cover a broad spectrum of difficulties, including poor childhood and developmental experiences, anger, shame, embarrassment, denial, poor impulse control, and acting out.

The second dimension focuses more specifically upon the child with FAS/FAE and his or her problems. Attention is directed towards helping the parents with specific behavioral, educational, and child management strategies or, when they are unable to provide these, seeing to it that their child receives the needed services. It is important to have a broad resource spectrum from which to draw. In my work, I have relied very heavily and successfully upon the following specific theoretical systems and intervention systems:

Adlerian psychology, STEP (Systematic Training for Effective Parenting) programs, active parenting, parent effectiveness training, reality therapy parenting and school approaches, common sense discipline, practical parenting, and general behavioral approaches both for intervention and monitoring of self and child. The names of parenting and child management materials that I have found very useful are among the resources identified in Appendix II.

The relationship of the counselor with the parents and child needs considerable attention. It is important to engage in discussion in a nonjudgmental way and allow family members to communicate at their own comfortable pace. Such a deliberate approach removes hostility and defensiveness that might be associated not only with being counseled but with having a special needs child. Further, parents are more likely to carry out and use effectively suggestions and strategies that are developed in this manner.

I have termed this process "structured information sharing" and "rapport building." It is directed towards gathering important context and problem information from the parents, identifying their specific problems and concerns about their child, and laying a foundation for implementation of future plans, needs, and expectations. Throughout this process, it is necessary to share some of one's own experiences, interests, ideas, and to identify common ground with the parent(s). This is a critical and most enjoyable process and often determines the success of future efforts. Consider the following case example, various aspects of which are referenced throughout this chapter.

A family was referred for assistance because they were having difficulties dealing with their two-year-old son who had fetal alcohol syndrome. The father and the boy's birth mother were divorced. The father had custody of his son. There were no other children in the home. The father worked as an office assistant in the tribal chairman's office. He was living with a recovering chemically dependent woman. She assumed the role of the boy's stepmother. She had lost a child of her own prior to her relationship with the father.

Neither parent was actively drinking although both had extensive histories of alcohol abuse. The father's partner first contacted social service specialists, because she was concerned about the father's anger, his tendency to become abusive and neglectful towards his son, and the increasing care and protective role she was having to assume. The social service specialists, in turn, placed pressure on the father to enter into counseling to secure guidance on how best to deal with his son.

The father resisted outside intervention or participating in the recommended counseling. The family kept its first appointment, however, and during the session a general history of the parent's relationship was taken, and the parents' concerns about their son were identified, as well as the specific problems they were having with their son and with each other.

Because of my extensive work history with Native Americans, it is usually easy to identify some shared experiences or experiences similar enough to provide a rapport. In this situation, the father had attended a Job Corps site at which I knew several of the staff. One of the staff members who had made a positive impression on the father was an Indian individual with whom I had worked. My positive views of this individual lessened the father's resistance, increased his motivation, and relieved his defensiveness. Their son's birthday was in November as is mine, so I shared with the family in a tongue-in-cheek manner that all "good and capable" people were born in November, however one of the serious consequences of a November birth date was a genetic tendency to lose one's hair. Because I am identifiably bald, this provided some humor, lessened the need for defensiveness, and also established another common base with the family. The stepmother had spent time in an institution as a child, and she and I discussed various institutional procedures and the impact they have upon residents, providing yet another common base of understanding and experience. Numerous other shared experiences or ideas came to light during this first session. Throughout this process, these common or shared experiences need always to be framed in a positive or favorable way so they can be easily accessed later to promote the family's efforts at change and problem-solving.

Humor is helpful throughout the process of building a relationship and intervention. Humor puts problems in context in a nonthreatening manner and generally puts family members at ease. Also, humor strengthens rapport and resolves existing differences between parents and the counselor. Counselors have mentioned their confusion and disapproval of the jokes families offer. But this joking, no matter how inappropriate, needs to be understood in terms of the family coming to realistic terms with the special problems of their child and as a means of testing the acceptance of the human service provider.

Family members may view the human service provider in a number of possible ways: (1) as an instrument of the authorities, (2) as a reminder of their possible personal dysfunctions and of their ineffectiveness as parents, (3) as someone in authority who can and may criticize or generate unpleasant feelings and reactions in them, and (4) as someone who views them as persons in need of help, which is not viewed as appropriate, for their special needs child. These beliefs need to be questioned if intervention efforts are going to be effectively utilized and internalized as lasting behaviors by parents and other family members. It is useful to identify the reasons for being seen, reframing the need for assistance as positive and as a demonstration of their responsible concern for their child. This is easily done by expressing the fact that their child was really a gift to help them become better people, better parents, and a better family.

This reframing can draw on the parents' beliefs, as appropriate. For example: "This is another indication that the spirits want you to become the good person you can be"; or "The creator has awarded you a special needs child to promote your development to a fully competent and authentic human being"; or "Eastern philosophy states that the universe always sends you what it is you need to learn and resolve and in your case, your son is a life task which you must confront, deal with, and be guided by and master." The message must be positive and understandable to the parents and family because it can become an unwavering strength and resource to direct and guide their efforts. It also gives them a palatable reason why they have a child with FAS/FAE while other actively drinking individuals appear not to. Self-esteem reinforces their acceptance of help and intervention and provides a foundation upon which later assistance can be more readily accepted and integrated into the family. In situations where the counselor is required to provide an evaluative report, this role needs to be clearly explained to the parents so that together the parent(s) and counselor can work out an honest and realistic report.

As the information gathering proceeds, it is important to capitalize upon every opportunity to provide the family or parents with needed information, resources, and skills to deal with their child more effectively. This requires the counselor or intervention person to possess a broad generalized base of information as well as a considerable amount of topical and specific information about the problem. It is helpful to have a variety of resources—books, pamphlets, or the names of local community agencies and support groups—to provide to the parents. This facilitates a feeling that one is not alone in dealing with the problems faced by having a child with FAS/FAE.

If you are successful in accomplishing these rapport and relationship building tasks, seldom, if ever, will you experience hostility or resistance. In my experience, each time I have encountered hostility, poor follow-through, or resistance, it has invariably been the result of my not following my own advice in building a positive and nondefensive helpful relationship. The error, for myself, has often been a due to rushing things and not allowing a relationship to develop and evolve to a point where the parents, child, and family can eagerly invest themselves in improving their skills and problem-solving capacities. Also, if I have been unclear as to what I am doing and who I am doing it for, and if I attempt to be a cold, detached, totally objective professional, I find I have the least success, and I experience increased resistance, hostility, and avoidance (of me, not the need for assistance). Almost all of the parents I have been fortunate enough to know professionally have worked with eager dedication to provide better care for their children, to improve their parenting abilities, and to become more of an advocate for their children's special needs. This, I believe, is attributed primarily to the quality of our relationship and my belief in their ability to lead more satisfying, enriched, and gratifying lives, enjoying even more their child, children, family, each other, and themselves.

## TWO-FOLD NATURE OF THE INTERVENTION TASK

The first step in effective intervention is to assess the specific child management problems and concerns and the family adjustment difficulties. At first parents will disclose more simple and obvious problems. The counselor needs to be able to make concrete the problem, the context in which the problem occurs, and its enduring nature. If parents understand their behavior in terms of what caused it and what the consequences are, this will help to form a clearer perspective on their drinking, partying, parenting, and developmental needs. This in turn leads to greater understanding of how to deal with their specific child concerns.

The father's problem in relating to his son with fetal alcohol syndrome provides an excellent example of employing this behavioral paradigm. His anger, hostility, and abuse were explored in terms of his previous feelings of guilt, powerlessness, and frustration. The stepmother's behavior was identified as a response to her need to be a good partner and as a response to the loss of her own child. The consequences of these behaviors was that the family was caught in a dysfunctional circle of behavioral exchanges for which there was no satisfaction or resolution.

Attention needs to be given to how the family responds to both internal and external stress and events. If the family does not respond constructively, then each member must be provided with specific stress management skills that will effectively address and resolve these problems. It is helpful to implement a structured schedule that includes eating at regular identified times, going to bed and getting up at agreed-upon times, establishing specific times throughout the day to interact and provide developmental stimulation to their child, and establishing some time each day for the parents to be together, not only to review and discuss personal concerns but also to enjoy each other and their efforts. When dealing with culturally different individuals, the counselor must be aware of specific cultural patterns and interactional modes so as not to suggest something which is culturally offensive.

Often a parent or the family needs a specific intervention, such as medical, alcohol, or psychological services. These services must be provided before further work can be undertaken on the problems associated with the alcohol-affected child. In general, facilitating structure and specific family routines help stabilize the family and provide a positive foundation upon which to continue specific problem-resolution strategies with the family's child. This can be a rather extended process due to the variety of complex problems often found in families with a child with FAS. If specific strategies are to be carried out by parents, it is critical to strengthen the family unit, the marital relationship, and the ability to deal effectively with stress. Otherwise further work with the child is likely to be fruitless and frustrating.

The second phase, which often coincides with issues addressed during the first phase, deals with the feelings, reactions, and frustrations of the parents in having a child with FAS.

This is a complex process and requires skill at dealing with parental feelings of guilt and the need to deny, minimize, avoid, or blame others for the problem. These issues must be confronted and resolved in order to integrate this reality into the parents' lifestyle in a balanced and adaptive manner.

It is generally difficult to identify feelings of guilt about having a child with FAS. If the counseling relationship is strong and secure, it is easier for parents to identify, address, and resolve guilt feelings. The guilt is often manifested in a variety of parental behaviors. These include over-attention and protection of the child, an inability to discuss openly the child and their concerns about the child, distancing themselves from the child, minimizing their child's difficulties, being over-critical or punitive to the child, or simply giving up on the child. Parents need to be encouraged to become more aware of their feelings and behaviors so they can more appropriately respond to the needs of their child. Numerous strategies are available to help address these specific problems, and the counselor or human service provider must be able to quickly acquire materials for the parent(s). Specific strategies employed by Rational-Emotive approaches, Reality therapy approaches, Meichenbaum's cognitive-behavioral approaches, Gestalt therapy, and insight-oriented therapies are most useful in providing a framework from which to address and resolve guilt feelings.

Hostility is often a reflection of guilt feelings and can be directed towards the other parent, the counselor, social service or educational agencies, and self. It usually helps to assist the parent(s) in identifying his or her anger and finding more constructive ways to express it. Many of the self-defeating behaviors exhibited by parents in regard to their child have roots in feelings of guilt. Each of these behaviors and feelings needs to be individually addressed and resolved.

In addressing the guilt issues, parents need to feel safe, secure, understood, accepted, and valued by the counselor. A counselor needs to be skilled at confronting rationalization and justifications for previous behaviors and questioning these in a manner that is not threatening to the parents. Often parents blame each other, and it is important to have the latest information at your disposal regarding the effects of alcohol on both males and females. It has been helpful to identify a more abstract reason for having a child with FAS. By this I mean that rather than having parents blame each other for their alcohol-affected child, they acknowledge and identify their partying, irresponsible behavior, and level of mismanaged stress as the primary contributors to having a child with FAS/FAE. This allows for the formulation of an understandable situation upon which to attach their guilt. It is almost mandatory to find such an understandable and identifiable reason. Parents often say they should have known better, and it is helpful to point out that they know more now than they did then and so, of course, they will not repeat those self-defeating, problem-inducing behaviors. It is always stressed that the more one knows, the better are the decisions one makes, and this truth can be repeatedly identified from their parental and personal experience.

The parents' guilt feelings are usually accompanied by a strong tendency to minimize or deny the problems of their child with FAS/FAE. They will often resist seeing the problem to be as serious as others view it, and project their difficulties onto others. "It was the doctor's fault" or "the school's fault" are common projections. These projections must be dealt with in a firm, nonintimidating manner by providing reality-based feedback and offering parents encouragement. As parents attempt to minimize their child's problems and their responsibility in addressing them, a supportive, encouraging but firm stance seems to work best. Parents need to be provided facts about their child, his or her performance gaps, what these performance deficits mean, and how they can teach the child skills to compensate for the deficits.

The father repeatedly projected his concerns about his child onto others. It was the doctor's fault, his partner's fault for not being a good mother and caretaker, and the white man's fault for introducing Indian people to alcohol.

In addressing these projections, it was necessary not to become defensive and to stress that although there probably was some truth in his projections, they were not categorically correct. Each of these projections needed to be addressed. In confronting the projection "it was the doctor's fault," he was asked how the doctor was at fault for the fetal alcohol syndrome of his son? He said that he was not but should have been able to do something. The father was unable to identify what it was the doctor should be able to do. For the second projection of the stepmother not being a good caretaker, the father was asked to identify specifically what it was his partner was not doing. He was asked if his partner chose to live with him so she would have a child to care for? He said no and was unclear as to what it was that was bothering him about his partner's caretaking activities. It was suggested that perhaps he would find something wrong with anything that she did as he was angry at his ex-wife, his son's natural mother, for drinking and giving birth to a son with

FAS. The father was encouraged not to vent this anger on his current partner. The third projection, white man is at fault for introducing alcohol to the Indian, was acknowledged and affirmed. Subsequent to this affirmation, it was pointed out that many Indian people had experience with alcohol prior to the arrival of the white man and even if they had not, how did this resolve the fetal alcohol syndrome problems of his son. This was discussed at some length with the positive outcome of the father becoming more aware of the need for improved prenatal care, responsible drinking, gaining ability to accept how things were, and accepting what needed to be done to minimize the fetal alcohol syndrome problems in his son.

In this segment of the discussion it was important not to become defensive, self-righteous, or condemning of the father and his struggle. It was necessary to be compassionately firm and unwavering in addressing unrealistic perceptions and expectations, and to do so in an accepting and encouraging manner. Parents often need to be asked that if all that they say is true, how does that change the situation they are confronted with by the child with fetal alcohol syndrome? Parents readily recognize that it will not change their situation, and this frees them from a tendency to lay blame and moves them towards problem-solving and management of their child.

It is important to stress with unwavering firmness the need for the parents to be responsible for ensuring that their child receives the best education, home stimulation, home consistency, and support possible.

In addressing specific blaming, parents need to be given the facts on how, generally speaking, the specific problems of the child are a function of the teratogenic effects of alcohol. This is difficult and must be done with much empathy and compassion. Often, parents spend a considerable portion of their time avoiding dealing with the specific needs of their child or simply not exhibiting much follow-through or identifiable concern about their child's difficulties. As parents become less guilty and defensive about having a special needs child, this type of behavior often recedes. Their avoidance is best understood in terms of their own guilt and self-consciousness about having a child with FAS. Parents need to be made aware of how their avoidance, lack of follow-through, or seeming disinterest is a function of their guilt and self-consciousness about having a child with FAS. This should be done gently, compassionately, and supportively. Identifying a nonthreatening cue that can be tossed at the parents during such times can be effective. This cue, that can be a word, a phrase, or specific facial expression, is one which has meaning to the parent(s) and symbolizes in a playful or humorous manner their avoidance or unwillingness to deal with their child's problem. Humorous cues seem to be most powerful in inhibiting avoidance behaviors and generating positive change, as the following example illustrates.

The father criticized his partner for not being a good mother to his son and not fulfilling her role. The father said he could not do this because he was working and also was a man. He was asked to identify specifically what he could not do in caring for his son, a task with which he had difficulty. I said maybe he himself wanted care, and humorously suggested that it was as if he was complaining that someone needed to change his Pampers. Throughout an eighteen-month period of working with this family, each time the father began to voice unrealistic or unreasonable concerns he was asked if "his Pamper was full and needed changing?" This invariably resulted in laughter and his dropping the criticism and becoming more active in solving the problem. In fact, late in work with this family the simple identification of "Is this a Pamper complaint?" was the cue that stopped the criticism and inaction and directed the family toward problem resolution.

As these issues are addressed, it is important to remember that each one needs to be reviewed on a regular basis with the parents. This review and affirmation helps strengthen the parents' ability to integrate their work and future plans and expectations into their personalities and world views. At this point, parents need to identify anticipated future difficulties, generate ways to respond to these difficulties, form plans to meet their personal and relationship needs with each other and their family, and identify developmental needs and weaknesses that must be confronted and adequately met. The review must be positive, encouraging and affirming for each of the parents and other nuclear or extended family members.

## SPECIFIC FAMILY INTERVENTION SUGGESTIONS

The provision of appropriate interventions and assistance to families with an alcohol-affected member depends upon the age of the individual: infancy, childhood, adolescence, and adulthood. At each of these arbitrary divisions, the family is provided a different set of specific guidelines.

A number of general guidelines should be provided parents and family members with an alcohol-affected child. These general guidelines include:

1. Develop and establish structured family routines. This includes regular and consistent meal times, bedtimes, and times to get up.
2. Always provide prompts with respect to what you want done. Tell your child what he or you will be doing and what is to happen next. Example: "We will make your bed, then we will pick up your room. After we've made your bed and picked up the room, we will have breakfast."
3. Keep down the number and variety of distractions. Try not to do multiple things at the same time.
4. Structure consistently both with respect to activities and the expectations and consequences for inappropriate behaviors.
5. Demonstrate acceptance and empathy, and facilitate development in all areas: interpersonal, social, family, personal, and community. Example: "How will you deal with your child when attending a powwow, community meeting, educational performance review at school, or when shopping?" "How will you respond to requests from parents of other alcohol-affected children?" and "What do you have to offer other parents of other FAS/FAE children?"
6. Observe the parent and child for any health or adjustment problems.

### INFANCY AND PRESCHOOL

When parents have been informed by their physician that they have a child with FAS/FAE, they require considerable empathy, understanding, and support. It is more helpful to identify the positive aspects of their child and future with the child and use this base to create an awareness of the forthcoming responsibilities and possible problems.

Parents need to be informed of the general identified effects that can be expected in an alcohol-affected child. It is helpful to identify the more concrete and observable aspects of children with FAS. These include low birth weight and height, a failure to gain weight, facial abnormalities such as a short upturned nose, short eye openings, a thin and flat upper lip, small chin, drooping eyelids, extra folds of skin in the corner of the eye, eyes not always able to track or focus together, malformed ears, and flat cheeks. Not all of these features are present in each child; however, children with FAS will show more of this group of facial abnormalities than children who are not alcohol affected.

Creases in the palm of the child's hands may not be normal. Fingers and toes may show some bending and the child may have problems in the joints of both hands and feet. The infant may have limited movement of the elbows and knees. Central nervous system abnormalities include jitteriness, tremulousness, weak sucking response, poor feeding response, irregular sleep patterns, hyperexcitability in response to lights, noise, new people or sounds, and muscle spasms producing a rigid back and neck.

Individuals with fetal alcohol syndrome have an increased incidence of heart defects, cleft lip and palate, and other structural abnormalities. These need to be identified by the family physician. Remember that not all FAS children will have all of these structural abnormalities. Rather, children with FAS experience a higher incidence.

The child and mother need to be followed closely after they are released from the hospital. This is especially vital if the mother continues her drinking, placing the child at increased risk for neglect. In such cases, extended family members and community support systems can be invaluable in protecting and providing appropriate care to the infant. Faced with such a situation, the counselor must assume a more direct role in confronting the mother with the specific necessity of remaining sober, dealing with her alcohol abuse in a constructive manner, and becoming involved in local support groups such as Alcoholics Anonymous, 12-Step groups, etc.

As infants, children with FAS need regular medical visits. A more frequent medical problem of these children during the preschool years is middle ear infections. It is very important to monitor the child's hearing during infancy and the preschool years. The various birth defects common in children with FAS require attention. Common birth defects include dislocated hips and curvature of the spine, probable skeletal handicaps, and problems with the teeth. The basic problem is a displacement of the secondary teeth, which results in abnormal contact between upper and lower teeth. Astigmatism and nearsightedness are the most common visual problems experienced by children with FAS, and these need to be monitored regularly by the parents and medical personnel during infancy and the preschool years. Parents need to be provided with this information so they will recognize the problem and seek treatment.

Most children with FAS have delayed development, at least to some degree. Parents need to be provided with strategies to encourage normal development. The child needs help with fine and gross motor coordination, visual tracking, and orientation in space. Language stimulation and vocabulary building are often required and parents need to learn how to respond appropriately to misarticulations in the child's speech. Sensory stimulation activities, as well as a learn-by-doing approach, appear to work best in minimizing developmental delays. Listed below are a few concrete examples of sensory stimulation and learning-by-doing activities:

1. Teaching colors: Yellow
   • Wear yellow clothes
   • Find yellow-colored household articles
   • Identify foods which are yellow
   • Make or cut-out pictures with yellow construction paper
   This can be done for each of the colors and one can employ a variety of tasks with each color as the basis for the task.

2. Teaching Concepts: Square
   • Find squares throughout the house
   • Make squares out of construction paper
   • Identify squares in magazines, books, and television programs
   • Make square cookies or cake
   • Find snack food items that are square: cereals, crackers, cookies, etc.

   This can be done for all the various forms and other concepts you would like to teach.

   Concept: Under and over
   • Have child crawl under chair, sit under table, or hide under blanket or pillow.
   • Stand over toy or sit on top of toy.

3. Teaching Activities: Staying in yard
   • Have child stand in front of a house, stay within designated area in the house. A space can be designated by four chairs, boxes, etc.

   This identified or partitioned area can be expanded to incorporate more and more space within which the child needs to learn to stay and this learning can be transferred to the front or back of the house or yard.

These activities help parents work actively with their alcohol-affected child and improve their ability to understand and deal with the specific problems. Since many children are hyperactive, parents need to be taught how to respond in a helpful way to the hyperactivity. Behavioral management strategies are generally the most effective. Often, the parent has unintentionally rewarded the child by giving constant attention to the hyperactive behavior either verbally or nonverbally. Parents need to be made aware of how these management efforts reinforce the hyperactivity rather than resolve it and they should be encouraged to ignore it as much as possible, providing positive reinforcement for nonhyperactive behavior. Efforts to improve the child's ability to remain on task for as long as possible are necessary. Again, behavioral strategies appear to be most effective in accomplishing this goal. Parents can be taught a simple behavioral-shaping program with the target behavior being an increase in the time their child can remain on any given task. The behavioral strategies provide individuals with an easily understood way of identifying and working with a broad spectrum of behavior in their child. They also provide for a consistent and effective tool for changing behaviors.

The parents should be encouraged to enroll the child in Head Start or other preschool day care programs. It is worth noting that often parents are unclear or tend to overlook developmental delays, apparently feeling the child is somewhat slow in a given area but will catch up or outgrow it. Parents and other family members need to be made aware of the severity of the delay and the need to respond with more stimulation and skill building with their child to minimize the gaps generated by these developmental delays.

Attention needs to be given to the parents to ensure their child is receiving the best stimulation and management skills available. When parents have not yet been able to resolve their own dysfunctions, this process is short-circuited, with the child suffering the resultant negative effect. The counselor needs to try to maximize the parents' ability to deal effectively not only with their problems but with their child's problems.

I recommend that parents consider techniques found in appropriate child management programs. My personal preference is the STEP program, which is grounded in Adlerian psychology. The STEP program provides parents, Indian and non-Indian, with a model from which to analyze, understand, and deal effectively with their child's behavior. The communication portion of the STEP program, however, is not culturally appropriate to many Native American tribes and needs to be modified to ensure culturally appropriate and sensitive communicative styles. The STEP program also provides an excellent model for discipline and for improving family functioning in general.

## CHILDHOOD

As their child enters school, parents need to be ready for the accompanying problems the child is likely to experience. Especially when the child looks different and has poor speech abilities, he or she may experience stress. These problems identify the child as someone not like most others, and he or she can be the brunt of childhood teasing and harassment.

Educational problems encountered by the child with FAS/FAE include attention deficits, hyperactivity, poor impulse control, memory problems, restlessness, difficulties with problem-solving, difficulty in identifying dangerous situations, and difficulty with learning from past experiences. Teachers and parents often believe the child is smarter than he or she actually is and attribute poor scholastic performance to laziness. Reading and writing appear to be more easily learned by children with FAS than arithmetic. Children with FAS generally possess good social skills. They tend to be exceedingly friendly, outgoing, and overly tactile in their interactions with others. These social skills will often mask poorer academic abilities so the children are not dealt with effectively.

Parents need encouragement to inform their child's teachers of the child's special needs. They also need to learn how to teach socially appropriate behaviors and responses. This can be done at home by repeatedly demonstrating and "play-acting" age-appropriate experiences where their child must learn to respond appropriately. Here, parents can act as someone who wants to be a friend, or play, fight, argue, or tease. Then they can coach their child on how to respond better to these interpersonal exchanges. Parents can be encouraged to demonstrate how to respond when one's feelings are hurt and when one is made fun of. Often it is necessary to role-play these situations in counseling as parents frequently have difficulty in managing these interpersonal exchanges as well. It helps to have the child explain the reasons for his or her choice and then provide a summary of the appropriate response to instill more deeply in the child what the appropriate response is and why.

Parents need to be taught how to respond helpfully to the behaviors of lying, stealing, temper tantrums, and disobedience. Behavioral strategies have been useful in establishing a base from which parents can effectively operate. The counselor needs to repeatedly stress to the parents that consistency is important in their responses to the child's disruptive and inappropriate behaviors. It is useful to provide parents with information regarding their child's development, age-related psychosocial behaviors and needs, and physical development. This information can be a base from which parents can promote development and stimulation for their alcohol-affected child.

### ADOLESCENCE

During adolescence, children with FAS generally reach their academic ceiling. During these years, attention needs to be directed towards skills development and vocational training. Self-sufficiency skills and the ability to manage oneself appropriately need to be strengthened. One general educational goal should be towards daily living skills and the ability to manage one's life with a minimal amount of support and guidance.

Sexual behavior appears and needs to be dealt with directly. Alcohol-affected individuals are often easy marks for others, so attempts must be made to make these individuals less exploitable and less likely to be victimized. Girls and boys both need to be given guidance with regards to identifying and normalizing their sexual feelings and needs for expression. This requires the ability to provide families and the alcohol-affected individual with sound sexual education. This demands attention to both the physiological as well as the attitudinal and value dimensions of sexual behavior. Individuals need to understand the normalcy of the increasing sexual feelings and how these feelings are best expressed. Because parents are often uncomfortable with this dimension of their parenting, it is helpful to work with the entire family in addressing and providing adequate sexual education, sexual expression, and value solidification. The materials which I have found most helpful in this regard include the *SARguide* developed by the National Sex Forum, and *The Sex Handbook: Information and Help for Minors*, by H. Handlin and P. Brennen. These materials need to be presented in a casual, matter-of-fact manner and should not be presented in a moral, fear-inducing, or judgmental style. The counselor needs to be comfortable with this approach so as to make the parents and family feel comfortable with discussing and dealing with sexual issues. Birth control measures are generally recommended by professionals, and each family must decide how comfortable they are with these methods and, if not, what the possible consequences might be.

Concern needs to be given to the person's ability to manage his or her money and resources effectively. Alcohol-affected individuals are, for the most part, unable to manage money effectively and as a consequence need some assistance in this regard. Parents or someone else must be a protective payee or record keeper and money dispenser.

Assistance also must be given to the management of the person's health, hygiene, and daily living requirements. For individuals who had good training and management from birth forward, less attention needs to be given to these matters. As with all previous stages, a consistent and stable environment helps the alcohol-affected individual to benefit from these interventions and guidance.

## ADULTS

Adults with FAS/FAE almost always require a guardian to be appointed to manage money and resources. If the adult lives in a specialized residential or subsidized living situation, attention needs to be given to the person's ability to manage health needs, clothing, and housekeeping. Involving the adult with FAS in various community support groups and activities is always helpful. Concern needs to be directed towards continued management of sexual drives and interest. Frequently, alcohol-affected adults are encouraged to employ birth control methods as they are not able to provide adequately for an infant. Often, sterilization is considered for both males and females. It is vital that whatever method is chosen fits with the values of the person and the person's family or caretaker.

Alcohol-affected adults often need help in appropriately managing their free time. Involvement in town sports leagues, clubs, or other community activities is beneficial. The development of personal hobbies or projects is also valuable. If and when an adolescent or adult with FAS/FAE is experiencing psychological problems, attention needs to be given to ensuring he or she receives treatment. Occasionally the adult with FAS will have legal, educational, or medical needs, and the caretaker or guardian must ensure that these needs are appropriately met.

The Indian and non-Indian adults with FAS/FAE I have worked with are now in a variety of settings. Some live independently with an agency such as a mental health center or adjustment training center available to help them when needed. Two of these individuals manage their own money, shopping, and medical needs with little or no need for prompting or guidance. Others require more direct supervision. A couple of individuals hold full-time positions, one with the county and the other with the city, and are employed as general semiskilled or clerical workers. Work responsibilities include snow removal, city and county maintenance duties, and general office and clerical duties. Some of the adults live in sheltered homes and are employed in sheltered-work situations. These people will always require some direct supervision to do well. Two individuals have become street people and exist by panhandling and borrowing or begging from others as well as occasionally working at spot jobs. Relatives provide them with shelter when the weather is too severe to be out.

With each of the general categories, it is necessary to be optimistic, encouraging, and positive about dealing with any specific issue that is confronting the family and the infant, child, adolescent, or adult with FAS/FAE. It is worth noting that alcohol-affected individuals generally remain socially outgoing, trusting, and enjoyable to be with. The major negative changes often seen in persons with FAS/FAE as they become older is an increase in inappropriate sexual behavior, increased social isolation, disappointment with education and work, loneliness, and depression. Many of these problems can be minimized with good training from infancy forward, the establishment of clear guidelines and structure, immediate and understandable consequences for inappropriate behaviors, and an attitude of support and encouragement. As counselors, the foundation can and must be laid early to help offset the deficits associated with fetal alcohol syndrome. Success with these efforts will ensure that an individual with FAS can live an enjoyable and satisfying life.

# Overcoming the Cycle of Failure and Frustration
## Art and Other Therapies

*Antonia Rathbun, M.A., A.T.R., cofounded the FAS/Drug Effects Clinical Programs in Portland, Oregon, where she and Diane Malbin, M.S.W., facilitate parent education and support groups for birth, foster, and adoptive parents of children with FAS/FAE. She has consulted for Portland Public Schools, Beaverton School District, the Council For Prostitution Alternatives, education service districts, public health departments, and other community service agencies throughout the Northwest and Canada. She is a registered art therapist using visual and kinesthetic approaches to enhance cognitive, perceptual, emotional, and social development in affected children and adults. She is the birth parent of a child with FAE.*

IN A FAST-PACED INFORMATION SOCIETY, we expect a normal person to be well behaved and controlled. Our world demands a lot— initiative, drive, staying with tasks, dependability, flexibility, and a high pain threshold for mental and bodily discomfort. Children and adults with alcohol-related birth defects strain to meet these cultural expectations while trying to overcome the serious difficulties caused by organic brain damage.

Caregivers of alcohol-affected children find themselves stuck in a cycle of frustration and burnout, feeling responsible for the child's success while utterly worn out by the gap between what they hoped for and what is happening at home and school. Guilt and hopelessness mount as they attempt to bring order, force solutions, and prevent failure. Parents, teachers, and other professionals lose touch with their own strengths and those of the person with FAS/FAE.

These ideas are offered as a springboard to help parents and professionals develop successful approaches to the education of people with alcohol-related birth defects. We have no pat answers due to:

- the range and complexity of alcohol-related birth defects
- the need for local communities to develop strategies that fit their own cultural contexts and that are rich in symbolic and community-relevant teaching approaches
- the need to shift from a model of teaching and problem solving based on control to a new model based on collaboration. This new model stresses structure rather than control, diversity of educational approaches, and building on the children's strengths.

We need to revise our stance from "what to do about FAS/FAE" to "what to do along with individuals with FAS/FAE." We need to build solutions with them where they are, instead of where we wish they would be.

## Reversing the Downward Cycle of Deterioration: A Mother's and Daughter's Mask

Art therapy helps parents and children reveal their emotional states through such activities as painting masks. This first mask was made by the birth mother of an eight-year-old child before the child was diagnosed as having FAE (see figure 1a, following page 308). This parent lived out the family dynamics of the three generations of alcoholics she came from. She is the only one sober. This mother in the midst of denial cannot speak her pain. Confused and frustrated about how to help her child, she feels shame, anguish, and fear over what her alcoholism has done. The tumult of dark and bright colors clamp over the mouth of the masks, rising like a flood. The mother indeed talks about "drowning" in her parenting. Scarves of red and black, like plumes of anger and depression, seem to be coming out of her ears. She is afraid of the child's anger and grief and afraid she has failed. In reaction, she tries to control more, struggling to fix her impaired daughter. Even though she uses recommended parenting techniques, the deterioration between her and her child gets worse.

Inside the mask, a cartoon painted in sky blue shows Charlie Brown reading aloud to himself, "In the fifth chapter of Thessalonians, it says 'without ceasing'" (referring to prayer). With this one image, she comforts herself in her confusion, fear, and terrifying silence.

Her child has just entered therapy.

Her daughter Gwen entered therapy for children of alcoholics. Her first mask, like her mother's, indicates repressed anger, hurt, loss, and pressure (figure 1b). The bilateral split of the face, one half of the face black and the other half white, is a familiar symbolic element often linked to internal conflict. The dark half of the mask represents the child's shame and confusion, her sense of badness, arising from the judgments of her parents and teachers whose expectations she can meet only inconsistently. The dark, bruised-looking colors (blue, black, and purple) and pressured strokes convey how hurt and burdened this child feels. Frustrated to the point of despair, she was getting Ds and Fs in school. Since no one knew she was suffering from organic brain damage, she was viewed as unmotivated. Trying to be good while being seen as bad wore her out. This mask conveys her feeling of pressure and sense of defeat.

The mouth, a thick, pouting red rectangle, has orange Xs across it, as if sewn shut. Gwen got in trouble when she talked back, yelled, argued, and had tantrums. Adults feared the child's feelings and controlled her even harder. The eye sockets are rimmed with red, a sign of rage ("seeing red").

Many parents and professionals see children with FAS/FAE as angry and out of control. They do not recognize this anger as a signal of the children's hurt and sadness. The children feel something is wrong with them, and yet adults encourage them to "buck up, try harder, and just get down to business." All of the ways they attempt to please fail.

Two more years would pass before her mother would recognize her daughter's problems as FAE and understand that subtle brain damage was contributing to her daughter's difficult behavior. After two years of effort, the mother gained the assistance of recognized specialists in the field, and Gwen was finally identified as having FAE. But teachers, other professionals, and family members even then discounted the diagnosis. Gwen looked normal and was so verbal.

Gwen's own response to finding out about FAE was relief: "So it's not my fault!" She no longer felt blamed. During the following months she grieved, spilling her anger and hurt at her mother: "How could you let this happen to me?" But the second mask, made two years later, shows the gradual disappearance of the dark line down the middle of the face, as Gwen's internal conflicts began to diminish (figure 2a). The dark colors and compressed composition break up and the mouth opens, as the child speaks her pain. Half the mouth turns down but the other half turns up in a smile, capturing her grief but also her relief at things finally making sense. Gwen now got help when she got stuck, and once she gained understanding and support, she responded with increasing relief. The light side of the second mask has brighter colors and softened lines.

The last mask, made at the end of the third year in therapy, shows a dramatic improvement in Gwen's psychological health (figure 2b). The line splitting the center of the face is gone. The smooth horizontal lines, peaceful mouth, and open quality to the composition express the child's acceptance. She has freed her energies for coping, instead of defending against constant misunderstandings and despair. As adults began to capitalize on her strengths, she grew more active in creating her own solutions when things went wrong at home or school. This mask shows hope and confidence in its harmony of composition and its sparkle. Gwen sprinkled it with glitter and spoke of how proud she felt.

## Conceptual Framework for Exploring FAS/FAE Symptoms and Strategies

A diagnosis of FAS/FAE means that prenatal alcohol exposure has damaged the child's central nervous system. The brain damage can range from mild to severe, but even subtle organicity interferes with the brain's ability to relate one piece of information to another. Brain damage interferes with learning, thus causing the developmental delays common in alcohol-affected children.

Practical intervention takes the form of creative detective work where parents and professionals invent strategies to fit the child and the situation. Three basic principles may be helpful in developing educational approaches for children with FAS/FAE.

1. *Adults and children with subtle brain damage typically require more external support, prompts, and cues than others might expect.* Instead of trying to control the children and setting up power struggles, parents and professionals need to provide external support for children, such as routines and visual pictures of what the child needs to do. Over time, children will internalize some of this external structure and make their way more efficiently without needing so many outside cues.

2. *Children with FAS/FAE tend to be visual and concrete in their thinking.* Parents and professionals need to appreciate how important it is to base education on the child's visual and concrete learning style. Children with subtle brain damage in general learn more easily when visual or kinesthetic cues are combined with verbal instructions. Visual or metaphoric thinking through art or role playing helps children with FAS/FAE express emotions and improves their ability to solve problems. Images are the language of the concrete, empowering the child's communication with us.

3. *Children with FAS/FAE may have strengths in areas like sports, dancing, painting, or sewing that parents and professionals can use to relieve their pent-up frustration and to provide experiences of ease and mastery.* Much of the tension between children and their caregivers results from a misreading of how brittle

the children's confidence becomes over time, how eroded and inadequate they feel, and how worn down they are by failing to meet everyone's expectations, including their own.

## Symptom Clusters and Remediation Strategies

Some of the problems of children with FAS/FAE, like memory deficits and distractibility, are the direct results of organic brain damage. Other problems, such as temper tantrums and over sensitivity to criticism, are better understood as secondary problems. The secondary layer of symptoms, typically problem behaviors, evolve when the brain damage is misunderstood as deliberate disobedience and children become consumed with frustration. Secondary symptoms evolve when families have no way to understand what is going wrong and how to relieve the tension building between adults and alcohol-affected children.

Dealing constructively with the problems created by the organic brain damage can reduce the need to treat secondary behavioral symptoms that have become entrenched when the subtle signs of brain damage are overlooked and misinterpreted.

The following sections present typical examples of the clusters of problems common among alcohol-affected children, along with recommendations suggesting ways to approach them.

### Memory Deficits, Distractibility, Sporadic Mastery, and Avoidance

*Case Example*

A twelve-year-old child with FAE sat in her social studies class. The teacher announced the class would watch a film, take notes on it, and report what they had learned aloud after the film was over. The child barely completed writing down a single point she had heard before the film had made several other points.

She could not tell which points were the important ones and she could not write them all down. She could not just listen, because she knew she would forget much of it, maybe even the most important parts. She struggled through the film, ashamed and in dread.

In front of all the other students, the teacher made remarks about the child's "needing to pay closer attention and really listen to the film." The teacher did not realize that the child could hear but she could not differentiate, prioritize, sequence, and organize what she was hearing. She had writing difficulties as well. The child was humiliated in front of her classmates once again.

In literature class, the child faced the same problem. She was asked to read a paragraph and write a summary to read aloud. The child went home and enjoyed reading the paragraph but did not know how to render her responses in written form. "I read it and I follow the story," she said. "It's like I am inside of it. I can't be outside of it and understand it. When I'm done, I'm outside of it and can't say what it was like inside again."

In her school reading, this child swims from detail to detail, immersed in the story or events. In general conversation, the child also acts this way while others get impatient and want her to "just get to the point." She has problems organizing information and digests it much more slowly.

Children with FAS/FAE are often accused of daydreaming, low motivation, and failing to pay attention. Their slow cognitive pace is often misinterpreted as lack of commitment and laziness. The child is just as confused as the adults about what makes learning so frustrating. The average child needs to be taught the material; the challenged child needs to be taught the approach to the material.[1]

### Recommendations

**Use Visual Images.** To help the child simplify the material she reads, show her how to use visual images to transform verbal material into understandable information. Here is how the child learned to write in summary:

1. She reads the paragraph or story.
2. She draws three pictures to show what was most important to her about the story. She could also draw three empty rectangles and then imagine a photographed scene inside.
3. She arranges the pictures in the order that best shows how the story went.

---

1. S. Smith, *No easy answers: The learning disabled child at home and at school* (New York: Bantam, 1980).

4. She then writes two sentences to describe what is in each picture, like a two sentence caption underneath the picture.
5. She then takes a clean sheet of paper and writes the two-sentence captions from each of the imaginary pictures in one paragraph, which results in a single paragraph summary.

By teaching children how to use such a visual story program, they can build on their visual thinking to pin down information.

**Recognize Children May Hide Memory Problems.** Due to their memory deficits, children with FAS/FAE seem to be forever starting over on schoolwork, homework, or household chores. They know that last week they learned and understood it, but now they are at a loss to remember it. Both children and caregivers feel mystified and frustrated when skills they learned a week ago disappear and have to be relearned over and over, especially when the children know that they knew it, but now they cannot do it.

The children need frequent and prolonged reteaching of concepts that teachers and other adults will take for granted that they know because the child appeared to be listening or said "Uh, huh" and did not ask questions at the time the concept was explained.

Keep in mind that the child may try to cover memory problems by such defenses as:

- Rationalization: "They said I didn't have to." (Meaning: "Don't ask me to think about it. I'm afraid I forgot, and I feel inadequate.")
- Denial: "I did that before," or "I know." (Meaning: "I don't want to go over it because then someone will know I don't quite know it, and I'll have to try to learn it which makes me feel hopeless and embarrassed because it feels too hard.")
- Makes a token response or repeats the response: the child repeats a phrase with urgency or frustration
- Gives superficial compliance but cannot follow through: the child seems to agree to the adult's proposal but has not understood what is expected.

Adults who use accountability techniques such as making spoken contracts with the child often find this method does not work because the child does not understand the contract and tries to cover up. The adult establishes the terms of the contract and the child appears to make a commitment. The adult assumes the child has understood the words and grasped the contract. But the child with FAS/FAE may or may not have grasped the point but will not say so. When the child fails to fulfill the contract, the adult feels cheated. The method backfires even though both the child and the adult are doing the best they know how.

Teach Children with Memory Problems to Cope With Stress. With children who have memory deficits, adults should avoid making accusations such as "Weren't you listening?" or "Why did you do that?" The child was listening and does not know why things are not working. The "why?" question shuts down communication and comes across as an accusation.

Instead, sift back through the events from the child's point of view. The adult should help the child find a way to talk concretely about what is going wrong and should teach the child how to cope with the mounting stress. Instead of cornering the child, the adult might say instead:

"I'm noticing that . . . (name the task) isn't working too well for you."

"I see you . . . (describe the behavior or body cue in a neutral tone of voice). Are you stuck?"

Then the child can say something like "You talked too fast," or "It all went away."

At this point, help the child understand her emotions and cope with them. You can use picture language.[2] The adult might ask, "What does it make you want to do?" Then the child can give a picture-answer like "I want to run away" or "I want to kick her."

Help the child understand the physical sensations they are experiencing so that they can recognize these sensations as a signal that they need assistance or a break. Many children have a typical sensation or behavior they can tell you about if you ask them (chest tight, hands clenched, holding their breath). Labeling the physical sensation leads to naming the emotion. Such labeling helps children

2. S. P. Randels, personal communication, 1990.

learn to solve problems.[3] Then the adult can say something like "You hear too many words and your stomach gets tight? Then come to me for help or . . . ." Identify a self-soothing behavior that the child can use to cope with the situation like sitting under the desk for a break or working a blob of silly putty in her hands until she feels calmer. This is not a time-out strategy or a punishment. It is a variation of a redirect strategy, based on the different way children with FAS/FAE respond to stimulation. Be sure to recognize the child's effort and progress at successfully using techniques for self-soothing. It is a first step to restoring the child's confidence at home and at school.

### Perseveration and Shutdown

*Case Example*

A twenty-six-year-old woman with FAS drew a cartoon sequence to describe a traumatic event that left her believing she could not be safe unless her case manager came to her rescue in person on demand twenty-four hours a day. Actually, the woman had shown adequate coping skills to handle the episode with the help of a phone conversation with the case worker. But a full month later she was convinced that the crisis was still going on.

Drawing a comic strip to describe the events helped her point to the places where she got stuck. She could also see, from the pictures, that she in fact made it through the events to safety by using her own resources and the guiding telephone call. Until she was able to see this ending visually, she remained adamant that she had not been safe (perseveration) because the case manager did not physically come to the scene and rescue her. What she herself had done was not real to her.

The woman drew an image from her childhood where she hid from her incest perpetrator in a nest of pillows. This image represented a way she had once solved the problem of how to handle fear and get to safety. Encouraged, she made a full, adult-sized nest of pillows to crawl into so she could soothe herself when she was overstimulated or emotionally out of control. She has now adapted the nest to a tent over her bed, which she relies on to help her manage overstimulation when trying to solve problems and cope with daily tensions.

---

3. E. P. Whitlock, personal communication, 1992.

Perseveration or engaging in the same behavior over and over often emerges in alcohol-affected adults and children. Sometimes the repetition indicates organic brain damage—the person has gotten stuck in a task. The problem is also that people misinterpret stuck behavior. Caregivers see the child as just wasting time and fiddling. Sometimes the repetition indicates that the child is overloaded with emotion or external stimulation and needs to calm down. The repetitive behavior can have a quieting effect.

When a conflict occurs, alcohol-affected children and adults appear to escalate from anger or panic into shutdown. They can lock up, short circuit, and experience jamming quite suddenly, becoming rigid or agitated the more others attempt to introduce facts or try to reason with them. They resist attempts to talk it out and repeat phrases over and over, sounding like a broken record. They may explode, yell, and glare or, alternatively, withdraw and look emotionally frozen. They may react with restricted breathing and talk in loud, flat, or robotic voice tones. They may lock themselves in their rooms and bolt the door or walk out of school or off the job. What they are doing is trying frantically to reduce outside stimulation while managing their chaotic internal emotions. Some children stay in their room for hours, falling asleep without food or without taking off their clothes. Some adults lock themselves into their rooms or apartments for days at a time.

### Recommendations

Caregivers typically feel defied or ignored and increase their efforts to communicate. This approach worsens the distress of the person with FAS/FAE, by increasing the stimulation and overload that alcohol-affected people may not be able to handle. Yet teachers and parents often do not realize what is going on and fall back on formulas that actually increase the mental demands on a child who is shutting down. The worst thing to say is, "You can if you put your mind to it. I know you are a very smart child. Let's see you try before you give up."

This approach puts more pressure on the child. What he or she is saying loud and clear is, "You are demanding I say or do or feel something. But I am stuck. Something is not working. I hate this!"

When the person's thinking has become rigid, do not try to solve the problem right then. That will overload the child's circuits even more. The child is saying that he or she cannot handle any more. "I can't do this" means "I can't do this right now." Back off.

The caregiver can:

1. Detach. Slow your own response time. Just say, "Well, let's stop here. Take a minute and just breathe for now."

2. Give the child the chance to wind down, or even hide out a bit if needed. Breathing techniques may help the child cope with frantic feelings. With young children, you can say something like "Take a deep breath and let's land your plane! It's coming in for a landing now." Using a soft oral sound along with the breathing and the visual imagery of the plane landing. That way you have taught the child a program for relaxation which she herself can use to calm down in escalating situations.

3. Honor the child's expressing what she cannot do. "So something's not working and that's okay. When you can, tell me what's hard."

4. When she is ready, let her complain and ventilate the anger or disappointment before solving the problem together.

## Poor Auditory Comprehension and Difficulty with Task Completion

### Case Example

A twelve-year-old child with FAE was stumped by her teacher's instruction to the class, "Do as many of these problems as you can in class, then finish the assignment for homework." She could only work four problems during her class time. She spent two hours on the rest of the problems at home, only to run out of time to complete the homework she'd managed to write down for the other four academic subjects. She gave up, deciding that she could not omit her other homework and she could not possibly finish. She did some of the problems but did not turn them in because she saw the work as uncompleted. It was not the assignment the teacher wanted, so she would get in trouble. The general principle—turn in the work done—did not occur to her.

Feeling guilty, she put off telling anyone of her dilemma until the end of the quarter when it became evident that she was missing twenty-nine assignments.

## Case Example

A sixteen-year-old girl with FAS was given a list of chores to accomplish. Whenever her parents reminded her of her chores, they made sure to list the chores in detail. They thought this clarification would spur her on but instead she could not differentiate between the masses of words and became totally lost after the third item. She did not want to be accused of not cooperating and so would go off to her room holding onto whatever stuck in her mind once their long instructions had subsided. She hoped she would somehow get by. Her parents scolded her for not listening and not paying attention. They said she did not care about helping out in the family.

Children with FAS/FAE have trouble with verbal instructions even though they do hear them. The children may appear to have understood more than they actually did but have both auditory processing deficits and poor auditory memory. They look, attend, and still remain confused about directions. They may not be able to understand the fundamental purpose of the instructions, as in the case of the homework.

## Recommendations

Reduce instructions to a single item at a time. Structuring one task into even smaller components may still be needed. While all children may avoid work, alcohol-affected children may not understand the directions. For tasks like homework, set up a repetitive format within a structure, such as "Do thirty minutes of math per night, and even three problems done is OK."

Once they do figure out how to master the tasks, the sense of control and pride gained is worth the effort for everyone.

## Ordering and Sequencing Difficulties: Dealing with Change and Transitions

## Case Example

A ten-year-old boy with FAS who had been in a special education classroom was now mainstreamed to three different classrooms as his performance levels varied considerably. His hyperactivity accelerated, his sleep disturbances grew more acute, and the entire household was kept up most of the night for weeks on end. He was swearing and sexually acting out more than ever, even though he had not been sexually abused.

Since this boy had been doing satisfactory work in his special education class, the next step seemed to be to move him to the "least restrictive environment," according to P.L. 94-142 guidelines (a public law assuring equal access to children with disabilities). But he could not handle all the changes in routines and overstimulation.

Children with FAS/FAE are very schedule dependent and have difficulty orienting themselves if unexpected changes in their schedules occur. The basis of this problem lies in organic brain damage, which creates ordering and sequencing impairments. Alcohol-affected adults and children may complain that "everything's wrong" when the external markers by which they orient are moved or changed:

> I am a bowling ball. Once I get rolling down one lane, I just can't switch over . . . it takes me forever to slow down or move on to another kind of activity even when it's something I can remember I liked doing.
> —Man with FAE, age thirty-five.

> Every day of my life, I'm starting all over. I have to fight myself to get up out of bed. If one thing goes out of place in the morning, like I run out of milk for my cereal or something, once a piece falls out of my routine, the whole day it's like nothing fits after that.
> —Man with FAE, age thirty.

> I'm like a train. Once I get going one way, I can't just suddenly go off in another direction 'cause there's this whole chain of things I'm holding together.
> —Child with FAE, age twelve.

When the external markers by which they orient themselves are moved, alcohol-affected children may try in vain to place themselves again and defend against panic, another internal stimulus that just adds to the roar of the external stimulus overload they have to handle. They can pick fights, clutch other people's chairs, and invade other people's space.

Figures 1a and 1b

Figures 2a and 2b

*Figure 3*

*Figure 4*

Figure 5

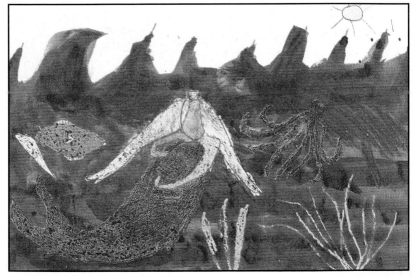

Figure 6

*Recommendations*

Just as it is impossible to turn a train at a sharp angle, the goal in preparing for change is to give alcohol-affected children and adults cues and structures, preparing a long smooth curve for their train of thought to change.[4] Provide cues ahead of time so that they can begin to wind down their attention and couple these verbal cues with enlisting the child's physical help in bringing the present activity to a close. Expect some distress and allow room for resistance.

Create an environment relatively low in stimulation, adding more items only after observing the child's tolerance level. Less is best—less furniture and less toys. For children with FAS/FAE who get easily overstimulated, simplicity is freedom. Let the schedule stay simple. If needed, keep the child in the same room rather than rotating classrooms each period. If the child prefers all one color of clothes, indulge his or her desire for uniformity. The same rules apply to food. No child ever died from eating the same kind of sandwich each day.

Predictability is a gift to alcohol-affected children. In their lives, something is always popping out of place or turning up missing—coats, hats, gloves, lunches. Make it easy by creating simple environments where things are not frequently rearranged and where there are strong environmental cues. Children can make small pictures of items, for example, and tape or glue the pictures on the cupboard or shelf where the object is stored as a reminder. Have alternate hats, coats, gloves, and plenty of humor. If the replacement items are not fancy, the child will not be so anxious over accidental loss. The child is what is important, not the belongings.

Keep in mind that children with FAS/FAE experience great fatigue from the ordinary demands and stimulation of a classroom and are often exhausted and unable to manage their frustration after a typical school day. Be careful not to overschedule the child. Provide physical and emotional spaces for disengagement. Children may want a nest of blankets piled in their closet or an exerciser on which to bounce. For children with sleep cycle disturbance, try a

---

4. L. Merrell, personal communication, 1991.

white noise machine; tapes with environmental sounds of rain, streams, or the ocean; or earplugs to keep out other sounds. Given time to cocoon after school or work, they may show greater resilience in handling their day's schedule.

### Poor Social Skills, Touching Difficulties, and Intrusiveness

*Case Example*

> A foster mother reports that her six-year-old foster child with FAS does not express feelings to her and does not seem to be emotionally attached to her. Yet he physically forces himself up to the mother's face, pushes wet kisses on her mouth, and shoves hugs on her despite frequent instructions otherwise.

Children with FAS/FAE are often invasive and intrusive with other children and adults. They often do not understand the idea of other people's body space. Their needs to touch make them appear exceptionally immature.

*Recommendations*

The notion of body space is abstract until the adult can find a concrete way to make body space real to a child. Find ways to make the concept of social space clear to alcohol-affected children through dramatic play or visual cues:

- Create "body halos" by using butcher paper. The adult and child take turns lying down and drawing an outline of their bodies. The second body outline should be drawn several inches away from the first outline. This space between the body outlines gets filled in like an aura with a particular color and can be called the person's "halo." Now the child has a concrete representation of what bodily space is. The adult can say, "I don't like it when someone pokes into my halo without asking me first. Will you ask me first?" Take turns asking and giving permission to enter someone else's aura.

Keep in mind that sometimes children with FAS/FAE have been victimized sexually. Talking about body space can be done by putting a sock on your hand and the child's hand to turn them into puppets. Talking through the puppets provides a language for discussing boundaries and safe contact. Be alert to gaze aversion, flat and terse voice tones, and other signs of anxiety which may indicate sexual abuse.

Adults can use other visual methods to teach the concept of personal space. Children can create their own space visually, for example, by putting duct tape around their desk and chair to mark their territory.[5] Animal imagery can be used to communicate the concept of territory. "Lions share the grasslands with other animals, but still have a territory when they want to watch or rest. You have to share the classroom but you can have a territory to be in when it is time for you to watch or be still."

## Stealing and Lying

*Case Example*

Imagine two scenes:

Scene 1: A cup sits on a desk. It belongs to someone but that someone is not in the room. No visual cue shows that some person owns the cup. The alcohol-affected person may walk in and see only the cup. He likes it. He takes it. That is not stealing. It is taking.

Scene 2: A person sitting at a desk holds a cup. The alcohol-affected person sees the cup in the other person's hand. He wants it so he walks over and rips it out of the individual's hand. That's stealing—taking something away from somebody directly that you know is not yours.

When the link between the object and its owner is not directly visible, children with FAS/FAE may not understand the relationship. Due to developmental delays, alcohol-affected children may also be acting from the self-centered orientation of a younger child. We do not accuse toddlers of stealing when they are attracted to some bright object. Children with FAS/FAE need help in understanding the concept of ownership, especially with unattended objects. Stealing often shows up when there is another difficulty causing them stress that they are unable to process and articulate to people.

5. S. Smith, *No easy answers: The learning disabled child at home and at school* (New York: Bantam, 1980).

Alcohol-affected children may also have difficulty with lying. Children and adults with FAS/FAE often appear to be lying when the facts are so glaringly obvious that no one can help but catch them. This picture does not exactly fit our ordinary picture of lying, devious deception.

The concept of confabulation may be helpful in understanding this behavior. Confabulation is "a symptom in which the patient supplies ready answers to questions without regard for the truth. The patient who confabulates appears to fill in gaps in memory with plausible facts."[6] Children with FAS/FAE may confabulate not because they are trying to deceive deliberately but because it is "just easier than having to push my mind into gear to sort through the facts."

*Recommendation*

Avoid asking questions that put the child in a position to lie. Rather than begin a cycle of blame and accusation, look at the lie as the child's attempt to even the score in a game beyond his level that is easy for others but hard for him. It is so hard for him to think, process information, and put words on things.

## Conclusion: Concrete Thinking and Building on the Child's Strengths

*Case Example*

A child with FAE, identified as gifted and talented in the visual arts, chose a fairy as her personal metaphor (figure 3). The fairy wings could communicate her wishes for ease (school was hard), speed (she had a slow cognitive pace), and the ability to rise above things (she felt weighed down by her handicap).

In some drawings, she was a struggling bird trying to fish from the difficult sea. She pictured her environment as a stormy sea with craggy waves (figures 4 and 5).

When FAE was finally identified, the ocean scene took a whole new turn (figure 6). The mermaid became her personal symbol, still magical like the fairy but one who can swim through the sea.

---

6. R. Berg, M. Franzen, and D. Wedding, *Screening for brain impairment. A manual for mental health practice* (New York: Springer Publishing, 1987).

Now she understands her own needs better and can begin to address these needs for herself with her parents and teachers. "I used to feel like I was drowning," she said. "I had to learn how to swim in the sea of my life."

The measures we use to evaluate children with FAS/FAE often underestimate the presence of substantial creative intelligence, curiosity, and a rich fantasy life. Our measures do not reveal the fairies, the mermaids, the birds, and the sea. We too often ignore the gifts of alcohol-affected children in such areas as music, the performing arts, or athletics.

We who work with alcohol-affected children need to understand the reality of the organic brain damage. Rather than rail at this reality, we need to see it as a mandate for our own creativity, our responsibility to help children with FAS/FAE create ways to succeed at school or work. Successes take place when we stop trying harder and start trying differently.

The goal of helping people with FAS/FAE learn is best served by building upon their strengths and adjusting the environment around them to support them better, just as we do with their other handicaps of a physical nature.[7] Together with the alcohol-affected individuals we work and live with, we must build solutions in the context of our communities:

> The alcohol-affected child is like a garden. Some seeds need to be planted year after year, like the carrots and the radishes. The seeds the birds carry away have to be replaced almost immediately. But there are bulbs that grow in the garden and every year they come up almost without tending. It can be too easy to see what failed to come up this year and step on the crocuses close to the ground. The important thing is to be thankful that there is a garden. It is not a wasteland.[8]

---

7. S. Clarren, personal communication, 1992.
8. L. Merrell, personal communication, 1991.

# Conclusion

JUDITH KLEINFELD

THIS BOOK OFFERS THE *WISDOM OF PRACTICE*—the expertise of parents, teachers, and professionals who have many years of experience working with alcohol-affected children. Their experience suggests three optimistic messages:

1. The negative stereotypes of alcohol-affected children so common in our society are highly misleading.
2. Early diagnosis, early intervention, nurturant homes, and education tailored to their distinctive problems in processing information—Such conditions make an enormous difference to the success and the happiness of alcohol-affected children.
3. We can identify specific educational strategies that help alcohol-affected children learn in the home and the school.

---

*The negative stereotypes of alcohol-affected children so common in our society are highly misleading.*

A one-sided picture of alcohol-affected children pervades our society. The media tell the most tragic tales, the worst-case scenarios, with the spotlight passing by those children who succeed. Most of the research we now have describes the most severely affected children who did not receive the benefits of early intervention or the specific educational techniques parents and teachers have described in this book.

This lopsided view creates a false and destructive picture of what the children are like and what we can hope for. This book represents a step towards a more balanced view of the spectrum of damage and an exploration of a range of outcomes, including successes previously thought to be unattainable.

Some children with FAS/FAE do fit the stereotype of hopeless brain-damage, depression, and failure. But many others are thriving. They are happy in their families, have good friends, and are succeeding in school, some in regular classes and others in special programs.

The negative stereotype of children with FAS/FAE is inaccurate for two important reasons. First, prenatal alcohol abuse has very different effects on different children. Some children have indeed suffered severe damage to the brain and central nervous system, are mentally retarded, or have severe learning problems, despite average IQ scores. But other children have been much less affected and have only subtle learning problems. Moreover, some children appear to escape entirely, even though their mothers abused alcohol during pregnancy. Ironically, as we become more attuned to the subtle effects of prenatal alcohol abuse, we will identify more and more children who have only mild problems.

Second, as we learn how to help children with FAS/FAE, we can create a different future. The stereotype of the past comes from a time when FAS/FAE was not understood and methods of intervention had not been identified. The best of homes and schools cannot undo the damage and make the children whole. But parents and teachers have been able to create situations which build on the strengths of children with FAS/FAE and where they live happy and successful lives.

At this time, we do not know what the future holds for alcohol-affected children. We have no research on what happens to children with different degrees of biological damage who receive the most appropriate attention and care. We have no research on the effects of specific intervention programs. The follow-up studies we have now focus on children with FAS/FAE who are very likely the more severely affected and who have not received the benefits of early diagnosis, early intervention, and education tailored to their needs.

We cannot overemphasize the importance of creating new images of what children with FAS/FAE can achieve. We need the image of Antone, in the top reading group in a regular school class, with a best friend the same age, and who dreams of a future helping other people. We need the image of Cindy, who has graduated with honors from the American Institute of Indian Arts, a junior in college, and a talented artist and designer. We need the image of Lisa, who relishes her family, friends, and pets, who is active in youth groups, and who insists that her parents help out a small boy worried that his own family cannot afford a donation to the YMCA campout. We need the image of Danielle, a teenager with severe FAS, who works as a preschool aide and a tutor to another child with FAS and who sees herself as just what she is—a fine and valuable person.

We do not intend to minimize or trivialize the biological damage done to children by alcohol abuse during pregnancy. Many children, impulsive and lacking in judgment, are at serious risk for running afoul of the law, for being victims, or for victimizing others. Many will continue to need special assistance and care throughout their lives.

The image of the hopelessly brain-damaged child with FAS doomed to jail or the streets is both false and destructive. What the social worker told Michael Dorris—"Nothing can be done"—is not the case. Such images and beliefs sap the will of parents, teachers, and policymakers to exert the intelligent effort needed to create a different future.

*Such conditions as early diagnosis, early intervention, nurturant families, and education tailored to their distinctive problems in processing information make an enormous difference to the success and happiness of alcohol-affected children.*

With alcohol-affected children, we do not yet know the limits of what we can accomplish when we know what we are dealing with, when we start early, and when we create home and school environments adapted to their needs.

The diagnosis is crucial, say the parents who have written these chapters. "Without identification or diagnosis," as Malbin[1] puts it, "parenting a child with FAS/FAE is like trying to find your way around Denver with a road map of Cincinnati." Unless the parents understand the effects of prenatal alcohol abuse, they are apt to cause additional psychological problems by constant anger at their children for behavior the children cannot help. Once they know what they are up against, they can carefully observe their children's patterns of behavior and devise ways to help their children overcome problems.

When parents do summon the courage to tell their children of the diagnosis, the children's response is often relief. "Good, I thought something was wrong with me!" said Malbin's daughter when her mother told her about FAE. Many children are relieved to hear of the diagnosis because it means that they are not at fault. They can take pride in how much they have overcome. They can enjoy inventing their own solutions to problems, as when Malbin's daughter figured out how to tell whether it was time to head for the school bus by pasting a Post-it with the bus time next to the digital clock.

Getting the diagnosis does not mean that everyone must be given the diagnosis. The parents writing these chapters are cautious about the label, about whom they tell of the problem. They usually want their children's teachers to know about the problem. They want the teachers to use in the classroom some of the techniques that are working for the children at home. They want the teachers to understand that their children cannot be treated just the same as other children when they misbehave because they are not just the same, their brains and central nervous systems have been damaged by prenatal alcohol abuse. Thus, it is fair to treat children with FAS/FAE differently. But at times, parents think it best not to tell other people about the diagnosis. One parent explained why she did not tell the Sunday school teacher about her son's diagnosis of FAS. She had watched this teacher work with two boys, her own son and another boy diagnosed as FAS. The teacher worked with her son

---

1. The parents and teachers named in this conclusion have written chapters in this book that readers may refer to. For ease of reading, we have not used formal citations.

and ignored the child with the diagnosis of FAS. That child was left to play without instruction.

Once families have the diagnosis, they can intelligently proceed down what Groves calls the "FAS Path." This path usually begins with early intervention. Parents can use many strategies to build their children's attention span, reduce their sensitivity to touch, and teach them how to play in productive and educational ways. "When parents follow through at home with strategies we teach them," Hinde writes, "we have seen dramatic development." Indeed, the unfortunate consequence of excellent early intervention is that some children leave the program so close to their developmental level when individually tested that they no longer qualify for the special services they still need.

Early education creates a firm foundation. But early intervention is not an inoculation that protects the child forever more. Most children continue to need special help if they are to maintain their gains. They need special preschools which emphasize structure and routine and focus on skills like speech development. Children with FAS/FAE thrive in preschools where teachers carefully supervise children all the time, routines are clear and unvarying, classroom spaces are clearly marked, and visual information supplements verbal directions. What is effective for alcohol-affected children is not simply good teaching.

When alcohol-affected children reach school age, parents report great difficulty getting the school to adapt the program to what their child requires. Even when they tell teachers of the diagnosis and discuss exactly how to work with their children, the information sometimes fails to register. Teachers must divide their time among many children and find it difficult to give sustained attention to children with FAS/FAE. Nor do many teachers see why they should change their entire classroom for just one child and a child with little potential anyway. Many teachers end up sending schoolwork home to overburdened parents who must then cope with yet more demands.

Few school districts offer the special classroom for alcohol-affected children that Tanner-Halverson developed on the Tohono

O'Odham Indian Reservation. In this setting, teachers could invent a wealth of concrete techniques to help alcohol-affected children pay attention or wait their turn. But many school districts are committed to a philosophy of mainstreaming. School personnel also worry that special programs for alcohol-affected children will end up singling out children from certain cultural groups.

Some teachers, like Patrice Winick in a small rural school, do have the freedom to reorganize their entire classroom with alcohol-affected children in mind. She emphasizes projects and role-playing activities rather than lectures. She takes children out into the community to make fish traps or camp at traditional sites, rather than teaching them entirely in classrooms removed from the world. "Rather than pandering to the needs of one child," Winick says, "all of the students gain from the clarity of the directions, consistency of the schedule, and the usefulness of real-life related lessons."

Some parents of children with FAS/FAE have been able to make appropriate arrangements for their children in the public schools. Some insist that academic requirements that their children cannot meet be waived. But other parents have turned to home schooling or have created alternative schools. Michele Saiz, for example, took leave from her teaching position to home school her kindergarten-age son with FAS. He is rapidly acquiring the vocabulary, lengthy sentences, small muscle control, and ability to sit still that he will need when he enters regular kindergarten the next year. Nancy Harrison persuaded a retired teacher, Beulah Phillpot, to start an alternative school in her living room. The school flourished, moved into a light and airy apartment, and developed sources of funding and cooperative arrangements with the local public schools so that children could move back and forth.

When parents advocate for their children, when they organize, when they rage and insist and refuse to give up and go away, they can achieve results. Political action, Lutke emphasizes, not just family change is necessary to create the world alcohol-affected children need. "The decision to become an advocate for your child," she writes, "arises out of the love you feel for your child and the pain you experience as you watch your child struggle every day in a world that he does not understand, with expectations he cannot meet, and which turns him into a bad person when he fails. Advocacy gives the parent some measure of control over her child's life as well as the knowledge that a situation is not hopeless and the parent and child are not helpless."

Parents of alcohol-affected children know that their own love and intelligent devotion is not enough. They cannot undo the biological damage that prenatal alcohol abuse has done. But they can observe and invent and help their children achieve everything possible.

*We can identify specific educational strategies that help alcohol-affected children learn in the home and in the school.*

Bathing the fetal brain in alcohol is a lot like spilling a drink on a computer, the electrical circuitry gets scrambled in unpredictable ways. Much of the behavior that parents and teachers find so aggravating, Morse points out, can be understood as problems the child's brain is having in processing information.

In essence, alcohol-affected children suffer from organic brain damage that makes it difficult for them to take in information, distinguish the signal from background noise in their environments, organize the information in an integrated or sequential fashion, and respond to the signal with the right routine. As in a computer gone awry, sometimes the information does not get put into memory. Sometimes the child perseverates, as when a single letter repeats again and again across the screen. Sometimes the child makes odd noises or does strange things, like a malfunctioning computer that goes blank and then flashes random symbols.

The specific techniques that parents and teachers find helpful in educating alcohol-affected children fundamentally simplify the information that the child must deal with at any one time. These techniques reduce the load of information the child must handle and make it easier for children to distinguish the signal from the background noise. Over and over again, parents and teachers emphasize the importance of creating structured and routine environments where the child does not have to deal with large amounts of new information at any time. They emphasize the importance of helping the child see the signal by presenting it visually, as well as in words, through pictures, labels, and broad facial expressions. Help children see the signal, they say, by walking over to them when giving them a message or using a specific cue to get their attention. Some parents and teachers help children focus on the message and screen out distracting noise by using computers or tape recorders with earphones.

Since many alcohol-affected children do not learn spontaneously from their experience, many parents and teachers have found it valuable to provide them with programs—essentially structured routines which guide them through tasks. To teach her alcohol-affected children to dress or take a bath, for example, Lutke routinized each activity and turned it into a song, "Socks, left foot, right foot; undies, left leg, right leg; pants, left leg, right leg." In her Learning Centre, Phillpot taught children routines for guiding themselves through an arithmetic problem and encouraged them to talk out loud as they went through each step of the routine. Rathbun taught her daughter relaxation programs so she could control her frantic feelings. "Take a deep breath and let's land your plane!" she would say, making a sort whirring noise. "It's coming in for a landing now." Gradually, children learn the program and use it on their own.

## A Concluding Word

Not all knowledge and certainly not all wisdom come from formal academic research. Parents who have devoted themselves to the children they love can be the most sensitive and astute of observers. Teachers who have worked for many years with alcohol-affected children have a wealth of knowledge and inventions. Experienced therapists have come to understand the emotional landscape and have learned how to create trust and rapport so they can help the families help the children.

We have chosen to present the wisdom of practice in the form of stories of people's lives, rather than lists of educational techniques. Only through story can we do justice to the human emotions and do honor to the human will and spirit.

# Appendix I
## Education Techniques for Children with FAS/FAE

VALBORG KVIGNE, JUDY STRUCK, ELLEN ENGELHART AND TRACY WEST

THIS APPENDIX LISTS EDUCATIONAL TECHNIQUES FOR preschool children, elementary students, and junior and senior high school students. These techniques were developed by the South Dakota Affiliated Program, University of South Dakota School of Medicine.

Some information is repeated from list to list. The intent is to provide a hand-out suitable for parents or workshop presenters to give teachers at a particular grade level.

### EDUCATION TECHNIQUES FOR PRESCHOOL CHILDREN WITH FAS/FAE

I. Environment
   A. Calm and quiet.
     1. Soft music may be calming.
     2. Tone down classroom so rooms are not overly stimulating.
       a. Keep a minimal number of objects hanging from the ceiling and on the walls.
       b. Use calm colors of paint on the walls.
     3. Use headphones for quiet time. (Students with FAS/FAE are not always able to block out other noises.)
   B. Structure.
     1. Establish a few simple rules.
     2. Enforce the same rules in the same way.
     3. Use the same language when enforcing the rules.

323

C. Transition from one activity to another activity.
   1. Tell the children what they will be doing: "We'll finish painting then we'll eat a snack."
   2. Give the child an object to help make the transition. The child could carry a book to story time, a puppet to the puppet story, or a toothbrush after snack time.

II. Language Development
   A. Children who are not talking.
      1. Begin with simple story books.
      2. The teacher can touch an object and name the object for the child. The teacher touches a table and says to the child "table."
      3 Use real objects like "trees, cars, dog" and name the objects.
   B. Children who are talking using single words.
      1. If the child says "drink," say to the child, "more drink" to stimulate more words in the child's vocabulary.
      2. Expand the child's vocabulary slowly. When the child starts using two words at a time, start using three words "want more drink."
      3. Talk with the child at the child's level. Use short sentences.
   C. Poor articulation.
      1. A speech therapist would be a good resource for the child and teacher.
      2. The teacher needs to model proper pronunciation.
      3. Go around the classroom, touch objects, and name the object. Have the child do the same thing.
      4. Meal time. Have the child say what he/she wants rather than just giving the child what one thinks the child wants.
      5. Music activities can help children learn vocabulary.
         a. Good morning song.
         b. Song before the children eat.
         c. Name songs.
         d. Circle game songs—sit down, stand up, name games.
   D. Sign language may be helpful in teaching children with FAS even when they do not have a hearing loss. Sign language is concrete and visible and can be used along with verbal language.

III. Mathematics
   A. Memorized counting from one to ten does not mean the child understands the numbers.

    B. Teach the child what the number "one" means before any more numbers are taught to the child: "Give me one crayon." "Put one napkin on the table."

    C. Cut numbers out of paper. Glue oatmeal, rice, glitter, etc. to the number so the child can see, feel, and hear the number.

    D. Touch and count objects.

IV.   Alphabet

    A. Make letters with paper and glue objects to the letter.

    B. Match letters and words to pictures.

    C. Use the sounds of the letters repeatedly: *J*, "juice," "jump," "jacket," etc.

    D. Cut out a letter out of sandpaper and have the child follow the sandpaper letter with his/her finger.

    E. Write a letter on the blackboard and have the child trace the letter on the blackboard.

    F. Make dots on a paper in the shape of a letter and have the child connect the dots to make the letter, gradually decreasing the number of dots to connect to make the letter.

    G. Make letters with jiggler jello.

    H. When a child is learning to write his/her name, the child may find it easier to use all capital letters at the beginning.

V.   Sensory Stimulation to Teach Each Concept

    A. Teach a concept through different sensory methods: Teaching the color "orange."

       1. Wear orange clothes.

       2. Paint with orange paint.

       3. Use orange construction paper for projects.

       4. Serve oranges for a snack.

       5. Sit on an orange rug.

    B. Use objects as much as possible to teach concepts such as teaching about "circles."

       1. Laminate polka dot fabric.

       2. Use a cookie cutter to cut circle sandwiches.

       3. Cut circles from construction paper and glue Cheerios on the paper.

    C. Use "concrete" teaching activities.

       Example: Child is told to stay in the yard but continuously wanders into the street. Parents obtained four large orange cones and had the child stay inside the four cones. Parents gradually expanded the cones.

Example: "What do you want?" This question is very abstract. Give child choices he/she can see, feel, touch, and hear.

VI. Managing Hyperactivity
   A. Keep the environment structured.
   B. Make a picture calendar.
      1. Make a board with hooks.
      2. Laminate pictures of activities for the whole day. Examples: Have a picture of a child taking jacket off and hanging up the jacket. Have a picture of a child putting puzzle together.
      3. As the child completes each activity during the day, the child takes the picture off the hook, turns it over, and hangs the picture back on the hook. The child knows that he/she has completed the activity.
   C. Give the child a choice from two or three toys and plenty of time to make a choice.
   D. Place each activity in two baskets.
      1. Have two baskets for a puzzle, two baskets for a pegboard, two baskets for a matching activity, two baskets for lacing cards, two baskets for scissors and paper activity, etc.
      2. Take the activity out of the "start" basket. When the child has finished the activity, the child puts the activity in the "finish" basket.
   E. Keep the designated activities in the same place.
   F. Hyperactive children should sit on a chair rather than on the floor. The chair helps keep the child in a specific space. Show the child how to sit in the chair, if necessary (feet flat on the floor, hands on the side, sitting up straight).
   G. Have the activity at the table ready. The child probably will not sit at the table very long waiting for the teacher to bring an activity.
   H. Structure the day alternating quiet time and active time.
   I. Help the child control tantrums.
      1. Take the child to a different room. Lullaby music in this room may help calm the child.
      2. Hold the child.
      3. Teacher's body language should not get the child excited. Talk in a calm voice and walk slowly. If the teacher is relaxed, this will help the child relax.
      4. Determine what happened before the tantrum occurred. Look for antecedents, what caused the child to lose his/her temper.

     5. Look at different ways to eliminate the chances of the child throwing a tantrum. If the child has an extremely difficult time with loud noises and lots of activity, the child should be taught in a relatively quiet and calm area.

     6. Reduce the likelihood of the child having a tantrum by teaching the child new ways of dealing with his/her stress. Teach the child to say, "I'm mad."

J. Determine whether the child's diet could be a contributing factor for the behavior.

K. Observe the child for any contributing health problems. For example, with an ear infection, child may pull at his/her ears. Ask the child to "Show me where you hurt."

L. Ignore negative behavior whenever possible and avoid overreaction.

M. Build in positive reinforcement, like hugs. When the child finishes an activity or does a good job, let the child know he/she will get a hug. Often children with FAS/FAE like to be hugged.

N. If the child does not need sleep at nap time, the child may benefit from having activities such as riding a tricycle in the hall.

VII. Short Attention Span

    A. Determine how long the child is working on an activity.

    B. Ask the child to do "one more." Example: If the child is drawing circles on a paper and the child decides to quit, have the child draw one more circle. The teacher should never make the child do the activity more than once if the teacher said "draw one more circle."

VIII. Social Behavior

    A. Show the child how to share toys. You may need to use a timer to share the most popular toys.

    B. Teach the child how to be a friend, demonstrating with puppets or dolls.

    C. Teach the child how to sit with a friend at the table.

    D. Pair children for a week so the child with developmental disabilities can learn from the other child.

IX. Eye-Hand Coordination Activities

    A. Use puzzles with knobs on the pieces, lace cards (may need masking tape on the end), clothes pins to squeeze, pegs to pound in pegboard.

B. The teacher may need to guide the child through the activity and then encourage the child to do the activity on his/her own. The teacher could pick up the puzzle piece for the child and put in the right place in the puzzle or lace the first two holes of the lacing board.

X. Other Considerations
  A. The following evaluations may be helpful in learning more about the child's development and assist in planning the teachers activities.
    1. Speech and language evaluations.
    2. Psychological evaluations.
    3. Motor evaluations.
  B. Children with FAS/FAE usually need more one-to-one teaching.

## EDUCATION TECHNIQUES FOR ELEMENTARY CHILDREN WITH FAS/FAE

I. Environment
  A. Calm and quiet.
    1. Soft calm music may relax the classroom during breaks.
    2. Tone down classroom so rooms are not overly stimulating.
      a. Keep a minimal number of objects hanging from the ceiling and on the walls.
      b. Use calm colors of paint on the walls.
      c. Reduce classroom clutter.
      d. Use bulletin boards as teaching tools and soft colors. (Bulletin boards could be covered when not in use.)
    3. Use headphones for quiet time. (Students with FAS/FAE are not always able to block out other noises.)
  B. Structure.
    1. Establish a few simple rules.
    2. Enforce the same rules in the same way.
    3. Use the same language when enforcing the rules.
  C. Transition from one activity to another activity.
    1. Give the student reminders for the ending and beginning of activities. Use a tactile signal. Touch shoulder, tap elbow, and say, "The bell will ring in five minutes, you need to finish up. We will go to lunch when the bell rings."
    2. Have the student follow a fairly consistent routine every day.

3. Provide notebooks which have all the students' classroom activities in order for the day. This gives the student a concrete item with which to structure his/her day.
4. Have the students carry the book to the reading area, or a puppet to the puppet story.
5. Give students several breaks during the day. Students may need sleep during the day or some may need to get up and move around more frequently than other students, and may need food snacks. Plan activities to facilitate movement and creative work between seat work assignments.
6. Class periods should not exceed twenty minutes.

II. Language Development
   A. Talk with the student at the student's level. Use short sentences.
   B. Poor articulation.
      1. A speech therapist would be a good resource for the student and teacher.
      2. The teacher needs to model proper pronunciation.
      3. Articulation errors are common. Accept students' communications without correcting them but repeat their sounds correctly.
      4. Music activities can help student learn vocabulary.
         a. Good morning song.
         b. Song before the students eat.
         c. Name songs.
         d. Circle game songs—sit down, stand up, name games.
   C. Encourage high quality of speech.
      1. Be aware that quantity does not indicate quality. Students with FAS/FAE often use a large quantity of speech.
      2. Listen for the number of words per sentence.
      3. Listen for the number of new words the student uses.
      4. Stress concept development through concrete examples encouraging the student to demonstrate understanding. Example: Talk about temperatures so the child would know what to wear on a hot day and what to wear on a cold day.
   D. Sign language may be helpful in teaching students with FAS even when they do not have a hearing loss. Sign language is concrete and visible and can be used along with verbal language.

III. Mathematics
   A. Memorized counting from one to ten does not mean the student understands the numbers. Stress concept development of numbers, encouraging students to demonstrate knowledge.

B. Teach the student what the number "one" means before any more numbers are taught to the student: "Give me one crayon." "Put one card on the table."

C. Cut numbers out of paper. Glue oatmeal, rice, glitter, etc. to the number so the student can see, feel, and hear the numbers as well as manipulate objects that represent the number.

D. Touch and count objects.

E. Teach functional math—money, time, and practical uses of addition and subtraction.

F. Use the student's fingers for addition and subtraction or a calculator. These methods should not be the first choice but should not be ruled out. A calculator may be necessary for the student with FAS/FAE to do multiplication and division.

IV. Alphabet

A. Make letters with paper and glue objects to the letter.

B. Match letters to objects. Example: A—Apple." Next, match letters to pictures.

C. Follow the above sequence with words. Match words to words: "Apple"— "Apple."

D. Invent new words into other activities, other class work, and home activities. Have a "Letter for the Day." Use the sounds of the letter repeatedly: *J*, "juice," "jump," "jacket," etc.

E. Use green and red clues to indicate the beginning and ending of a letter and to encourage proper writing of letters.

V. Reading

A. Teach left to right direction. Some students may have difficulty focusing their eyes on the left side of the page and moving their eyes to the right.

1. If a student uses a piece of paper to follow the line across the page, the student may have an easier time reading.

2. Use a green marker at the left side changing to red at the right side for written work.

3. Use colored arrows to signal starting points and left to right direction.

B. Use books with simple, plain pictures. Small detailing marks in a picture can distract the student.

C. Provide the student with books that follow student's interest and independent reading levels. (Independent reading levels means the student can read 90% of the words in the book.)

D. Read aloud to the students daily and provide uninterrupted silent reading periods.

VI.  Use Sensory Stimulation to Teach Each Concept
    A.  Teach a concept through different sensory methods: Teaching the color "orange."
        1.  Wear orange clothes.
        2.  Paint with orange paint.
        3.  Use orange construction paper for projects.
        4.  Serve oranges for a snack.
        5.  Sit on an orange rug
    B.  Use objects as much as possible to teach concepts. Example: Teaching about "circles."
        1.  Laminate polka dot fabric.
        2.  Use a cookie cutter to cut circle sandwiches.
        3.  Cut circles from construction paper and glue Cherrios on the paper.
    C.  Use concrete teaching activities.
        1.  Example: Child is told to stay in the yard but continuously wanders into the street. Parents obtained four large orange cones and had the child stay inside the cones. Parents gradually expanded the cones.
        2.  Teacher sets a work-play schedule by using pictures, nesting cups, and so on. The teacher would set out six nesting cups to show the student he/she has six activities to complete before taking a break.
        3.  Make abstractions concrete. Example: "What do you want?" This question is actually very abstract. Give child choices he/she can see, feel, touch, and hear.

VII.  Managing Hyperactivity
    A.  Provide structure, routine, and as few rules as possible.
    B.  Make a picture calendar.
        1.  Make a board with hooks.
        2.  Laminate pictures or take Polaroid pictures of the student doing activities to occur during the day and during work time. Examples: Have a picture of a student taking jacket off and hanging up the jacket. Have a picture of a student putting puzzle together.
        3.  As the student completes each activity during the day, the student takes the picture off the hook, turns it over, and hangs the picture back on the hook. The student knows that he/she has completed the activity.
    C.  Make lists of assignments for the student to follow during the day. (Students may need a list taped to their desk. Some

students with FAS/FAE may have difficulty relating chalk board instructions to their own behavior.)

D. Place each activity in two baskets.

1. Have two baskets for a puzzle, two baskets for a pegboard, two baskets for a matching activity, two baskets for lacing cards, two baskets for scissors and paper activity, etc.

2. Take the activity out of the "start" basket. When the student has finished the activity, the student puts the activity in the "finish" basket.

E. Keep the designated activities in the same place.

F. Enclose shelves and book cases if possible to eliminate visual distraction.

G. Use vivid colors, sound, and movement to emphasize important concepts.

H. During organized activities, give hyperactive students structure. They need to know the sequence of the activity, what is expected of them, and what behaviors will be acceptable. Example: "During this activity we will stay in our chairs. There will be no talking. Keep your eyes on your own paper. If you want help, raise your hand and I will come to help you."

I. Balance loosely structured activities with highly structured activities to give the students opportunity to move about, visit, and relax.

J. Structure the day alternating quiet time and active time.

K. Help the student control tantrums.

1. Remain calm and quiet. Teacher's body language should not get the student excited. Talk in a calm voice and walk slowly. If the teacher is relaxed, this will help the student relax.

2. Let the student know there is a protocol for loss of control. Taking the student's hand and holding it a short time will give the student a signal that the teacher thinks the student is losing control. If restraint is necessary, the teacher needs to exercise care and control. Talk to the student, telling him/her that you are helping him/her to control his/her behavior. Example: "I am going to hold on to you until you are calm. Are you feeling better? Let me know when you are ready for me to let go."

3. Take the student to a different room if necessary. Soft music and soft colors in the room may help calm the student.

Talk to the student in a calm, soft voice. Ask the student to tell the teacher when he/she is ready to go back to the classroom.
   4. Determine what happened before the tantrum occurred. Look for antecedents, what caused the student to lose his/her temper.
   5. Look at different ways to eliminate the chances of the student throwing a tantrum. If the student has an extremely difficult time with loud noises and lots of activity, the student should be taught in a relatively quiet and calm area.
   6. Reduce the likelihood of the student having a tantrum by teaching the student new ways of dealing with his/her stress. Teach the student to say, "I'm mad."
   L. Determine whether the student's diet could be a contributing factor for the behavior.
   M. Observe the student for any contributing health problems. For example, with an ear infection, the student may pull at his/her ears. Ask the student to "Show me where you hurt." Look for behaviors which may signify visual problems: abnormal head posturing, squinting, holding paper close to face, obvious errors made when working from the chalk board.
   N. Ignore negative behavior whenever possible and avoid overreaction.
   O. Build in positive reinforcement.
   1. As the student finishes each activity on the picture calendar, give student positive reinforcement for his/her efforts in completing the activity.
   2. When the student does a good job on a project, tell the student he/she did right. Example: "I really like the way you wrote your Ks."

VIII. Short Attention Span
   A. Determine how long the student is able to work on a given activity.
   B. Expand this time by one more try and reinforce the student.
   C. Determine what activity the student can attend to longest. What is it about that activity that allows him/her to attend. Generalize these features to other activities.

IX. Social Behavior
   A. Show the student how to share playground equipment. You may need to use a timer to share the most popular equipment.

B. Teach the student how to be a friend.
   1. Use puppets or dolls.
   2. Emphasize the feelings of others.
   3. Practice using manners, consideration statements, and apologies.
C. Teach the student how to sit with a friend at the table. Emphasize conversation, sharing, and courtesy.
D. Use peer tutoring.
   1. Pair children for a week so the child with FAS/FAE can learn from other children.
   2. Allow students with FAS/FAE to help other students. Example: "Jane will bring the basket around to pick up your papers. Have them ready when she gets to your desk."
   3. Capitalize on academic strengths of the student with FAS/FAE.

X. Eye-Hand Coordination Activities
A. Use puzzles with knobs on the pieces or lace cards.
B. Let student help with tasks that require sorting, stapling, putting things in place, etc.
C. The teacher may need to guide the child through the activity, and then encourage the student to do the activity on his/her own. The teacher could pick up the puzzle piece for the student and put in the right place in the puzzle or lace the first two holes of the lacing board.

XI. Other Considerations
A. The following evaluations may be helpful in learning more about the student's development and assist in planning the teachers activities.
   1. Speech and language evaluations.
   2. Psychological evaluations.
   3. Motor evaluations.
B. Children with FAS/FAE usually need more one-to-one teaching.

## Education Techniques for Junior and Senior High School Students with FAS/FAE

I. Environment
A. Calm and quiet.
   1. Soft calm music may relax the classroom during breaks.
   2. Tone down classroom so rooms are not overly stimulating.

   a. Keep a minimal number of objects hanging from the ceiling and on the walls.
   b. Use calm colors of paint on the walls.
   c. Reduce classroom clutter.
   d. Use bulletin boards as teaching tools and soft colors. (Bulletin boards could be covered when not in use.)
  3. Use headphones for quiet time. (Students with FAS/FAE are not always able to block out other noises and may be distracted by a teacher talking with another student and even a ticking clock.)
 B. Structure.
  1. Establish a few simple rules.
  2. Enforce the same rules in the same way.
  3. Use the same language when enforcing the rules.
 C. Transition from one activity to another activity.
  1. Give the student reminders for the ending and beginning of activities. Use a tactile signal. Touch shoulder, tap elbow, and say "The bell will ring in five minutes, you need to finish up. We will go to lunch when the bell rings."
  2. Have the student follow a fairly consistent routine every day.
  3. Provide notebooks for students that have all the students' classroom activities in order for the day. This gives the student a concrete item with which to structure his/her day.
  4. Have the students carry the book to the reading area.
  5. Give students several breaks during the day. Students may need sleep during the day, to get up and move around more frequently than other students, and may need food snacks. Plan activities to facilitate movement and creative work between seat work assignments.
  6. Class periods should not exceed thirty minutes.

II. Language Development
 A. Recognize that students with FAS/FAE may have delayed language development. Use concrete basic language when giving instructions. Use simple sentences and avoid giving more than one instruction per sentence.
 B. Sign language may be helpful to teach students even when they do not have a hearing loss. Sign language is concrete and visible and can be used along with verbal language.

III. Mathematics

A. Teach functional math—money, time, practical uses of addition and subtraction.

B. Encourage students to use strategies for counting, such as fingers or counting tools, such as a calculator. These techniques should not be the first choice but should not be ruled out.

Note: Math seems to be the most difficult subject for the students with FAS/FAE. Memorizing the multiplication table may not be successful with all students who have FAS/FAE. Division may also be difficult.

IV. Reading

A. Teach left to right direction. Some students may have difficulty focusing their eyes on the left side of the page and moving their eyes to the right.

1. If the student uses a piece of paper to follow the line across the page, the student may have an easier time reading.

2. Use a green marker at the left side changing to red at the right side for written work.

3. Use colored arrows to signal starting points and left to right direction.

B. Provide the student with books that follow student's interest and independent reading levels. (Independent reading levels means the student can read 90% of the words in the book.)

C. Encourage reading for enjoyment and developing independence.

1. Incorporate popular magazines, newspapers, and school paper into reading program.

2. Emphasize reading as a means to communications—note writing, letter writing, memos, posters, etc.

D. Read aloud to the students daily and provide uninterrupted silent reading periods.

V. Sensory Stimulation and Concrete Activities to Teach Each Concept

A. Provide hands-on materials whenever possible.

B. Take students to actual site to teach learning objectives.

C. Allow students to make concrete choices. Instead of asking the abstract question "What do you want?" give the student choices he/she can see, feel, touch, hear.

VI. Managing Hyperactivity and Attention Deficits
  A. Provide structure, predictable routine, and as few rules as possible.
  B. Allow students to sit in their chairs as comfortably as possible. Rapidly growing students are often unable to maintain strict posture and enforcing it can be frustrating for both teachers and students.
  C. Limit time frames for one activity to no more than thirty minutes if possible.
  D. Help the student control tantrums.
    1. Remain calm and quiet. Teacher's body language should not get the student excited. Talk in a calm voice and walk slowly. If the teacher is relaxed, this will help the student relax.
    2. Let the student know there is a protocol for loss of control. Taking the student's hand and holding it a short time will give the student a signal that the teacher thinks the student is losing control. If restraint is necessary, the teacher needs to exercise care and control. Talk to the student, telling him/her that you are helping him/her to control his/her behavior. Example: "I am going to hold on to you until you are calm. Are you feeling better? Let me know when you are ready for me to let go."
    3. Take the student to a different room if necessary. Soft music and soft colors in the room may help calm the student. Talk to the student in a calm, soft voice. Ask the student to tell the teacher when he/she is ready to go back to the classroom.
    4. Determine what happened before the tantrum occurred. Look for antecedents, what caused the student to lose his/her temper.
    5. Look at different ways to eliminate the chances of the student throwing a tantrum. If the student has an extremely difficult time with loud noises and lots of activity, the student should be taught in a relatively quiet and calm area.
    6. Reduce the likelihood of the student having a tantrum by teaching the student new ways of dealing with his/her stress. Teach the student to say, "I'm mad."
  E. Enclose shelves and book cases if possible to eliminate visual distraction.

F. Use vivid colors, sound and movement to emphasize important concepts.

G. During organized activities, hyperactive students need structure. They need to know the sequence of activity, what is expected of them, and what behaviors will be acceptable. Example: "During this activity we will stay in our chairs. There will be no talking. Keep your eyes on your own paper. If you want help, raise your hand and I will come to help you."

H. Balance loosely structured activities with highly structured activities to give the students opportunity to move about, visit, and relax.

I. Balance active and quiet activities.

J. Structure the day, alternating quiet time and active time.

K. Observe the student for any contributing health problems. For example, with an ear infection, the student may pull at his/her ears. Ask the student to "Show me where you hurt." Look for behaviors which may signify visual problems: abnormal head posturing, squinting, holding paper close to face, obvious errors made when working from the chalk board.

L. Ignore negative behavior whenever possible and avoid overreaction.

M. Build in positive reinforcement.
   1. As the student finishes each activity on the picture calendar, give student positive reinforcement for his/her efforts in completing the activity.
   2. When the student does a good job on a project, tell the student he/she did right. Example: "I really like the way you read the whole story."

VII. Social Behavior
   A. Teachers needs to consult the school counselor. It is important that teachers and counselors work together using complimentary techniques to best serve the student in the following areas:
      1. Inappropriate sexual behavior.
      2. Depression.
      3. Loneliness and isolation.
      4. Inappropriate expectations for work, school, and independence.
   B. Be emphatic, firm, and realistic about expectations and performance from students.
   C. Treat students with FAS/FAE as valuable, worthwhile human beings with gifts to share.

VIII. Vocational Education

A. Continue practicing the basic skills necessary to live independently as adults, especially daily living and survival skills.

B. Help student learn how to transfer their skills using a variety of settings and people.

C. Curriculum should focus on recognizing and coping with being labeled as "different."

D. Curriculum should focus on assisting students to function as social human beings.

    1. Understanding the rules of social interaction.

    2. Taking on responsibilities.

    3. Making decisions and realizing their consequences.

    4. Developing and practicing independent living skills within a group setting such as getting along with others in the same living space, sharing, responsibilities, cooking, and personal hygiene.

E. Curriculum should assist students function in the world of work.

    1. Identify individual interests and aptitudes.

    2. Develop self scheduling skills, community mobility skills, rule-governed behavior, etc.

    3. Develop and practice job related skills.

IX. Other Considerations

A. The following evaluations may be helpful in learning more about the student's development and assist in planning the teachers activities.

    1. Speech and language evaluations.

    2. Psychological evaluations.

    3. Motor evaluations.

B. Students with FAS/FAE usually need more one-to-one teaching.

*—University of South Dakota*
*Affiliated Program*
*USD School of Medicine*
*414 E. Clark*
*Vermillion, SD 57069*
*1-800-658-3080*

# Appendix II
## Sources of Special Interest for Families and Educators
### DAVID A. AND GAIL S. HALES

*David A. Hales is professor of Library Science and head of the Alaska and Polar Regions Department at Elmer E. Rasmuson Library, University of Alaska Fairbanks, Fairbanks, Alaska 99775-1005.*

*Gail S. Hales is training specialist, Resource Center for Parents and Children, 1401 Kellum Street, Fairbanks, Alaska 99701.*

THE PURPOSE OF THIS RESOURCE LIST IS TO HELP parents, educators, and others locate useful information on fetal alcohol syndrome and fetal alcohol effects (FAS/FAE).* As adoptive parents of two children experiencing fetal alcohol effects, we have been alert to sources of useful information. Many that we have found especially informative, such as newsletters of parent groups or special videotapes, are difficult to locate but quite valuable. Brief descriptions of each title are included to make it easier to identify material suitable for specific needs.

Since 1973 when the term fetal alcohol syndrome (FAS) was first used in the scientific literature, thousands of articles have explored various aspects of the phenomenon. New information comes forth at an increasing rate. This resource list does not include all

---

*The resource list has been brought up to date for this printing.

341

material written on the subject of FAS/FAE. Rather we have included sources particularly useful to parents, siblings, teachers, child care providers, Scout leaders, coaches, and social service workers, focusing mainly on materials produced from 1989 to 1993. Several comprehensive bibliographies compiled as recently as 1991 are also listed, as well as titles of significant merit to educators. In addition, this listing includes the names of sources recommended by chapter authors.

This resource list is composed of four sections:

1. Audio/video tapes are especially useful for workshops and in-service education programs. The videotapes provide visual images of what the problems are and how to go about helping children.

2. General sources direct users to the enormous and various literature on FAS/FAE. They include books and articles of special interest to those concerned with education and policy initiatives to prevent FAS/FAE and to assist affected children.

3. Newsletters keep people informed of recent developments, upcoming conferences, legislation, and other matters.

4. Organizations listed have a national scope with special focus on fetal alcohol syndrome.

## AUDIO/VIDEO

*Adolescence and the future.* Evanston, Ill.: Altschul Group, 1991. (22-minute video.) Available from Altschul Group, 1560 Sherman Avenue, Suite 100, Evanston, Illinois 60201. Tel. 800-323-9084 or 800-232-3263.

Parents, educators and health professionals focus on the problems facing two young people experiencing FAS. The video addresses skills and attitudes necessary for parents to effectively help their children develop positive self esteem as well as acquire job and life skills.

*Alcohol and pregnancy: Fetal alcohol syndrome and fetal alcohol effects.* Chatsworth, Calif.: AIMS Media, 1992. (20 minute video.) Available from AIMS Media, 9710 DeSoto Avenue, Chatsworth, California 91311-4409. Tel. 800-367-2467. Fax 816-341-6700.

This video shows how alcohol adversely affects the developing fetus. Interviews with children, teenagers, biological parents and foster parents deliver a strong preventive message underscoring the life-long physical, behavioral and central nervous system impact of FAS. That FAS/FAE knows no racial, cultural or economic barriers is stressed, and women and men are encouraged to take responsibility for their baby's health before it is born.

*Assessment and the early years.* Evanston, Ill.: Altschul Group, 1991. (21-minute video.) Available from Altschul Group, 1560 Sherman Avenue, Suite 100, Evanston, Illinois 60201. Tel. 800-323-9084 or 800-232-3263.

Educators, psychologists and medical doctors discuss the special needs of FAS/FAE children and offer strategies for working with them in the home, at preschools and in elementary schools.

*The biomedical aspects of alcohol use.* Timonium, Md.: Milner-Fenwick, Inc. and Project Cork Institute, Dartmouth Medical School, 1992. (Slides and text.) Available from Milner-Fenwick, Inc., 2125 Greenspring Drive, Timonium, Maryland 21093. Tel. 800-432-8433. Fax 410-252-6316.

This set ten separate units discusses the biomedical aspects of alcohol use. Unit 5, "Pregnancy and Fetal Alcohol Syndrome," consists of 46 slides and 24 pages of text. The contents highlight the historical perspective, types of fetal alcohol effects, risk of alcohol use during other periods, and prevention of fetal alcohol effects. The information was compiled by Ruth E. Little and Ann Streissguth.

Brekke, B. *Sex education for the lower functioning developmentally disabled.* Santa Monica, Calif.: Stanfield Film Association. (No date.) Available from Stanfield Film Association, P. O. Box 1983, Santa Monica, California 90406. Tel. 310-820-4568.

This film provides an understanding of sexual needs and behavior of lower functioning developmentally disabled persons. It is open, candid, and direct about the problems and issues surrounding sexuality in this population and provides a foundation upon which to examine and perhaps modify one's own beliefs in this area.

*The clinical diagnosis of fetal alcohol syndrome.* Albuquerque, N.M.: Flora & Co., 1994. (31-minute video.) Distributed by Flora & Co., P.O. Box 8263, Albuquerque, N.M. 98198-8263. Tel. 505- 255-9988.

This video is designed to provide health care professionals with sharpened skills, enhanced diagnostic confidence, and improved patient services. Special information regarding growth, central nervous system manifestations, and physical features are included.

*Cocaine kids training tape: New strategies, new solutions.* Evanston, Ill.: Altschul Group, 1991. (23-minute video.) Available from Altschul Group, 1560 Sherman Avenue, Suite 100, Evanston, Illinois 60201. Tel. 800-323-9084 or 800-232-3263.

Although the title of this video refers to cocaine-affected children, the information is also applicable to FAS/FAE children. The video gives an enormous amount of information regarding the manifestations of prenatal exposure to these damaging substances as well as precise teaching strategies for working with affected children. Strategies include modifying the learning environment, play therapy, social/emotional development, effective communication, motor skill development and home/school teamwork.

*Fetal alcohol syndrome/fetal alcohol effects: A community perspective.* Lethbridge, Alberta: Lethbridge Community College, 1993. (30-minute video.) Available from Lethbridge Community College Bookstore, 3000 College Drive South, Lethbridge, Alberta, Canada T1K 1L6. Tel. 403-320-3341.

This video emphasizes the importance of having early diagnosis with appropriate interventions, in understanding the unique differences of individuals experiences FAS/FAE. It focuses on abilities rather than disabilities. Information is illustrated in vignettes of families living successfully with children who experience FAS/FAE. "The focus of this video is upbeat and deals with success."

*Fetal alcohol syndrome and effects: Stories of help and hope.* Center City, Minn.: Hazelden, 1994. (25-minute video.) Available from Hazelden, 15251 Pleasant Valley Road, P.O. Box 176, Center City, Minn. 55012-0176. Tel. 800-328-9000. Fax 612-257-1331.

This video presents a balanced view of FAS/FAE issues. It includes a factual definition of FAS/FAE and vividly illustrates the positive prognosis possible for children with FAS/FAE.

*Fetal alcohol syndrome and effects: What's the difference?* Evanston, Ill.: Altschul Group, 1992. (23-minute video.) Available from Altschul Group, 1560 Sherman Avenue, Suite 100, Evanston, Illinois 60201. Tel. 800-323-9084 or 800-232-3263.

This program provides a candid overview of the physiological effects of FAS/FAE and resultant the behavior problems. A mother who abused alcohol during pregnancy speaks about her guilt. A clinical psychologist discusses permanent damages including learning disorders, speech and living problems, heart problems and damage to the central nervous system. Potential challenges and handicaps faced by persons with FAS/FAE are also discussed. This is an excellent introduction to FAS/FAE and would be a good program for schools and the general public.

*Fetal alcohol syndrome. Family practice update. Episode No. 9013. September 9, 1990.* New York: Lifetime Medical Television, 1990. (30-minute video.) Available from Lifetime Medical Television, Box 5913 GPO, New York City, New York 10084. Tel. 718-482-4155.

In this videocassette, Ken Jones, who coined the term "Fetal Alcohol Syndrome," Ann Streissguth, a psychologist, and Larry Culpepper, a professor of family medicine, discuss FAS/FAE. Two case studies showing degrees of severity are presented. The importance of diagnosis and acquiring help for all concerned is emphasized.

*Healing the broken cord*. Washington, D.C.: National Organization on Fetal Alcohol Syndrome, 1992. Available from National Organization on Fetal Alcohol Syndrome, 1815 H Street NW, Suite 750, Washington, D.C. 20006.

Highlights of workshops and speeches presented at the 1991 National Organization on Fetal Alcohol Syndrome conference are the part of this audio visual package. A four-hour audio tape and a 45-minute video tape, address topics such as "Education Perspectives on the FAS Child," "Legal Perspective," "A Mother's Experience," and "Next Steps to Healing" and discussions by those on the cutting edge of FAS prevention and service among American Indians and Canadian Native communities.

*Influences: Innocence betrayed. The long term effects of prenatal substance exposure*. Santa Monica: Pyramid Film and Video, 1993. (24-minute video.) Available from producer, 2801 Colorado Ave., Santa Monica, Calif. 90404. Tel. 800-421-2304.

This video explores the devastating societal impact from a growing population of children and adolescents permanently disabled by prenatal substance abuse. With clarity and compassion the film follows children and their guardians as they attempt to cope with baffling learning and behavioral disabilities. Interviews with educators and profiles demonstrate how various treatments are providing these children with hope for the future.

Kempton, W. *Sexuality and the mentally handicapped*. Santa Monica, Calif.: Stanfield Film Association. Available from Stanfield Film Association, P.O. Box 1983, Santa Monica, California 90406. Tel. 310-820-4568.

This is a film which explores the sexual needs and behaviors of mentally retarded persons. The film is very clear, open, and addresses issues surrounding the confusion and discomfort often experienced by parents of mentally handicapped persons and the general public.

LaDue, R., Randels, S., and Burgess, D. *Fetal alcohol children in the classroom*. Portland, Oreg.: Northwest Regional Educational Laboratory, 1989. (Audio tape.) Available from Northwest Regional Educational Laboratory, P.O. Box 414, Portland, Oregon 97207. Tel. 503-257-1515.

This tape includes information about the growth deficiencies, behavioral and cognitive effects of FAS. It also includes recommendations for appropriate educational curricula.

*One for my baby*. Chatsworth, Calif.: AIMS Media, 1983. (28-minute video.) Available in English or Spanish from AIMS Media, 9710 DeSoto Avenue, Chatsworth, California 91311-4409. Tel. 800-367-2467. Fax 816-341-6700.

This video defines the dangers of maternal alcohol consumption for the unborn child through interviews with parents of children with FAS, physicians, and other health care workers. Although the production is ten years old, the material is factual and especially useful to the Spanish-speaking audience.

*Preventing FAS.* Evanston, Ill.: Altschul Group, 1990. (21-minute video.) Available from Altschul Group, 1560 Sherman Avenue, Suite 100, Evanston, Illinois 60201. Tel. 800-323-9084 or 800-232-3263.

Public education is the focus of this program which includes ways to assist high-risk women to stop drinking.

*Training tapes for living with FAS and FAE: The early years, birth through age 12.* Evanston, Ill.: Altschul Group, 1992. (32-minute video.) Available from Altschul Group, 1560 Sherman Avenue, Suite 100, Evanston, Illinois 60201. Tel. 800-323-9084 or 800-232-3263.

Focusing on techniques for providing positive behavioral programming for young children and pre-adolescents, this program offers encouragement to individuals living with FAS/FAE.

*Training tapes for living with FAS and FAE: Independence, ages 12 to adult.* Evanston, Ill.: Altschul Group, 1992. (32-minute video.) Available from Altschul Group, 1560 Sherman Avenue, Suite 100, Evanston, Illinois 60201. Tel. 800-323-9084 or 800-232-3263.

Strategies to help adolescents and adults with FAS/FAE develop social and adaptive living skills are presented in clear, easy-to-follow steps.

*What is FAS?* Evanston, Ill.: Altschul Group, 1990. (24-minute video.) Available from Altschul Group, 1560 Sherman Avenue, Suite 100, Evanston, Illinois 60201. Tel. 800-323-9084 or 800-232-3263.

The cause, treatment, and prevention of alcohol-related birth defects are examined. Commentaries from FAS/FAE experts and families with children with FAS/FAE are included.

*What's wrong with my child?* Deerfield, Ill.: Coronet MTI Film and Video, 1990. (26-minute video.) Available from Coronet MTI Film and Video, 108 Wilmont Rd., Deerfield, Illinois 60015. Tel. 800-621-2131.

This is a segment of the television program 20/20 that aired March 30, 1990. It includes interviews with Sterling Clarren, M.D. and psychologist Ann Streissguth, Michael Dorris, author of the book *The Broken Cord,* and others. They present an interesting perspective from professionals who are very involved with FAS/FAE issues. A transcript is available from Journal Graphics.

## GENERAL

Abel, Ernest L. *Fetal alcohol syndrome.* Montvale, N.J.: Medical Economics Books, 1990.

Presented in this work is an overview of FAS including the historical background, growth in study, research and literature, worldwide incidence of FAS, pharmacology, effects, diagnostic features of FAS, cost, attitudes and prevention.

———. *New literature on fetal alcohol exposure and effects: A bibliography, 1938–1988*. Westport, Conn.: Greenwood Press, 1990.

This bibliography is a supplement to the bibliography cited above and gives references for 1983 through 1988. There is some overlap with the years covered in the earlier bibliography due to the large number of items found after the first bibliography was published. Some 1,818 citations are included. The entries are in alphabetical order by author.

———. *Fetal alcohol exposure and effect: A comprehensive bibliography*. Westport, Conn.: Greenwood Press, 1985.

Arranged alphabetically by author, this work lists 3,088 journal articles relating to alcohol effects on reproduction. No abstracts are included. Although many of the entries are not in English, translated titles are included. The introduction includes a summary of alcoholic beverages and their alcohol content and a layman's explanation of how alcohol is absorbed into the body and transmitted to the fetus. This is a valuable listing for articles from 1973 to 1984.

Adams, C. *No more secrets: Protecting your child from sexual assault*. San Luis Obispo, Calif.: Impact Publishers, 1981.

This is a supportive, conversational guide for parents who would like to teach their children how to prevent sexual advances. It encourages open discussion with one's child or children and stresses the importance of no secrets with regard to sexual advances and inappropriate sexual behavior from others.

Adams, C., Fay, J. and Loreen-Martin, J. *No is not enough: Helping teenagers avoid sexual assault*. San Luis Obispo, Calif.: Impact Publishers, 1984.

This book provides parents with a guide through proven realistic strategies to help teens avoid sexual victimization. The book deals with topics such as date rape, peer pressure, and exploitation by adults.

*Alcohol and other drugs can harm an unborn baby: A resource list*. Rockville, Md.: National Clearinghouse for Alcohol and Drug Information. (No date.)

Brief explanations of the effects of alcohol, illegal drugs, over-the-counter drugs, prescription drugs, cigarettes and caffeine on the unborn begin this resource list. This list also includes brochures, pamphlets, fact sheets, books, journals, posters, videos, curriculum guides and Spanish language publications. The material is not copyrighted and duplication is encouraged.

Allen, R. B. *Common sense discipline: What to say and do when children misbehave*. Tyler, Tex.: Common Sense Publications, 1984.

This booklet contains a variety of specific childhood problems and provides a means to respond to them in a problem-solving, constructive manner. The book is based on behavioral principles and tends to be very practical and somewhat of a cookbook of children's misbehavior and how a parent might better handle and respond to these.

Ayers, T., Lyons, P., McIlvenna, T., Myers, F., Rila, M., Rubenstein, M., Smith, C., and Sutton, L. *SARguide: A self-help program for sexual enrichment/ education.* San Francisco: National Sex Forum, 1975. (Available from National Sex Forum, 1525 Franklin Street, San Francisco, California 94103. Tel. 415-928-1133)

This book is designed to increase the reader's understanding about sexuality and the sexuality of oneself and others. It is structured in a step-by-step manner to increase sexual knowledge and enhance one's senses with the goal of reaching a sexually healthy attitude and existence.

"Birthmark of the Bottle." *Northland News* 10, No. 1 (January 1994): 6–19. $1.50 includes shipping and handling. Available from *Fairbanks Daily News-Miner*, P.O. Box 70710, Fairbanks, Alaska 99707. Tel. 907-456-6661.

The *Northland News* is a monthly compilation of articles from the *Fairbanks Daily News-Miner* and is sent to northern Alaska's rural residents. This issue includes a series of articles regarding FAS/FAE. For the series, reporter Kristan Kelly took a candid look at the scope of maternal alcohol abuse and the effects of prenatal drinking on children, mothers, and adoptive parents in interior Alaska. Prevention programs and information on how alcohol affects a developing fetus are included. The series was recently presented the Public Service Award, the highest honor from the Alaska Press Club. The information centers around families in interior Alaska, with the personal accounts and information valuable to everyone involved with FAS/ FAE issues.

Blume, Sheila B. *What you can do to prevent fetal alcohol syndrome: A professional's guide.* Minneapolis, Minn.: Johnson Institute, 1992.

This book provides basic information about the cause and effects of FAS/ FAE and moves on to discuss prevention through education, screening, treatment referrals, needs for pregnant alcoholics, and public policy. It is specifically designed to help the professional motivate others to seek out early and adequate prenatal care.

*Building solutions for educational services: A topical update on children exposed prenatally to substance abuse.* Eugene, Oreg.: Western Regional Resource Center, 1991. Available from Western Regional Resource Center, Center on Human Development, University of Oregon, Eugene, Oregon.

This information is compiled for educators who deal with children prenatally exposed to substance abuse. The guide's eight sections cover special education and early intervention. Each section lists issues, statistics or strategies and one or two exemplary articles or papers. A resource and reference section provides additional contacts, such as agencies, programs, etc., followed by an extensive bibliography.

Burgess, Donna M. and Streissguth, Ann P. "Educating students with fetal alcohol syndrome or fetal alcohol effects." *Pennsylvania Reporter* 22, no. 1 (November 1990): 1–3.

Material in this article is presented in a short, easily read format including a description of the physical and neurological characteristics of FAS/FAE as well as achievement and behavioral characteristics. Suggestions for teaching strategies include targeting functional skills, focusing on cultural relevance, developing effective communication, and designing community based curricula.

————. "Fetal alcohol syndrome and fetal alcohol effects: Principles for educators." *Phi Delta Kappan* (September 1992): 24–29.

Characteristics of children prenatally exposed to alcohol are discussed and educational programs specifically designed to meet their special needs are described. Educators must be prepared to recognize the possible behavior profile of students with FAS/FAE in order to make necessary referrals. Children with FAS/FAE tend to be concrete thinkers, thus performing fairly well during early school experiences but the more abstract the material becomes, the more difficulty they may have. Educational strategies should include early intervention, targeting functional skills, teaching communication and social skills, and managing challenging behaviors.

Cole, Carol K., Ferrara, V., Johnson, D. J., Jones, M. W., Schoenbaum, M. B., Tyler, R., Wallace, V. R., and Poulsen, M. K. *Today's challenge: Teaching strategies for working with children prenatally exposed to drugs/alcohol.* Los Angeles, Calif.: Los Angeles Unified School District, Division of Special Education, 1989.

Guidelines for adapting preschool programs to the special needs of children with alcohol related birth defects are provided in this booklet. The manual includes teaching strategies in the areas of learning, play, social/emotional development, communication, motor skills and home/school partnership. For each of these areas, descriptions of normal development, at risk development and teaching strategies are provided.

Coles, Claire D. and Platzman, K. A. "Fetal alcohol effects in preschool children: Research, prevention, and intervention." In *Identifying the Needs of Drug-Affected Children: Public Policy Issues*. OSAP Prevention Monograph 11, 59–86. Washington, D.C.: U.S. Health and Human Services, 1992.

Developmental and behavioral effects of prenatal alcohol exposure on children as they reach the preschool and early school age years are described. Needs of alcohol exposed children are defined, as well as barriers to services and the need for further research. The most critical section for educators addresses intervention, which includes professional training specific to FAS/FAE, program development, family support, treatment coordination, and additional service development.

Cook, Paddy Shannon, Petersen, R. C., and Moore, D. T. *Alcohol, tobacco, and other drugs may harm the unborn.* Rockville, Md.: U.S. Department of Health and Human Services, 1990.

Written for health care providers and others, this publication alerts and motivates young women and men to drug-free lifestyles to insure a healthier lives for themselves and their offspring. It includes an overview of approximately 300 scientific books and articles on prenatal drug exposure. An excellent listing of various resources and a bibliography are also included.

Davis, Diane. "The FAS/FAE child in the classroom." *Iceberg: An Educational Newsletter* 1, no. 2 (May 1991): 1, 3.

Parents and teachers are urged to adapt their expectations of a child with FAS/FAE to an appropriate level for the child's ability. Routine, consistency, less stimulation and more one-on-one contact are successful teaching strategies. Acknowledgment of accomplishments is also vital.

Dinkmeyer, D. and McKay, G. D. *STEP: Systematic training for effective parenting.* Circle Pines, Minn.: American Guidance Service, 1983.

This is a parenting skills manual which is clearly structured, sequential, and arranged to provide parents with issues for discussion, exploration, and resolution. It is based in Adlerian psychology and provides specific ways in which to build positive relationships with children and to understand children's misbehavior, communication, encouragement. A logical consequences-discipline system is presented. The book also provides a way to hold and conduct regular family meetings.

Dorris, Michael. *The broken cord.* New York: Harper Perennial, 1989.

This is a true story of Dorris' plight with his adopted son, Adam, who experiences learning disabilities, behavioral and medical problems. It recounts the discovery of these problems resulting from Adam's birth mother's alcohol abuse during pregnancy. This story brought about significant public awareness of FAS/FAE. Written before many teaching strategies and resources were developed, the book leaves the reader with a bleak impression. The book has been made into a movie.

Engelmann, Jeanne. *A woman's loss of choice, a child's future: How alcohol and other drug use during pregnancy affects our children.* Center City, Minn.: Hazelden, 1994. 24 p. $1.75.

This highly illustrated booklet clearly explains the basics of fetal alcohol syndrome and fetal alcohol effect. The contents focus on myths and truths about using alcohol and drugs during pregnancy. It gives information on how prenatal use may have affected a child and how it may affect its continuing physical and mental development. It details some places where help is available.

*FAS/FAE Information and resource packet.* Vermillion: University of South Dakota, 1989. Available from University of South Dakota Affiliated Program, USD School of Medicine, University of South Dakota, 414 E. Clark, Vermillion, South Dakota 57069-2390. Tel. 605-677-5311 or 800-658-3080.

One of the most basic and valuable resources available for educators and care takers is this packet of information. It includes copies of special reports to the U.S. Congress on alcohol and health, brochures and pamphlets with excellent illustrations and photographs, and handouts of about six pages each prepared by Valborg Kvigne and others. Some is based on Ann Streissguth's research, some of which is referenced in this resource list. Information in the packet includes education techniques for children, adolescents and adults with FAS/FAE. All materials can be copied and distributed freely as there are no copyright restrictions.

"Fetal alcohol syndrome." *The Harvard Mental Health Letter* 7, no. 5 (November 1990): 1–4.

FAS and FAE are widespread problems affecting as many as 80,000 children born each year. Retarded growth, physical deformities, and brain function abnormalities are the most serious manifestations of the problem. Learning disabilities including low IQ, poor judgement, inability to perceive cause and effect and lack of moral understanding are a few of the difficulties encountered. Long-term special education, vocational training, medical treatment, and speech therapy are only a few of the special services required by children and adults with FAS/FAE. Women with FAS or FAE often give birth to children with FAS or FAE because of alcohol use during pregnancy. No known level of alcohol consumption is safe during pregnancy. Often children of alcoholic mothers end up in foster care or other placements due to the drinking mothers' inability to care for their children.

Giunta, Carole Q. and Streissguth, A. P. "Patients with fetal alcohol syndrome and their caretakers." *Social Casework: The Journal of Contemporary Social Work* (September 1988): 453–459.

Characteristics of FAS are reviewed and both patient and caretaker needs are explored. The article concludes that medical, educational, familial and community assistance is necessary for children and adults experiencing FAS. Caretakers of FAS patients have special needs including medical information, peer support, financial assistance and respite care.

Glasser, W. *Reality therapy for parents.* Los Angeles, Calif.: Institute for Reality Therapy, 1978.

This booklet provides parents with a basic understanding of reality therapy and how to use these concepts in dealing with their children and family members.

Handlin, H. and Brennen, P. *The sex handbook: Information and help for minors.* New York: G. P. Putman's & Sons, 1974.

This book is written for adolescent males and females. It is designed to provide information needed to resolve sexual questions and confusion and how to enjoy sex and take care of oneself. The book concentrates on practical information about one's body, obtaining birth control, pregnancy, abortion, and venereal disease.

Houlton, Betsy. *Tad and me: How I found out about fetal alcohol syndrome.* Center City, Minn.: Hazelden, 1991.

Tina realizes that Tad has some learning problems in school and as she researches FAS for her health class she realizes Tad is a child with FAS. Her friendship and feelings about Tad make FAS a personal experience for all who read the story and reinforce why alcohol is so dangerous to the developing fetus. This story includes facts about FAS and its effects on the body, growth, senses and intelligence. It also heightens sensitivity to the issues of FAS and provides insights as to some of the feelings and concerns of the classmates of FAS students.

Levin, Toby. *Rainbow of hope. A guide for the special needs child.* Starlight Publishing Company, 1893 NE 164th Street, Suite 1090, North Miami Beach, Florida 33162. Tel. 305-944-8446. $12.95.

Contains a brief overview of a wide range of disabilities and suggestions on living and growing with a disabled child. Each chapter appendix includes a list of national and local organizations that provide information on a variety of issues.

Kleinfeld, Judith. Fetal alcohol syndrome in Alaska: What the schools can do. A background paper prepared for the Alaska Department of Education. Fairbanks: University of Alaska Fairbanks, Fairbanks, Alaska, 1991. Available from the author, 601A Gruening Building, University of Alaska Fairbanks, Fairbanks, Alaska 99775.

Basic intellectual, physical and behavioral characteristics of children with FAS/FAE are outlined and rates of incidence in Alaska regions and elsewhere are provided. Information about educational issues at various age levels and the potential role of schools in educating affected children and prevention of further FAS/FAE births is given. Most of the document focuses on Alaskan concerns, but much information is pertinent for others.

Kleinfeld, Judith and Siobhan Wescott, ed. *Fantastic Antone Succeeds! Experiences in educating children with Fetal Alcohol Syndrome.* Fairbanks: University of Alaska Press, 1993.

This book offers the practical wisdom of parents, teachers, and therapists on raising and educating children with FAS/FAE. Parents describe how they organize their family life and deal with the schools. Teachers offer descriptions of classrooms where children with FAS/FAE thrive. Especially important are the stories of children with FAS/FAE who are doing well at school and home. This book emphasizes the message that the future of children with FAS/FAE is more hopeful than existing stereotypes portray.

Kvigne, Valborg, Engelhart, E., and Burke, K. *Fetal alcohol syndrome resource list.* Vermillion: University of South Dakota Affiliated Program, Center for Developmental Disabilities, 1991. Available from University of South Dakota Affiliated Program, USD School of Medicine, 414 E. Clark, Vermillion, South Dakota 57069-2390. Tel. 605-677-5311 or 800-658-3080.

This bibliography includes approximately 350 journal articles, books, videos, handbooks, curriculum packets, booklets and chapters in books regarding fetal alcohol syndrome published or produced from the mid-1970s to 1991. The items are arranged in alphabetical order by title. Each entry includes author, publisher, publication date, type of material, and a short abstract.

Malbin, Diane B. "Why bother to identify these kids? Identifying fetal alcohol syndrome and effect: Barriers and potentials." Available from the author, FAS/Drug Effects Clinical Program, 9450 SW Barnew Road, Suite 220, Portland, Oregon 97225.

This fifty-seven-page paper is an elaboration of the chapter Malbin wrote for *Fantastic Antone Succeeds! Experiences in Educating Children with Fetal Alcohol Syndrome,* edited by J. Kleinfeld and S. Wescott. The paper includes nine appendices with information on intercultural communication, a survey of caregivers, samples of FAS fact sheets, a resources list, a bibliography, and two listings showing the importance of identifying children with FAS/FAE and the consequences when they are not identified.

Marlin, K. *The basics of practical parenting.* Columbia, Md.: Practical Parenting Publications, 1973.

A booklet that embraces Adlerian concepts and applies them to basic positive parenting strategies. It is very practical and provides a variety of rules to employ to effectively deal with and manage your child.

Nanson, J. L. and Hiscock, M. "Attention deficits in children exposed to alcohol prenatally." *Alcoholism: Clinical and Experimental Research* 14, no. 5 (September/October 1990): 656–661.

Twenty children with FAS/FAE were compared with twenty children experiencing attention deficit disorder (ADD) in four major attention components: hyperactive behavior, response to treatment, extent of ADD and behavior problems. Subjects also completed IQ tests. Results indicated significantly greater intellectual impairment among the FAS/FAE group but attention deficit and behavior problems were similar to the ADD group. Researchers deduced that treatments known to be successful in increasing learning ability in children with ADD may also be successful for those with FAS/FAE.

National Institute of Alcohol Abuse and Alcoholism. *Program strategies for preventing fetal alcohol syndrome.* Rockville, Md.: U.S. Dept. of Health and Human Services, 1987.

This manual provides basic information and serves as a guide for developing community programs aimed at reducing alcohol-related birth defects and increasing awareness that alcohol consumption during pregnancy can be harmful to the fetus. It is divided into three parts. Part I is a review of the scientific research on the teratogenicity of alcohol and information on the prevalence and economic implications of alcohol-related birth defects. Part

II focuses on ways to reduce alcohol-related birth defects through such means as training health and other professionals, public education and client services. Part III emphasizes strategies for planning and developing community-based programs. Photographs, drawings, tables and additional references are found throughout the publication.

*National Organization on Fetal Alcohol Syndrome Directory: A directory of treatment centers, prevention programs and support groups nationwide.* Washington, D.C.: National Organization on Fetal Alcohol Syndrome, 1993. $35.00 + $3.00 shipping and handling.

This directory provides an alphabetical listing of the FAS/E resources in each state. Included are support groups, newsletters, treatment centers, and resource agencies. This is a helpful reference tool for referring individuals to available resources in their particular geographic region.

Olson, Heather C., Burgess, D. M., and Streissguth, A. P. "Fetal alcohol syndrome (FAS) and fetal alcohol effects (FAE): A lifespan view, with implications for early intervention." *Zero to Three/National Center for Clinical Infant Programs* 13, no. 1 (August/September 1992): 24–29.

This article helps care providers develop new and useful ideas for providing services to children with FAS/FAE and their families. Information covers historical background, long-term prospects, understanding behavior and reframing expectations, guidelines for interventions, recommendations and an excellent listing of information sources. Continuing care, beyond childhood, is vital to continued positive outcomes for children and adults with FAS/FAE.

Olson, Heather C., Sampson, P. D., Barr, H., Streissguth, A. P., and Bookstein, F. L. "Prenatal exposure to alcohol and school problems in late childhood: A longitudinal prospective study." *Development and Psychology* 4 (1992): 341–359.

Children's classroom behavior and achievement difficulties at age eleven are examined in this research. The 458 participants in this study had been followed since birth. Central nervous system deficits, such as attention and memory difficulties were the most widespread manifestations across the spectrum of prenatal alcohol exposure. Binge drinking during pregnancy (five or more drinks on any one occasion) appeared to have the greatest negative influence on children's ability to perform in school. Mathematical ability was most noticeably affected, while reading, spelling and written expression were also significantly affected. Attention deficits, hyperactivity, impulsivity, immaturity and inability to get along with others were also manifest.

Popkin, M. H. *Active parenting handbook.* Atlanta, Ga.: Active Parenting, Inc., 1983.

This book is directed towards training parents to be more active as opposed to reactive to their children's behavior. It stresses to parents the importance of active involvement with your child. Exercises are included for parents to practice the concepts and strategies. The material is based on the works of Alfred Adler and Rudolf Dreikurs.

Resource list: Birth defects—fetal effects of maternal polydrug use. Portland, Oreg.: Western Regional Center for Drug-free Schools and Communities, 1991.

The Center has added an extensive appendix to the National Clearinghouse for Alcohol and Drug Information Resource List. This includes FAS information sources from throughout the United States, not just those limited to the western region.

Slinn, Jim. FAS/FAE: A practical guide for parents. Anchorage, Alaska:self-published, 1994. 47 pages. $2.50 for postage and handling. Available from Jim Slinn, Parents Resource Network, 540 West International Airport Road, Anchorage, Alaska 99518-1110. Tel. 907-564-7489. Fax 907-564-7429.

This booklet is filled with helpful hints for parents of children with FAS/FAE. The information is based on the author's own experiences and information he has gathered for working with his two adopted children with FAS. A resource list and a brief bibliography are also included.

Sorensen, R. C. and Abrams, H. N. Adolescent sexuality in contemporary America: Personal values and sexual behavior ages 13–19. New York: Harry N. Abrams, 1973.

This is more of a textbook on adolescent sexuality and behavior. It is directed primarily for adolescents between the ages of thirteen to nineteen and focuses on sexual behavior, issues, concerns, and problems.

Spohr, H. and Steinhausen, Hans-Christoph. "Follow-up studies of children with fetal alcohol syndrome." Neuropediatrics 18: 13–17.

Data from a multidisciplinary study of children with FAS is reported. These individuals underwent pediatric, neurological, and psychiatric assessments, EEG recordings and psychological testing. Examinations three to four years later revealed that with increasing age, dysmorphic signs became less apparent, neurological performances improved, and EEG records revealed less pathological patterns. Observations also showed improved psychiatric status and cognitive function. Children did not become normal in all psychiatric areas. Hyperactivity and distractibility seem to be major handicaps for these children in school. The study concluded that biological maturation significantly determines the outcome of FAS.

Streissguth, Ann P., Aase, J. M., Clarren, S. K., Randels, S. P., LaDue, R. A., and Smith, D. F. "Fetal alcohol syndrome in adolescents and adults." Journal of the American Medical Association 265, no. 15 (April 17, 1992): 1961–1967.

The term, fetal alcohol syndrome, applies only to the severest manifestations of disabilities caused by a mother's drinking during pregnancy. A study of sixty-one adolescents and adults diagnosed with FAS found characteristic facial malformations grew less distinctive after puberty. Growth deficiency was still evident in head circumference and height but weight deficiency was less significant. Central nervous system damage was most evident in academic functioning (second to fourth grade levels) and in maladaptive behaviors such as poor judgment, distractibility, and inability to perceive social cues. The study concludes FAS has predictable, long-term effects extending into adulthood.

Streissguth, Ann P. "Fetal alcohol syndrome and fetal alcohol effects: A clinical perspective of later developmental consequences." In *Maternal Substance abuse and the developing nervous system,* edited by I. S. Zagon and T. A. Slotkin. San Diego, Calif.: Academic Press, Inc., 1992.

Childhood FAS developmental disabilities continue into adulthood. Physical manifestations decrease with physical maturity but still remain evident. Attention deficits, evident in seventy-five to eighty percent of FAS patients, continue in school and in the work place. Adaptive behaviors such as independent living skills, social skills, and effective communication skills are significantly low. Educators and mental health professionals should recognize the need for systematic information on the effects of specific remedial programs or intervention efforts throughout the life span.

Streissguth, Ann P. *A manual of adolescents and adults with fetal alcohol syndrome, with special references to American Indians,* 2d edition. Seattle, Wash.: Dept. of Psychiatry and Behavioral Sciences and U.S. Dept. of Health and Human Services, 1988.

Following FAS and FAE information, this work discusses basic research then presents recommendations for helping adolescents and adults with FAS/FAE. Although the follow-up study is primarily of American Indians, the publication is applicable to all. Illustrations, graphs and photographs of people with FAS, along with a bibliography of some forty references are also included.

Streissguth, Ann P., Barr, H. M., and Sampson, P. D. "Alcohol use during pregnancy and child development: A Longitudinal Perspective Study of Human Behavioral Teratology." In *Longitudinal studies of children at psychological risk: Cross-national perspectives,* edited by C. W. Greenbaum and J. G. Auerbach, 174–200. Norwood, N.J.: Ablex Publications, 1992.

The effects of prenatal alcohol exposure on a group of infants over a seven year period is described, including neonatal, infancy, preschool and school age findings. At each stage subjects were given behavioral, developmental, and intelligence tests. Neonates were found to have difficulty maintaining either an alert state or a good sleep state. Also, the sucking reflex was negatively affected. Older infants displayed feeding problems as well as mental and motor delays. Preschool and early school age children continued to display deficits in attention, fine and gross motor function, memory, intelligence, and achievement.

_____. "Moderate prenatal alcohol exposure: Effects on child IQ and learning problems at age 7 1/2 Years." *Alcoholism: Clinical and Experimental Research* 14, no. 5 (September/October 1990): 662–668.

This research report describes one facet of a longitudinal study of nearly 500 children prenatally exposed to alcohol. The research focus was the long term effects of moderate levels of prenatal alcohol exposure. A seven-point IQ decrease for children was associated with maternal consumption of an average of two drinks per day. Binge drinking (five or more drinks on at least one occasion) was associated with learning problems.

Strong, B. and Reynolds, R. *Understanding our sexuality*. St. Paul, Minn.: West Publishing, 1982.

This book attempts to provide a foundation of sexual knowledge. It deals with issues of both heterosexual and homosexual preferences and attempts to remove sexuality from emotional reasoning by presenting more objective and scientific facts regarding human sexuality.

Tapahonso, Luci. *Bah's baby brother is born*. Washington, D.C.: National Organization on Fetal Alcohol Syndrome, 1993. $15.00 plus $3.50 postage and handling.

This book is designed for young school-age children. Bah, whose mother is expecting a new baby, explains in simple and direct terms why drinking during pregnancy is dangerous. The story guides the young reader through the days before the birth and during the first few days of the baby's life. A worksheet helps enforce the main concepts of the book.

Tiefer, L. *Human sexuality: Feelings and functions*. (Part of the Life Cycle series.) New York: Harper & Row, 1979.

This book attempts to provide a factual summary of human sexuality. It examines what is known and accepted with regards to the human sexual response, how sex is viewed in various cultures, sexual development across one's life span, and sexual problems and their treatment. It also provides a simple format for one to assess his or her own sexual beliefs and behaviors.

Villarreal, Sylvia F., McKinney, L., and Quackenbush, M. *Handle with care: Helping children prenatally exposed to drugs and alcohol*. Santa Cruz, Calif.: ETR Associates, 1992.

Useful and practical suggestions are outlined for front line workers. In addition to specific information about prenatal drug and alcohol exposure, the book includes excellent suggestions for classroom applications. Case studies give examples of the broad range of experiences and challenges found with children born to drug/alcohol involved parents and profile good results when these children receive positive adult care and attention. Also included is a glossary of related terms, listings of resource agencies; treatment and training programs, state organizations, a bibliography of further readings, and an index. This is a valuable resource for educators of children, from preschool through age ten.

Waxman, S. *Growing up feeling good: A child's introduction to sexuality.* Los Angeles, Calif.: Panjanrum Books, 1979.

This book is for children and provides sexual information in a format which lends itself to discussion. Topics of love and human sexuality are blended in an illustrated book to provide a straightforward presentation. Photographs are tasteful and enhance the material being covered.

Weiner, Lyn and Morse, Barbara A. "Facilitating development for children with fetal alcohol syndrome." *Brown University Child and Adolescent Behavior Letter*, 1992. Available from Manisses Communications Group, Inc. P.O. Box 3357, Providence, Rhode Island 02906. Tel. 401-831-6020.

FAS/FAE affects children in a wide variety of ways. This article discusses some major developmental concerns and provides specific parenting techniques to help children with FAS/FAE grow to their full potential. Major topics are restlessness, growth, feeding, skill levels, and parent issues.

Will, Linda and Will, Hank. "FAS Primer. Part One: Physical characteristics of the FAS child." In *FANN: Fetal Alcohol Network Newsletter* 3, no. 2 (February and March 1992): 1–3.

This first article of a three-part series discusses the physical characteristics of the child with FAS and the diagnostic criteria by which these children are identified. Excellent basic illustrations and details are included.

_____. "FAS Primer. Part Two: Emotional and behavioral characteristics." In *FANN: Fetal Alcohol Network Newsletter* 3, no. 3 (April and May 1992): 4–7.

The second article of a three-part series focuses on the emotional and behavioral characteristics of the child with FAS. It outlines the type of behavior educators and parents can expect during early childhood, early and middle school years, adolescence and adulthood. Recommendations for improving the odds are also given.

_____. "FAS Primer. Part Three: Intellectual functioning, education and strategies." In *FANN: Fetal Alcohol Network Newsletter* 3, no. 4 (June and July 1992): 8–13.

Although there are no major cures for FAS/FAE, this final article of a three-part series outlines strategies which can facilitate the learning process. Specific strategies are outlined for daily living, general behavior problems, learning and memory problems, and thought processes. It also discusses guiding principles for education programs and outlines specific proactive actions school districts can undertake.

## NEWSLETTERS

*FANN Newsletter.* 1990–. Bimonthly. Gratis (contributions welcome). The Fetal Alcohol Network, 158 Rosemont Avenue, Coatesville, Pennsylvania 19320. Linda and Hank Will, editors.

This newsletter helps parents, teachers, and caretakers of individuals with FAS/FAE. It includes detailed information about conferences and workshops, including speakers, topics, and background of speakers. Information about organizations and support groups is also given. Although the newsletter is national in scope, some of the agencies mentioned are based in the mid-west and east. The 1992 issues features an outstanding three-part series entitled "FAS Primer." Part one presents the physical characteristics of the FAS child, part two discusses the emotional and behavioral characteristics of the FAS/FAE children, and part three discusses intellectual functioning and educational strategies. Excellent illustrations are included.

*FAS and Other Drugs Update.* 1981–. Biannual, gratis. Prevention Resource Center, 822 South College St., Springfield, Illinois 62704.

Designed specifically for counselors, care providers, health practitioners, and educators, this newsletter helps those working with women realize that healthy mothers produce healthy babies. Each issue includes a short article of about three pages such as "Prenatal Care: A Birthright," and "Helping Caregivers Services." Many articles include bibliographies and some material is written in Spanish.

*FAS/FAE Newsletter.* 1990–. Quarterly, gratis (contributions welcome). Newsletter comes with a $5.00 membership in the FAS/FAE Support Group. FAS/FAE Newsletter, P.O. Box 74612, Fairbanks, Alaska 99707, David and Gail Hales, editors.

The FAS/FAE Support Group at Fairbanks, Alaska, produces this newsletter in an effort to communicate FAS/FAE issues and information with others. The newsletter includes announcements of meetings and conferences, new publications, feature articles (original and condensed from other sources), and tips to parents, professionals, and caregivers.

*FAS Times: Fetal Alcohol Syndrome/Adolescent Task Force Newsletter.* 1992–. Quarterly. Comes with membership of $15.00 per year family rate, or $25.00 per year professional rate. Copies are gratis the first year without membership. Back issues are available for $1.00 each. Bob & Bonnie Crawford and Carol Wilburn, editors. P.O. Box 2525, Lynnwood, Wash. 98035.

This newsletter is packed with information helpful to parents, care providers, educators, and professionals who deal with FAS/FAE. Included are summaries of articles and reports from other publications, short articles and outlines from parents, caretakers, and individuals with FAS/FAE, notice of new publications, and letters to the editors and the task force. Also included are notices about group meetings, support groups, and hot lines available in Washington State.

*Growing with FAS.* 1989–. Bimonthly, $2.00. *Growing with FAS,* 7802 SE Taylor, Portland, Oregon 97215. Pamela Groves, editor. (Sample copy gratis. Include self-addressed stamped envelope.)

This helpful newsletter contains a variety of information for parents of individuals with FAS/FAE and for professionals. Over the years issues have included excerpts from professional papers, comments on the special strengths of children with FAS/FAE, a guide to summer camps appropriate for children with FAS/FAE, a "Question of the Month" calendar with answers, summaries of conferences, and reader comments

*Iceberg.* 1991–. Quarterly. $5.00 per year family rate, $15.00 per year professional rate. Fetal Alcohol Syndrome Information Service, P.O. Box 95597, Seattle, Washington 98104. Dale Leuthold, editor. (Sample copy gratis.)

This is an educational newsletter written for people concerned about FAS/FAE. It includes letters requesting help and assistance with answers, personal narratives from parents and caretakers of children with FAS/FAE, poetry, names and addresses of support groups, successful tips for working with affected individuals, upcoming events, and much more. Much of the information centers on activities in Washington state and the Pacific Northwest, but efforts are being made to become more national in scope and coverage.

*Notes from NOFAS—The National Organization on Fetal Alcohol Syndrome.* 1991. Gratis. Quarterly. Available from the organization, 1815 H Street, N.W., Suite 170, Washington, D.C. 20006. Cynthia Richardson, editor.

This is the organization's official newsletter and includes information about the organization's activities, interviews with its department heads and other professionals concerned with FAS. Advertisements of recent books, pamphlets and other materials are included.

## ORGANIZATIONS

National Association for Prenatal Addiction Research and Education
11 E. Hubbard Street, Suite 200
Chicago, Illinois 60611

This multidisciplinary society of professionals is devoted to addiction treatment and prevention for pregnant and postpartum women and their children. Memberships fees for individuals are $55.00, affiliate memberships are $300.00, and corporate memberships are $1,000.00

National Information Center for Children and Youth with Disabilities
P.O. Box 1492
Washington, D.C. 20013
800-999-5599

Provides state resource lists, free printed materials and a copy of their news digest.

National Information System and Clearinghouse
Center for Developmental Disabilities
Columbia, S.C. 29208
800-922-9234

Provides information on services and agencies for children with developmental disabilities in every state.

National Organization on Fetal Alcohol Syndrome
Washington, D.C. 20006
202-785-4585

This is a nonprofit organization dedicated to eliminating birth defects caused by alcohol consumption during pregnancy and to improving the quality of life of those affected by FAS/FAE. An important organization for educators, one of its major functions is to disseminate FAS/FAE information. Contributions are welcome.

Their goals and objectives are:

1. Reduce the rate of alcohol-related birth defects in the United States through better public awareness education.

2. Establish an annual conference regarding FAS/FAE.

3. Assist in the promotion of better prevention education, and community empowerment.

4. Train educators, community members, and health care professionals in issues regarding FAS/FAE.

5. Serve as a national clearinghouse for local, state and regional FAS/FAE organizations so that resources and information can be disseminated and exchanged more effectively.

# Literature Cited

Abel, E. "Incidence of anomalies among siblings of FAS cases." *Neurotoxical Teratol* 10 (1988): 1–2.

Abel, E. and Sokol, R. "Incidence of fetal alcohol syndrome and economic impact of FAS-related anomalies." *Drug and Alcohol Dep.* 19 (1987): 51–70.

Aronson, M. and Olegard, R. "Fetal alcohol syndrome in pediatrics and child psychology." In *Alcohol and the Developing Brain*, edited by A. Ryberg and E. Engel. New York: Raven Press, 1985.

Aronson, M., Kyllerman, M., Sabel, K. G., Sanin, B., and Olegard, R. "Children of alcoholic mothers." *Acta Paediatr Scand* 74 (1985): 27–35.

Barlow, N. A. *Charles Darwin's diary of the voyage of the H.M.S. Beagle.* Cambridge: University Press, 1933.

Berg, R., Franzen, M., and Wedding, D. *Screening for brain impairment. A manual for mental health practice.* New York: Springer Publishing, 1987.

Berliner, D. C. "The nature of expertise in teaching." In *Effective and responsible teaching*, edited by F. K. Oser, A. Dick, and J. Patry, 227–248. San Francisco, Calif.: Jossey-Bass, 1992.

Dorris, M. *The broken cord.* New York: Harper and Row, 1989.

Feuerstein, R. *Instrumental enrichment: An intervention program for cognitive modifiability.* Baltimore, Md.: University Park Press, 1980.

Greene, T., Ernhart, C. B., Ager, J., Sokol, R. J., Martier, S., and Boy, T. "Prenatal alcohol exposure to alcohol and cognitive development." *Neurotoxicol Teratol* 13 (1991): 1.

Jones, K. L. and Smith, D. W. "Recognition of the fetal alcohol syndrome in early infancy." *Lancet* 2 (1973): 999–1001.

Kleinfeld, J. S. "Getting it together in teacher education: A 'problem-centered' curriculum." *Peabody Journal of Education* 65, no. 2 (1988): 66–78.

_____. "Fetal alcohol syndrome in Alaska: What the schools can do." Prepared for the Alaska Department of Education. Northern Studies Program, University of Alaska Fairbanks, Fairbanks, Alaska, 1991.

Kaestle, C. F. "The awful reputation of education research." *Educational researcher* 22, no. 1 (1993): 23–31.

LaDue, R. A., Streissguth, A. P. and Randels, S. P. "Clinical considerations pertaining to adolescents and adults with fetal alcohol syndrome." In *Perinatal substance abuse: Research findings and clinical implications*, edited by T. Sonderegger, 104–131. Baltimore: The Johns Hopkins University Press, 1992.

Lemoine, P., Harousseau, H., Borteyru, J. P., and Menuet, J. C. "Les enfants de parents alcooliques: anomalies observees. Apropos de 127 cas." *Ouest Med* 21 (1968): 476–482.

Levine, M. D., and Melmed, R. D. "The unhappy wanderers: Children with attention deficits." *Pediatric Clinics of North America* 29, no. 1 (February 1982): 105–119.

Petrakis, P. L. *Alcohol and birth defects: The fetal alcohol syndrome and related disorders*. Rockville, Maryland: U.S. Department of Health and Human Services, Public Health Service, National Institute on Alcohol Abuse and Alcoholism, 1987.

Polanyi, M. *The tacit dimension*. Garden City, New York: Doubleday, 1967.

Riley, E. "The long-term behavioral effects of prenatal alcohol exposure in rats." *Alcoholism Clin Exp Res* 14 (1990): 5.

Rosett, H. L. "A clinical perspective of the fetal alcohol syndrome." *Alcoholism Clin Exp Res* 4 (1980): 119–122.

Rosett, H. L. and Weiner, L. *Alcohol and the fetus: A clinical perspective*. New York: Oxford University Press, 1984.

Silko, Leslie Marmon. *Ceremony*. New York: Penguine, 1977.

Smith, S. *No easy answers: the learning disabled child at home and at school*. New York: Bantam, 1980.

Sokol, R. J. and Clarren, S. K. "Guidelines for use of terminology describing the impact of prenatal alcohol on the offspring." *Alcoholism Clin Exp Res* 13 (1989): 597–598.

Spohr, H. L. and Steinhausen, H. C. "Clinical, psychopathological and developmental aspects in children with the fetal alcohol syndrome: a four-year follow up study." In *Mechanisms of alcohol damage in utero*, Ciba Foundation Symposium 105. London: Pittman, 1984.

Streissguth, A. P. "What every community should know about drinking during pregnancy and the lifelong consequences for society." *Substance abuse* 12, no. 3 (1991): 114–127.

————. "Fetal alcohol syndrome: Early and long-term consequences." In *Problems of drug dependence 1991: Proceedings of the 53rd annual scientific meeting*, edited by L. Harris. (NIDA research monograph number 119.) Rockville, MD: U.S. Department of Health and Human Services, 1992.

Streissguth, A. P., Aase, J. M., Clarren, S. K., Randels, S. P., LaDue, R. A., and Smith, D. F. "Fetal alcohol syndrome in adolescents and adults." *Journal of the American Medical Association* 265, no. 15 (1991): 1961–1967.

Streissguth, A. P., LaDue, R. A., and Randels, S. P. *A manual on adolescents and adults with fetal alcohol syndrome with special reference to American Indians*. 2nd ed. Seattle: Dept. of Psychiatry and Behavioral Sciences and U.S. Dept. of Health and Human Services, 1988.

Streissguth, A. P. and Randels, S. "Long term effects of fetal alcohol syndrome." In *Alcohol and child/family health*, edited by G. C. Robinson and R. W. Armstrong. Vancouver, B.C.: University of British Columbia, 1988.

Tversky, A. and Kahneman, D. "Judgment under uncertainty: Heuristics and biases." *Science* 185 (1974): 1124–1131.

West, J. R., Goodlett, C. R., and Brandt, J. P. "New approaches to research on the long-term consequences of prenatal exposure to alcohol." *Alcoholism Clin Exp Res* 14 (1990): 674–689.

# Index

The letter "n" following a page number indicates that the reference is a footnote.

JUDITH KLEINFELD is a professor of psychology at the University of Alaska Fairbanks. She developed and now directs the UAF Northern Studies Program, an interdisciplinary masters program for students interested in the circumpolar north. In 1987 she created and became the first director of the Teachers for Rural Alaska Program, an innovative teacher education program using the case method to prepare excellent teachers for village schools. Since 1969 she has done research on educational and northern policy issues. Her findings have been published in numerous professional journals and in a biweekly column in Alaska's major newspapers as well as many outside the state. In recognition of her work, she received in 1993 the UAF Emil Usibelli Distinguished Research Award. Dr. Kleinfeld received her Ed.M. in 1967 and Ed.D. in 1970 from the Harvard Graduate School of Education.

SIOBHAN WESCOTT is currently working towards a Masters in Public Health with an emphasis on behavioral sciences and health education. She first became interested in fetal alcohol syndrome while a legislative assistant for Senator Tom Daschle of South Dakota. Ms. Wescott, an Athabascan from Fairbanks, Alaska, has published several articles on various aspects of FAS/FAE. She is a member of the board of directors of the National Organization on Fetal Alcohol Syndrome. After completing the requirements for her degree, Ms. Wescott plans to pursue her interest in finding creative solutions for educating women about the effects on children of alcohol consumption during pregnancy and on caring for children who are alcohol affected.